Networked Regionalism as Conflict Management

Networked Regionalism as Conflict Management

Anna Ohanyan

Stanford University Press

Stanford, California

Stanford University Press
Stanford, California

Library of Congress Cataloging-in-Publication Data

Ohanyan, Anna, author.
  Networked regionalism as conflict management / Anna Ohanyan.
    pages cm.
  Includes bibliographical references and index.
  ISBN 978-0-8047-9386-5 (cloth : alk. paper) —
  ISBN 978-0-8047-9493-0 (pbk. : alk. paper)
    1. Regionalism (International organization) 2. Conflict management.
3. Peace-building. 4. Pacific settlement of international disputes.
I. Title.
JJZ5330.O36 2015
  341.24—dc23
                                                          2014036160
  ISBN 978-0-8047-9494-7 (electronic)

Printed in the United States of America on acid-free, archival-quality
paper. Typeset at Stanford University Press in 10/14 Minion.

To ARAM

Contents

Tables and Figures

Tables

Figures

Preface

As a teenager in Armenia in the early 1990s—during the very early years after the dissolution of the Soviet Union—I recall standing in a tiny local shop, in a remote village near the shores of Lake Sevan, holding a packaged bar of exceptionally brightly colored orange hand soap, its floral scent so remarkable at the time that I can recall it to this day. There was nothing particularly special about that soap, as it turns out, except that it was manufactured in Turkey, was likely destined for Western markets, yet had somehow found its way into my hands in a faraway corner of Armenia.

I distinctly remember feeling guilty for liking that bar of soap. Wariness of all things Turkish was instinctive, a legacy of the genocide of the Armenians by Ittihadist Turkey in the pre-Soviet period. That legacy involved a genocide so successful and complete that it would be used a few short decades later as a template by Raphael Lemkin and the Allies in constructing the legal basis for the Nuremberg Trials. And that difficult legacy had endured, with Soviet Armenia comprising so many children and grandchildren of survivors of the Armenian genocide, and had been reinforced in the present day by a border unilaterally blockaded by a seemingly unrepentant modern Turkey.

But what puzzled me most as I stood in that tiny shop, handling that aromatic bar of soap, were not issues of physical security or existential threat, but rather more mundane logistical questions. How had this Turkish bar of soap come to find its way to the shores of this mountain lake in landlocked Armenia, across closed land and air borders. How had it taken the path it had, to land in Armenia, from a place whose government had severed all diplomatic links with the destination country? Who was setting the rules, if there were any, that consented to retail trade in minor consumer goods, no doubt conducted by myriad circuitous means, prevailing over a deep, painful, unresolved past, and an insecure present?

But trade did prevail. And even today, despite a now decades-long unilateral blockade and the absence of diplomatic relations, many more Turkish toiletries, along with a long list of other consumer goods, regularly find their way from Turkish factories to remote Armenian villages. Although the formal research for this book started in the summer of 2010, it is those memories from the early 1990s, in small shops across Armenia, that have tacitly shaped the work presented in this book.

In circumstances such as those of Turkish-Armenian relations, concepts of regionalism and nonstate actors are no substitute for human rights protections and long overdue mechanisms of reconciliation, atonement, and redemption. However, the idea of "networked regionalism" as a component of conflict management strategies—the theoretical and policy framework introduced in this book—offers a pathway toward building relations between societies and communities in parallel and concurrent with other processes of formal diplomacy between governments. In particular, this book has three messages. First, peaceful coexistence is too important to be left to politicians alone, particularly in regions with immature democracies and persistent authoritarian tendencies. At the same time, it is too optimistic to expect that flows of trade and capital alone can transform conflict management processes for the better. And it is equally unrealistic to leave the "business" of peace solely to economists and private enterprise.

This book is a call for careful calibration and more strategic deployment of economic forces in politically divided areas, with a focus on strengthening *regions* toward managing local conflict. It is an appeal for a deeper understanding of the ways that various economic and political stakeholders currently intersect, and should intersect, in politically divided areas, and in the regions to which they belong. It is also a quest to identify economic and political stakeholders that unfortunately fail to cross each other's paths, reflecting an unfortunate gap in the global conflict management infrastructure. It is a plea for humility to policy-makers, national or international, and an appeal to seek out populations across conflict lines and border areas who suffer in the shadows of unresolved and frozen conflicts. There is significant untapped potential, which needs recognition and utilization, for more effective peace processes in politically divided regions; regional approaches to individual conflicts should be a significant part of any peace process.

Second, networked regionalism as a conflict management strategy also upsets a belief dominant among international and national policy-makers in conflict regions: that some regions are just broken, and no regional integration can occur unless and until political conflicts between states and nations are resolved. I present here an alternative narrative: there are no broken regions, but only collections of weak states. Unresolved conflicts are often visible, and are erroneously and easily blamed for the lack of regional integration in conflict areas. The study in this book shows that regional integration is lacking primarily because of poor administrative and governance capacities of individual states, shortages of democracy, rudimentary business practices and information scarcities at a regional level. Most of all, this work highlights the need for regional institutions that can be true advocates for those stakeholders that stand to benefit from greater regional cooperation. Giving such regional groups a voice, and creating a forum to advance their interests, can go a long way both for the socioeconomic development of constituent states in the region, and for the management and resolution of precarious frozen conflicts.

Third, networked regionalism as a conflict management strategy represents a challenge for us all to rethink the global infrastructure of conflict management in the context of post-American hegemony and increasing degrees of nonstate violence worldwide. States, particularly in the developing world, are losing their monopoly over the means of violence. The contemporary conflict management infrastructure remains rooted in policies designed during the Cold War for interstate conflict. The multilayered and multiplayer realities in conflict regions today require other responses. Regionalism, and its promotion, are one such important component to a restructuring of global conflict management policies. And it is with the hope that this book makes a convincing case to that end that I present this work.

To end this Preface I recall here the words of my too-wise eight-year-old daughter, Elise Mariam. As I attempted to explain to her the purpose of, and my hopes for, this book (in my words, "to find new ways of solving some of the conflicts between states"), she exclaimed that an appropriate job title for me and my colleagues would be "peace engineer." I admit to never having thought of conflict management as "peace engineering," but that portrayal captures the new vision and the new spirit that is required of professionals in the field of conflict analysis and resolution. Thinking solely like a politician or an economist may no longer be sufficient for addressing many of the old protracted and newly emerging conflicts around the world. Indeed, perhaps it is time to think like an engineer, and to design peace systems that are varied, are rooted in communities, yet concurrently address collective, regional issues and problems. To address conflicts, especially frozen conflicts, we must no longer simply address the conflicting parties; it is by healing the regions to which those parties belong, and leveraging regional structures and dynamics, that peace can be maintained. Such regional approaches are importantly inclusive of diverse types of actors across politically divided areas, ranging from small communities to business leaders, direct parties to the conflict or not. It is these actors, such as those I found decades ago in that remote village store on the shores of Lake Sevan, that are key to addressing contemporary conflicts.

Acknowledgments

The book is the outcome of a wonderful, intercontinental network of friends, colleagues, and supporting institutions. In the United States, the Fulbright Program administered by the U.S. Department of State and the U.S. embassy in Armenia, and the International Research and Exchanges Board (IREX), provided the necessary funding that made possible fieldwork in Armenia, Georgia, and Bosnia and Herzegovina. Combined with additional research support and sabbatical leave from Stonehill College I was able to spend a full year in Armenia and the region. Writing this book while located in the South Caucasus, together with my young children, provided a very real sense of living in the shadows of multiple frozen conflicts, which proved a great source of stimulation and dedication.

In Massachusetts, I am indebted to my colleagues in the Department of Political Science and International Studies for indulging my work and accommodating my leave. Gerald Espinosa and Sarah Dickerson, my research assistants at Stonehill College, assisted with the literature review in early stages of the research, for which I am thankful. The encouragement and counsel of David Matz was essential for me to muster the courage to engage this research area and proceed with the year-long fieldwork. Richard Finnegan encouraged me to apply to the Fulbright program, and I am indeed glad I did. Heartfelt thanks to Susan Allen, Steven Weber, Caroline Lambert, Michael Needle, Julia Del Sobral, Fiona Stevenson, Lisa Lee Hansel, as well as to Dr. Malcolm Smith, Robin Sklar, Grigor Vardikyan, and Slav Stepanyan for their personal and professional support throughout this work.

In Sarajevo, I am indebted to the staff at the Regional Cooperation Council (RCC) for opening their doors to me and for providing me with much needed access to mid- and senior-level officials at that institution. Jelica Minić in particular was instrumental in connecting me with her colleagues at RCC. My time at RCC was indeed inspiring, as it stimulated me to think about a potentially invaluable export from the Western Balkans: a Regional Cooperation Council–inspired analogous regional institution for the South Caucasus region.

While in Armenia, I benefited from the similar hospitality of the Regional Environmental Centre for the Caucasus, which allowed me an in-depth look at the exciting projects that this institution is advancing in the South Caucasus. Eurasia International University in Yerevan and the Ohanyan School provided significant logistical assistance throughout the full year of my Fulbright tenure in Armenia, helping expedite the writing process. Brusov University in Yerevan served as the institutional host during my Fulbright experience. It was thrilling to share early findings of this work with my students and colleagues there. Their intellectual curiosity constantly stimulated and challenged my thinking, and resulted in many lively discussions.

I am grateful to my respondents and humbled by their wisdom, experience, and thoughtful insights. It is their generosity in sharing their expertise that has informed this research in more ways than I can enumerate. I am also thankful to the anonymous reviewers for their useful feedback, and feel privileged to receive their endorsement for this work. In addition, writing a book can be a solitary exercise, and in early stages, sitting in a small room in Yerevan, it was hard to determine whether I was headed in the right direction. Geoffrey Burn, Executive Editor at Stanford University Press, trusted this project early on, and his belief in this research and sage guidance were essential. Special thanks go to James Holt, the Editorial Assistant, for all his patience and professionalism in fielding my numerous questions.

I am forever indebted to my children for venturing with me to Armenia for a full year. I am so proud of the courage and open-mindedness that my young daughters, Isabelle and Elise, showed throughout this experience. Their ability to transcend real and imagined boundaries with ease has been inspiring and hopeful of a more peaceful future. I am thrilled that they enjoyed and grew during their time in Armenia as much as I did. My toddler, Helen, with her innocent yet mischievous ways, always provided me with the appropriate perspective throughout this work: no child should be deprived of safety or live in misery and constant fear. Going to school should not be a luxury. It is our obligation to bestow on them a better world.

All of this would have been impossible without the central node in my network, my husband, Aram, whose selflessness has made this "intercontinental year" in our family work well. You are my toughest critic, and I would not have it any other way.

Concord, Massachusetts, June 16, 2014
P.S.—Happy Birthday, Isabelle and Elise!

Networked Regionalism as Conflict Management

Introduction

Academics frequently use numbers of active and "frozen" conflicts as a proxy for capturing the state of war and peace around the world. Drawing from the Uppsala Conflict Data Program at Uppsala University, Themnér and Wallensteen (Themnér and Wallensteen 2012) identified thirty-seven armed conflicts in 2011, for which a minimum of twenty-five battle-related deaths were recorded, and they identified thirty-one armed conflicts in 2010. The authors claim that, despite the increase, the number remains relatively low compared with those during the peak years in the early 1990s. However, the numbers mask the often unrecorded and understudied negative externalities posed by conflicts that are active yet frozen. Even when some type of temporary agreement is reached by the parties in conflict, the remaining instability and uncertainty continue to tax the economies of the states and communities involved in the conflicts.

Meanwhile, the instability affects the flow of foreign direct investment, job creation, and tourism, just to name a few consequences. In addition, such regions generate a push for the states involved in the conflict to increase their military spending, thereby diverting much needed funding from social development. Such regions are also associated with disappointing efforts at democratic reforms in the countries involved in the conflict, and many analysts caution that conflict management efforts are delayed by the governments of those countries in order to consolidate their hold on power structures (Caspersen 2012). Indeed, domestic political challenges, the weak hold of the regime on power in particular, tends to complicate the prospects of effective conflict management (Barnett 1995; Mansfield and Snyder 1995; Acharya and Johnston 2008; Haacke and Williams 2011). All of these factors create a vicious circle that is hard to break with ad hoc networks of global conflict management that are deployed arbitrarily and unevenly.

The global infrastructure in conflict management has been more effective at freezing conflicts than finding sustainable solutions (Crocker, Hampson, and Aall 2011). The lack of sufficient financial resources for sustained involvement in conflict regions is one dimension of the problem. This is also in part the reason for the second, organizational set of problems within that infrastructure: most of the interventions are state-centric, even when conflicts have a pronounced regional dimension. Particularly in bilateral aid to conflict regions, donors focus on one country, and very few organizational tools are available to support cross-border activities (Francis interview 2012). Organizational factors are also the reason for the emphasis on political actors and stakeholders in thinking about interventions and negotiation processes. Unless a state that is party to a conflict has been completely engulfed by war and unless a full-blown humanitarian intervention has been initiated, tailored and targeted economic policies that are sensitive to the specifics of a conflict environment are rarely applied.

Indeed, heavily politicized and state-centric, the existing paradigm of international conflict management predominantly targets government authorities while seeking to mediate the conflict. Economic and civil society stakeholders are traditionally excluded from negotiation processes between the parties to a conflict. Instead, mediation and negotiation—the two most common instruments of conflict management—are geared toward finding a political solution, which in some conflicts is considered a precondition for the deployment of economic instruments. The narrow political emphasis and sovereignty bias drastically reduce the possibilities of innovative responses to frozen conflicts, as I argue later in this book.

Even when civil society actors are funded, the international community tends to produce two parallel and rather disconnected sets of networks, state-centric and civil society–focused, that are poorly coordinated. A good example of this problem is the "ostrich diplomacy" practiced by government officials. When asked whether the government was aware of civil society projects being carried out between Georgia and the breakaway regions of Abkhazia and Ossetia, a government official from Georgia's Ministry of Foreign Affairs indicated (anonymous interview 2012) that she was not aware and not eager to find out. In the conflict between Azerbaijan and its Armenian populated enclave of Nagorno-Karabakh, backed by neighboring Armenia, the fragile ceasefire has been holding since 1994. High-level officials from Armenia and Azerbaijan have been meeting for years since then, but the civil society contacts have been very rare. Even if there is a breakthrough between government authorities, they will struggle to sell any kind of negotiated settlement to their respective publics.

Another dimension of the problem of the global infrastructure in conflict management more effectively freezing conflicts than finding sustainable solutions is the power vacuum in conflict regions. In political terms, in an age of declining U.S. hegemony (He 2010; Shor 2012) the power vacuum in many conflict regions has not been filled in a way that provides security and a sustainable peace arrangement. Declining U.S. hegemony has been accompanied by a regional "revival," but it has been manifested in competing power struggles domestically and the greater vulnerability of regions to neighboring regional powers. As a result, the declining hegemonic stability has failed to give way to regional stability. Instead, it has set off a rather complex interplay of interests from groups in the domestic/regional/global spheres of politics and the political/economic/social sectors of societies. In short, the capacities of the global security infrastructure have been strained, and some analysts are questioning its effectiveness in addressing old and emergent ethnic wars and civil strife (Crocker, Hampson, and Aall 2011; Kirchner and Dominguez 2011). With the end of the Cold War, the bipolar system of conflict containment has disappeared without giving way to a new system of global or regional conflict management.

Like its practice, the theory of conflict management in the new post–Cold War security environment has been slow to adapt to the new security environment with modified, responsive analytical tools. Territoriality, this time in disciplinary terms, remains a crippling factor. The interdisciplinary boundaries between conflict management/peace and conflict studies, on the one hand, and international political economy, on the other, have bogged down study of the increasingly complex conflict environment, which would have animated and informed the practice of conflict management in conflict regions. Theories in conflict management have generated deep understanding of intervention processes, actors, and outcomes. However, because most of this scholarship continues to focus on the organizational level of analysis, the broader political underpinnings of conflict processes and intervention strategies have received only scant attention. The interplay between domestic politics and foreign policy strategies, extensively researched within comparative politics, has failed to generate informed studies in conflict management scholarship. Studies in political economy have produced solid scholarship on state-society relations but have failed to apply that research in politically divided areas. It is not clear whether the same theories on the dynamics between economic forces and political actors can be replicated in conflict regions. Understanding the peculiarities of politically divided areas (PDAs), where economic interest is as important as identity politics, is a fruitful yet poorly explored research direction. Against this backdrop, this study presents a regional networked peace paradigm as a response to a new security environment and the persistence of frozen conflicts around the world.

Research Goals

This study questions the underlying paradigm of international interventions, which are country-specific and ad hoc. The paradigm currently underpinning the international conflict management effort is poorly matched with the protracted nature of most contemporary conflicts. Most conflicts, interstate or intrastate, are caused by or associated with weak state institutions. Under conditions of poor governance and underdevelopment, poverty and unemployment, and corruption and lack of democracy, negotiated agreements are hard to consolidate. Pursuing a different approach, this study makes a case for using region building as a strategy for peace building—that is, adopting regional approaches to address interstate as well as intrastate conflicts. Fostering regionalism—political, economic, and social regional integration—can be an effective way of engaging societies with one another while a negotiated settlement is being sought.

The political economy literature on regional studies has produced very little specifically tailored to politically divided areas. Instead, the field has been preoccupied with definitional issues pertaining to regions and regionalisms, as well as the extent to which regions are independent ontological constructs with distinct institutional and political lives. However, this study on regionalism in PDAs looks into the specificities of regional integration, if any, in PDAs. It also looks at the role of great powers in shaping regional politics in PDAs and calls for greater understanding of the types of actors and their relationships at the regional level and of the roles they can play in the advocated regional systems of conflict management. In this respect, at the conceptual level this study seeks to spark an interdisciplinary dialogue between students of regional studies and political economy, on the one hand, and conflict management researchers and practitioners, on the other.

Introduced in this study, the network approach is a useful conceptual bridge between regional studies/political economy and conflict management scholarship. By focusing on the network composition supporting various types of regional arrangements in PDAs, one can understand peace and conflict dynamics at the granular level. Using networks as a lens, researchers and practitioners are able to identify the specific stakeholders that are inclined or disinclined to cultivate cross-conflict ties. The network approach allows one to open the "black box" of a state's government, which in traditional conflict management processes is considered the main site of institutional organization. The approach then allows a closer look at the greater complexity and diversity of actors and interest groups, which may or may not be visible through the state-centric view. The traditional approaches to conflict management paint the political reality in conflict regions in broad brushstrokes, whereas the network approach resembles finger-painting: it emphasizes each small stroke, which only at a distance melds into the overall picture. Most important, the network approach captures the institutional context in which the relationships between economic forces and their political outcomes play out. In conflict management, the network approach specifies the agency and the structure that can potentially support conflict management processes on a short- and long-term basis.

The book has two goals. The first is descriptive: to understand the processes of regional integration, even a minimal one, in politically divided conflict areas. This goal includes regions of active as well as dormant, or frozen, conflicts, and all the cases in between. What is the nature of regionalism in such areas? Which actors are pushing for contacts with the other side and why? What is the institutional composition of the relationships between these actors? The institutional makeup of regional networks is important in shaping conflict management processes and outcomes on the ground. The network approach to regional studies developed in this research distinguishes between networks that are externally introduced and those that are locally cultivated. And from that approach emerge the implications of this distinction for conflict management processes and outcomes. Study of the structural composition of the networks also reveals the interests driving region formation. Indeed, the role of the great powers in regional politics is cast in a new light: the institutional presence of great powers and the type of networks deployed by them produce varied outcomes in conflict management processes.

The second goal of this book is to explore whether processes of regional integration can have any impact on the prospects and opportunities for conflict management by communities and their respective governments. In particular, can the institutional infrastructure of regional integration condition the prospects and effectiveness of conflict management and peace building on the ground? If so, what kind of integration matters? What are the benefits of political, economic, and social integration, if at all? Special emphasis is placed on the role that regional organizations play in enhancing security and advancing peace building in conflict and politically divided areas. In particular, this study focuses on regional organizations, seeking to explore the level of their embeddedness in societal networks across conflict lines. Are regional organizations that have achieved a greater degree of networking more effective as actors in conflict management than those that have not? If so, what types of networks have been most consequential in advancing security and conflict management in a given region? Are top-down and vertical networks more effective than horizontal networks?

The relationship between the network composition of regionalism in PDAs and peace-building processes is explored in this study by developing concrete network attributes to describe the variance in regional forms of engagement. As Chapter 2 maintains, the regional forms can vary in terms of the following network attributes: the patterns of their mobilization (top-down/bottom-up), which reflects the main political or economic drivers of a regional arrangement; the extent of institutional density of the regional networks, which captures a network's level of institutionalization and formality; the degree of power concentration in the network, which assesses whether the key political, financial, and organizational resources are concentrated within one or two network members (centered networks) or are more spread out (stretched networks); and the level of heteropolarity, which evaluates the extent to which stakeholders and interest groups from a variety of sectors (state and nonstate, local, national, regional, and global) are represented in the network. As argued in the chapters that follow, these network attributes add up to describe the central institutional infrastructure of regionalism in a PDA, which creates both unique opportunities and limitations for the peace-building processes.

In turn, conflict management/peace building are defined in two dimensions: (1) the impact of regional arrangements on conflict management, and (2) the extent of interventions in the society, which can range from limited and cosmetic to extensive and structural. The first dimension is examined in terms of the type of "peace" that it creates or to which it contributes. Here the study builds on the emerging thinking on the type of peace that a particular intervention can create, which can range from "cold" (end of violence and establishment of cease-fire arrangements) to "warm" (resolution of the conflict and reconciliation between the conflict parties). As for the second dimension, interventions in society can range from limited and cosmetic to extensive and structural.

The creation of highly institutionalized peace-building systems in a PDA that can function on a long-term basis, even without creating reconciliation in the short term, is the ultimate measure of effective interventions. The effectiveness of third-party interventions should be judged on whether they create peace systems and conflict management infrastructure. Such a network, when applied at a regional level, allows one to determine the overall trends and patterns, if any, in the types of networks mobilized in the region. The empirical section of this study examines some of the specific networks in a region, but it is the aggregations of such networks at the regional level that are evaluated. These aggregations of networks, or networks of networks, ultimately constitute an infrastructure of conflict management in a region.

A Regional Networked Peace Paradigm

A paradigm for a regional networked peace is both a theoretical and a policy framework of analysis. In terms of theory, it introduces the relatively new conceptual machinery of network governance into the field of conflict management and peace building, calling for greater emphasis on the institutional effects of a given conflict management infrastructure, on the one hand, and the political outcomes it creates, on the other. As a theoretical research agenda, the paradigm developed here reflects the specific relationship between regional networks and the impacts they may have on peace patterns. As a policy framework, the paradigm moves beyond simply calling for regional solutions to frozen and active conflicts by specifying how such regional interventions should be organized on an institutional basis to yield the most output.

The paradigm for a regional networked peace developed in this study is characterized by (1) utilization of a domestic-international interface in the political and economic activities of governments and markets; (2) a multiplicity of actors and issue areas and the sectors they represent: (3) recognition of the institutional effects of conflict management infrastructure on political outcomes; (4) strategic cultivation of regional networks; (5) expansion of space for technocratic engagement across conflict lines, as opposed to political engagement; and (6) institutionalization of multiple tracks of engagement across conflict lines, as opposed to utilizing track II diplomacy and the grassroots as an auxiliary to track I diplomacy. All of these features add up to the creation of regional peace systems in PDAs. These systems require not only renovating and restructuring the conflict management capacities of regional and international organizations, as discussed in Chapter 3, but also completely rewiring the relationship between them, as well as with state actors, civil society, and the private sector.

Speaking in 2012 in the context of Europe's engagement in conflict management in the Balkans and the intricate regional networks created by the European Union, a representative of the Regional Cooperation Council compared the existing regional initiatives to multiple and unconnected tunnels: "We do not even know whether the people in those tunnels are moving in the same direction or at cross-purposes" (Ivan-Cucu interview 2012). A regional networked peace paradigm is first of all a policy framework aimed at systematizing the existing interventions and initiatives and at building passage ways between the tunnels. As a policy framework, it expands the number of actors directly or indirectly involved in conflict management efforts, which also entails creating complex interdependencies among domestic, regional, and international players. Although the state remains the central actor in carrying out diplomacy, with the implementation of the regional networked peace paradigm it benefits from new leverages and "policy entry points" (Ramsbotham 2012) in the negotiation process. The paradigm offers concrete tools for creating new spaces of technical engagement across conflict lines, which allows the third-party actors to depoliticize the negotiation processes as much as possible. As with any other effort in international development, the regional peace paradigm requires intensive coordination between various initiatives, but the theoretical framework introduced here also specifies more concrete institutional conditions under which the yields for conflict management and peace building will be most optimal.

In this study, the theory underlying the regional networked peace paradigm is applied in the comparative context to three regions: (1) Western Europe—Northern Ireland; (2) Balkans—Bosnia and Herzegovina; and (3) the South Caucasus—the Georgia-Abkhazia, Georgia–Ossetia, Georgia–Russia, and Nagorno–Karabakh conflicts. The study also presents an overview of regional approaches to conflict management applied elsewhere in order to address critics who assert that the EU is the only case of building peace and security by creating regional arrangements.

In exploring the link between the four network attributes and the political opportunities for peace they create—the core of the regional networked peace paradigm—one can use these cases to expose the existing variation in regional types of conflict management infrastructures and their associated outcomes. In particular, the cases are selected on the independent variable: all three regions stand out as having levels of regional integration that differ dramatically in terms of the scope of integration as well as the depth and breadth of institutional infrastructure supporting regional integration. The European Union is the most evolved institutionally in regional integration. Its impact on the Northern Ireland conflict is contrasted with the moderate levels of regional integration in the Balkans and its impact on the conflict in Bosnia and Herzegovina. Finally, a closer look is taken at the sparse institutional infrastructure supporting low levels of regional integration in the South Caucasus and its impact on the four conflicts in the region, in addition to the Turkey-Armenia political tensions.

The comparison between the Balkans and the South Caucasus is particularly instructive. In part because of its geographical proximity to the European Union, as well as its accession promises from the EU, the Balkans has turned into a virtual laboratory of regional integration in a politically divided region. A variety of institutional forms and types of networks are currently being deployed by both the EU and other initiators. In sharp contrast, the South Caucasus is an institutional desert in terms of regional engagement. The channels of communication between Azerbaijan and Armenia are sparse and rudimentary. There are some civil society contacts between Georgians and Abkhaz and Georgians and Ossets, but the scale of such initiatives is insignificant for generating any political pressure on governments to engage in conflict management.

Application of the network model indicates that Northern Ireland has adopted the sophisticated machinery of regional integration, which many analysts highlight as a key driver for the successful resolution of the conflict. The Balkan region also stands out with its emerging and highly institutional regional arrangements. The current peace, though not fully consolidated and by some accounts still contending with a "frozen conflict" (Perry 2009), does not threaten to break down. But this is hardly true in the South Caucasus, where the latest conflict was as recent as 2008 between Georgia and Russia, and the relationships between Azerbaijan and Armenia remain strained and vulnerable to accidental war (International Crisis Group 2011). By probing the relationship between the nature of regional arrangements present in a given PDA and the patterns of peace and stability, the empirical chapters of this book explore specific and varied network attributes that create diverse limits and political opportunity structures for conflict management and peace building. Ultimately, building on the theoretical foundations of the regional networked peace paradigm developed here, this study champions region building through strategic network cultivation as a conflict management and peace-building pathway, as opposed to relying on state building and state-centric approaches to find solutions to increasingly complex conflicts in a highly globalized world.

Organization of This Book

Chapter 1 is an overview of the literature on regionalism. It reviews the existing definitions of regionalism and regionalization from the dominant theoretical traditions in international relations. Building on the fieldwork conducted for this study, it then delineates a set of characteristics of regionalism in politically divided areas, with an emphasis on the Balkans and the South Caucasus, and defines regionalism in politically divided areas. Here the chapter identifies some of the key debates within the regionalism literature and contextualizes and applies them to the politically divided areas. The key debates examined in this chapter include: territoriality versus functionalism as regional markers; the importance of state versus nonstate actors in region formation; conflict or cooperation as a regional marker; and the issue of autonomy of regions from great power politics.

Chapter 2 examines the network-based dimensions of regionalism in politically divided areas. It discusses the theoretical rationale for the application of network approaches to regional studies. In this chapter, networks are defined and their constituent components are identified, including governments, nongovernmental organizations, and local and international organizations and donors, as well as business actors. Building on the fieldwork conducted, this chapter delineates four network attributes supporting regionalism that are dominant in politically divided areas. It is these specific network features and types of ties that are later assessed in terms of the limits and opportunities they create for peace and its consolidation in PDAs.

Chapter 3 builds on the network-based typology of regional arrangements developed in the previous chapter. It explores the second research question in the study—namely, whether the institutional infrastructure of regional integration can condition the prospects and effectiveness of conflict management and peace building on the ground. This chapter starts out by building on the existing contemporary literature in conflict management. It juxtaposes the traditional state-centric and country-based concepts of interventions with regional peace-building approaches. The chapter provides a brief review of existing proposals on reforming the global conflict management infrastructure. It presents peace building as a region-building approach, based on the networked regional peace paradigm developed in this study. While Chapter 2 clarified and defined the key network attributes that matter for effective conflict management and peace building in PDAs, Chapter 3 clarifies what are considered to be "successful outcomes." Departing from peace and conflict studies, it rejects the notion that reconciliation is the ultimate goal for interventions. Instead, at the regional level cultivating institutionalized peace systems for addressing current and future conflicts is considered the ultimate goal for interventions. This chapter examines how networks with particular attributes contribute to particular peace patterns—that is, whether a cold or a warm peace is created and whether institutionalized peace systems at a regional level are cultivated.

Chapter 4 presents the case of Northern Ireland within the regional framework of the EU as the institutionally most evolved case of regional integration. This chapter also covers isolated cases of regional networks that span regional approaches to conflict management around the world. Chapters 5 and 6 examine the cases of the Balkans and the South Caucasus, respectively. And Chapter 7 discusses the theoretical and policy implications generated by this study. The conclusion highlights areas of future research on regional approaches to conflict management.

1   Regional Theory for Conflict Areas

Sarajevo is a confusing place. Nearly twenty years after the war ended, the physical traces of war are still visible everywhere, side by side with the new, glitzy shopping malls. In fact, as I made my way to a state-of-the-art fitness club, I became accustomed to the traces of bullet holes on the sidewalks and buildings. The newly built memorials to the war victims create public spaces of reflection and melancholy, right across from cafes, fountains, and shopping centers. Actually, this scene is quite indicative of the many contradictions that characterize postwar societies engulfed by the rapid spread of the global forces of commerce and trade. The question remains, though, about whether the new forces of commerce can weave a blanket thick enough to cover up, contain, or, dare I say it, heal the deep wounds of war and violence in such multiethnic and politically polarized societies.

The state and extent of regional integration in southeastern Europe, and in Bosnia and Herzegovina in particular, stand out with similar contradictions that escape traditional theorizing from the top down or the ground up. The presence of the great powers is visible in Bosnia and Herzegovina but is not omnipresent by any means. Although European structures have made great strides in blanketing the region with integrative networks, it is crisscrossed as well with transnational criminal networks, thereby corroding the very structures of the administrative state the European Union is seeking to build. The country is seeking to enter the European Union, which would dramatically reduce the political and economic significance of its borders, but the secessionist moods, continually fueled by the ethnonationalist political parties in Republika Srpska, are still prevalent. As one governmental official put it, there is still an ongoing fight between the rational forces of integration and business, on the one hand, and the retrograde groups of ethnic nationalism, on the other (Kapetanovich interview 2012)

Against this backdrop, this chapter begins with a brief overview of the main theoretical pathways in defining "region" and "regionalism." Understanding the conceptual map of this research and clarifying definitional issues are important here because this study bridges interdisciplinary divides between international political economy and conflict resolution/peace and conflict studies.

This chapter also delineates the key debates within regional studies, tailoring them to the specific context of politically divided areas (PDAs), and it underscores the limits of the existing regional theories as they apply to these areas. The specific debates in regional studies examined here are the importance of territoriality versus functional ties in defining regions; the importance of state versus nonstate actors in region formation processes; the role of conflict or cooperation as a regional marker; and the issue of regional autonomy relative to great power influence over a region and its member states. Any effort to address the main debates within regional studies makes possible their translation into the field of conflict management. One of the main purposes of the next section, then, is to expose students of conflict management and peace and conflict studies to some of the existing fault lines in the regionalism literature within international political economy.

Political Economy of Regional Integration

The significance of regional studies, and the regional level of analysis, ebbed and flowed in the twentieth century. Although regionalism experienced a revival in the 1970s, analysts argue that it did not get much traction because researchers were unable to transcend the definitional issues. Kelly (2007) argues that the definitional wrangling slowed down the process of consolidating the subfield and building a coherent research program. In addition, the Cold War was blanketing the world, leaving little room, if any, for state independence and region formation. Today, regional studies are experiencing a revival, largely because of globalizing economies and the revolutions in communication technologies that are connecting people and communities in qualitatively new ways. However, getting into the definitional debate is not the purpose here. And yet understanding the key fault lines in the definitional debates is important for the purposes of this study: the ultimate goal of this research is to contribute to public policy in conflict areas, and understanding how regions are defined is important when developing a policy framework for conflict management. It is also essential for facilitating interdisciplinary dialogue between studies in international political economy and those on conflict management and peace and conflict.

Perhaps the biggest definitional challenge in regional studies has been identifying the variables of most use in defining regions, and geographic proximity has been one of the most contested ones. Are regions defined by their geography and the territorial proximity of the states to one another, or are they shaped in terms of functionality, be it shared security or environmental concerns?

Back in the 1970s, Thompson (1973) tried to produce an inventory of the most common characteristics of regions as highlighted by various analysts at the time. He constructed an index that he then applied to the literature on regionalism with the goal of listing the most commonly cited features of regions. The aggregate list is rather long, indicating that there was little consensus among the scholars on the definitional attributes of regions. Of the twenty-one characteristics most commonly cited by researchers, the top five were (1) proximity or primary stress on a geographic region; (2) regular and intensive patterns of interactions; (3) interrelatedness, indicating that a change at one point in the regional system would affect other points; (4) internal recognition as a distinctive area; and (5) external recognition as a distinctive area.

All of these factors revolve around either geography or functional ties as a major regional marker. The emphasis on geographic proximity as a regional marker elevates geopolitical interests and great power politics as important variables in regional studies. Territory and geographic location as fixed factors reduce the bargaining potential between the states in PDAs. Theoretical approaches that define regions as geographic constructs tend to reflect the neorealist position on interstate relations, which emphasizes the role of the great powers in shaping regional dynamics. By contrast, the importance of functional ties and the intensity of interactions between states are better explained through neoliberalism, which focuses on factors such as interpersonal, interorganizational, intersocietal, and interstate contact. The bargaining power of each state is not fixed, and when viewed through such functional lenses, the opportunities offered by regionalism for conflict management processes are varied. The fourth and fifth variables—the internal and external recognition of the region—indicate the importance of region building as a social construction project. Constructivism as a theoretical tool is valuable in this context, which in regional studies is represented by the critical theorists who call for region building as a normative initiative (Hettne 1999, 2000; Hentz and Bøås 2003; Pugh and Sdhu 2003; Farrell, Hettne, and Langenhove 2005).

In politically divided areas, the salience of each of the regional characteristics and markets as discussed by Thompson (1973) tends to be different from the regional dynamics in settings with no major political tensions and protracted conflicts. In particular, in PDAs the social construction of a region is very limited because the conflicts in such regions are often fueled by or facilitated by nation-building initiatives. As a result, the regional identity is of marginal value. This marginality is often reflected in the small number of civil society groups with a focus on regional initiatives. Moreover, identity politics matters as a force that hinders enhanced cooperation around economic issues. Constructivism as a theoretical tool can help to explain how social fragmentation and nation building develop and flourish in parallel with the integrative forces of commerce and trade. Indeed, in terms of regional identity, politically divided areas are understandably less integrated after a conflict than before. The social fabric of the geographic region is torn apart, and the nation-building processes associated with the conflict make it almost impossible for the societies to envision a broader and more comprehensive identity for their nation as well as the region. For example, currently there is much deliberation about whether the countries in the Balkans should be considered part of the Balkan region or part of southeastern Europe (Bechev 2011; Tamminen 2004). The war has stigmatized the Balkan region, and with European integration on the table, the economic and political needs of regional integration in the Balkans are still recognized unevenly across the society.

Although in terms of identity geographic regions in politically divided areas are poorly integrated, if at all, the real material interests and stakeholders for enhanced regional cooperation are quite solid. Indeed, the economic interactions can have a more pronounced regional dimension. In this context, the functional approach to defining a region in politically divided areas can be useful, whether for the study of international organizations involved in such areas for security management and economic development, or for the use of business sector stakeholders reaching out to counterparts across the border.

The fieldwork and prior research conducted for this study indicate that in PDAs the functional ties are easier to develop among neighboring states that have relatively evolved administrative structures and governance practices. Issue-based cooperation across conflict lines is largely subject to both the political will of the conflict parties and the strength of the administrative structures in the respective governments (Ohanyan 2007). Therefore, in PDAs the limits of functional cooperation as a regional marker should be acknowledged, and the power of territorial proximity as both a source of conflict and cooperation recognized.

In theoretical terms, in politically divided areas in the developing world the issue is not whether territory or functional interaction is the key regional marker. Instead, it is how territory and functionalism *interact* that matters in forming regions. In the aftermath of war, often the conflicting parties find themselves in a similar situation of physical destruction and weakened institutions of governance. War legacies engulf all states in the region. Therefore, territory and geography tend to remain an important marker of regions in PDAs. Geography matters in such areas as a source of conflict and a factor in insecurity. Territory is also often a factor in the solution in peace-building efforts. As I argue later in this chapter, international organizations with specialized agencies for peace building and governance often develop aid packages for whole regions as opposed to countries. The country offices of these organizations regularly share best practices and coordinate their programmatic efforts. At least externally, geography and territory emerge as important regional markers for international organizations and multilateral aid agencies.

The key characteristic of regions in politically divided areas is the cohabitation of integrative and fragmenting forces. The lack of a shared identity in PDAs and intense nation-building processes often emerge in the presence of the more subtle integrative forces from the economic sector. The theoretical tools need to reflect this duality.

Two working definitions of *regionalism* are proposed in this study, specifically developed for PDAs. Under the first definition, a region in a PDA is a system of geographically proximate states with deep security and economic interdependencies, but one that may not broadly be seen as a region from the respective populations in the member countries yet receives strong recognition as a region by outside actors. Such regions also possess a layer of international institutions engaged in state-building and region-building projects of various sorts. Such regions are characterized by a weak cross-border interface and yet are open to international actors for state-building purposes or are vulnerable to external power penetration. Often, having weak governance/administrative structures and poorly consolidated democratic institutions, states in a politically divided region have functional ties that are embryonic and uneven. Cooperation in "practical" and nonsecurity areas is more pronounced than ties related to the security environment (Andreev 2009). In short, the economic and political interdependencies realized at least by one state in the region, or an external power, are an important steppingstone toward greater regional integration.

This observation leads to a second definition of *regionalism* that is more normative. Regional cooperation "does not spring magically out of the existence of common interests even if there is compatibility between each country's perceptions of its interests as well as its neighbors" (Trimçev 2009, 32). Instead, the economic and political interdependencies among the states and societies become an important ingredient of effective regional collective action, either domestically nurtured or externally imported. From a normative perspective, such regions are the sites of the centrifugal forces of nation building and the centripetal forces of economic globalization. The dynamic interplay between the stakeholders supporting these forces provides a key opportunity for peace building as region building. *The critical perspective sees regions as dynamic constructs, effectively cultivated by internal or external action with the specific objective of enhanced security and peace in the region. Regionalism in this framework becomes a policy initiative rather than just an analytical concept.*

Within the critical framework of regional studies, regionalism becomes an important normative tool with a strong policy focus that is particularly relevant for PDAs. Regionalism is understood as a tool (1) to establish a regional order to mitigate local instabilities and conflicts (Pugh and Sdhu 2003) and (2) to prevent the possibility of new penetration into the region in the post–Cold War period (Falk 1999). Kelly (2007, 213), in defining regionalism, cites Fawcett (2004): "Regionalism is a policy and project whereby states and nonstate actors cooperate and coordinate strategy . . . to create an interlocking web of regional governance structures such as those already found in Europe." Others define regionalism as a tool of institutional cooperation (Swanström 2002), whether in the form of preferential trade agreements or in the form of other types of institutional integration (Soesastro 1994). Another definition highlights the changed political context in the post–Cold War period and the political nature of multifaceted regionalism (Hettne and Inotai 1994). In this context, regionalism is treated as a structure for cooperation that is cultivated by internal or external actors. Regionalism is understood to be institutionalized cooperation among states within a given region (Acharya and Johnston 2008; Swanström 2002). In all of these perspectives, regionalism is a process strategically cultivated by political actors.

This is in contrast to *regionalization*, which usually refers to the "largely uncoordinated consequence of private sector–led economic integration" (Beeson 2003, 253). Regionalization is characteristic of the uncontrolled and unmediated efforts led by the private sector and civil society to achieve greater regional integration. In PDAs, where intergovernmental links are weak or nonexistent, such regionalization efforts are likely to produce regional spaces that are even more fragmented than in regions without major conflict fault lines. This is not to underestimate the political and economic significance of regionalization, which in essence is built around the real and realized material interests of organized stakeholders. Instead, it is simply to highlight that on its own, without the support of state and state-centric international institutions, regionalization will remain limited in its added value.

Critical theories on regionalism assume that (1) regions are dynamic; (2) they can evolve along a continuum from less to more integration; and (3) such regional cooperation should be fostered in order to address conflicts and instabilities in PDAs. Considering the scholarship produced by critical theories, the second working definition of regionalism developed in this study treats it as a political project with the concrete policy aim of mitigating and addressing conflicts that are frozen or postwar societies that are still engulfed in war legacies and interstate and intrastate societal divisions.

Both definitions introduced here are intimately intertwined. Although the second definition highlights region building as a peace-building approach, to be elaborated later in this book, the first one underscores the importance of existing material interdependencies between the states and societies, patterns of enmity and comity, and flows of threats and friendship (Kelly 2007). The objective basis of interaction is crucial, and latent interests and passive stakeholders are characteristic of regional dynamics in PDAs.

As I argue in this study, *regionalization* is quite variable, and in PDAs it is likely to be quite low. However, *regionalism* is of crucial importance in supporting nascent efforts at regionalization. The comparative regional studies indicate the variance in regional arrangements around the world, and the levels of institutionalization are a key variable in this regard. Similar to domestic processes of institution building for the purposes of enhanced governance, the states in PDAs need to develop a regional strategy, which I argue they should view as the external dimension of internal state-building efforts.

Key Debates within the Regionalism Literature

This section reviews the literature on regionalism in terms of its relevance to politically divided conflict areas, such as the Balkans and the South Caucasus. The starting point in building a literature on regional studies focused on PDAs is the fact that, contrary to the assertions of the promoters of commercial pacifism, rapidly globalizing forces and the spread of commerce around the world have failed to pacify hot spots and suppress conflicts. Conflicts in the twenty-first century manifest themselves in a dramatically different context: intrastate and interstate conflicts in the contemporary world are unfolding against the steady spread and mobility of capital and production across boundaries and against a denser network of international organizations and greater global awareness of world affairs. Therefore, globalization presents new opportunities as well as challenges for managing contemporary conflicts. Regional integration as an analytical as well as policy framework (ibid.) offers a range of opportunities for conflict management, while regions as territorially fixed geopolitical constructs continue to remain potential sources of instability and insecurity in the developing world.

The four main issues that divide contemporary regional theorists are pertinent for regional studies in the context of politically divided areas. They are (1) the importance of territoriality versus the relational basis of region formation; (2) the importance of state versus nonstate actors; (3) whether a given region is defined by conflict or cooperation; and (4) whether regions are autonomous actors or spaces of great power projection. These issues are described in the sections that follow.

Territoriality versus Functionalism

The current research on regional integration differs as to whether territory is a constitutive element in understanding and conceptualizing regions. In a relatively recent study, Buzan and Wæver (Buzan and Wæver 2003) make a special point of highlighting the importance of geographical proximity as a regional marker. In doing so, they argue against the study conducted by Lake and Morgan (1997), pointing out that regional proximity is an important indicator for delineating the regional level of analysis from a global one. In contrast to territorial approaches to regional analysis, relational approaches tend to be issue-focused: regional boundaries are defined in accordance with the issue under consideration, ranging from environmental degradation to transnational criminal networks. Kelly (2007) argues that the search for definitions of regions that could encompass all factors of security, economics, identity, and integration was characteristic of the first regionalism wave, and he draws from Nye (1968) and Cantori and Spiegel (1973) in this analysis. By contrast, according to Kelly (2007) contemporary regional studies have withdrawn from this effort to find all-inclusive regional definitions and are moving closer to functionalist analysis (Alagappa 1995, 364; Väyrynen 2003).

Transcending cartography and geographical proximity in favor of shared characteristics according to a functional need is descriptive of new regionalist theories. Kelly (2007) maintains that in the contemporary scholarship regionalism has moved away from the territoriality as a regional marker. Instead, the theoretical frameworks of the so-called new regionalism are more multidimensional, calling for regional definition along various issue areas (ibid.). Regions are now seen as flexible structures that are highly dependent on social practices and interlocking social networks of collaboration and interaction, conflict and contestation (Solioz and Stubbs 2009).

As I argue in this study, territory matters for region formation. The governments of weaker, less industrialized states are often unable or unwilling to extend their administrative capacities beyond the major cities and the capital. As a result, the rural border areas remain peripheral to the center. Eastern Turkey and the western provinces of Armenia are quite underdeveloped, and the regressive border management on both sides, combined with political problems, prevents the citizens of eastern Turkey from taking advantage, for example, of the hospitals in Yerevan, Armenia, which is the nearest metropolis for them. In addition, the local levels of government are also poorly developed in administratively weak states, which is yet another factor in favor of territoriality as a persistent dimension of regionalism. In the developing world, pure functionalist approaches to regional integration, premised on the assumption of spillover cooperation from one issue to the next, are hard to apply, primarily because of the weak administrative structures and the paucity of efficient bureaucracies in such regions (Acharya and Johnston 2008). These factors elevate the importance of a territory as a factor that negatively affects the prospects of greater regional integration.

The cultivation of transnational networks by international organizations has offset the shortages in administrative power of the weaker states (Jayasuriya 2008; Söderbaum 2004; Reinicke et al. 2000). In most cases, such network cultivation has a clear territorial pattern of formation, particularly if it is driven from the top down by international and supranational institutions, such as the United Nations or the European Union (Ohanyan 2008). When seeking to offset or complement the administrative capacities of the state, developing countries tend to be grouped together by international organizations according to their geographical location. In a way, these organizations, in providing such assistance in administrative governance, tend to follow the logic of economies of scale. With some adjustments to each country, international donor organizations working in the developing world tend to develop "regional strategies," which, again, are reproducing the territorial patterns of region formation and reflecting strong external region recognition.

State versus Nonstate Actors

The political significance of state and nonstate actors in region formation was another dividing line within the emergent studies of new regionalism. In contrast to the previous studies, new regionalism offered a more comprehensive and multifaceted analysis of regionalism, underscoring both state and nonstate actors, in addition to the political, economic, and environmental forces within a region, to name a few (Mittelman 2000; Acharya and Johnston 2008). The studies in regionalism back in 1970s were much more focused on interstate relations, and the agreements and treaties signed between governments were the key indicators of region formation. Governments were conceptualized as very much in the driver's seat in advancing regional integration, if any. In this context, formal institutions were emphasized at the expense of informal ones, and the politics unfolding between nonstate actors and the business sector were considered rather marginal to regional studies.

The emphasis on state actors was also reflective of the analytical tendency at the time to assert "system-dominance" over regions as subsystems (Katzenstein 2005): regions were viewed as spaces where great power relationships were playing out, leaving little room for autonomous regional behavior. Such analyses were biased toward the state, without much analytical space left for nonstate actors. In the current discourse as well, the distinction between state and nonstate actors is still pervasive. That debate tends to unfold across the familiar neorealist/neoliberal fault lines. Realist approaches to regional studies emphasize security as an organizing force of regions, and statehood is considered the key player in security management. Alternative explanations consider the functional integration of regions, which expands the scope of analysis from political security to human security, thereby opening up the debate to issue areas beyond "hard power" to include the human dimension of security as well as nonstate actors. Analysts who underscore the importance of state also assert that state strength is a variable in understanding "regionness." Weaker states, the argument goes, are more susceptible to overlay and penetration by great powers (Buzan and Wæver 2003); stronger states with greater infrastructural power demonstrate greater independence of regional policy (Taylor 2005). Indeed, the issue of "stateness" in understanding regional integration is related to the one on regional autonomy—that is, whether a region possesses political autonomy relative to great powers (discussed later in this chapter).

The issue of state strength in regional politics challenges the neat dichotomy of the state versus nonstate actor debate, around which neorealism and neoliberalism are centered. Some respondents from the South Caucasus pointed to the great power influence in the South Caucasus as one of the factors preventing greater regional cooperation (Gegeshidze interview 2012). Yet the case of the Balkans, also a politically divided region with relatively more settled great power dynamics and heavy European support for regional integration, represents a challenge of the notion of great power influence as a factor preventing regional integration. Instead, it appears that weak administrative resources and low infrastructural power are equally, if not more, consequential in shaping levels of regional cooperation.

Indeed, even if there is no overlay or the great power interest in a given region has been diminished, it is premature to expect revitalized regional cooperation efforts in PDAs in the developing world, as the Balkan case illustrates. Forging regional links and relationships, even if such relationships are in the interests of a given state, often requires strategic political calculation by intermediary actors because perceived shared interests do not produce enhanced cooperation on their own (Trimçev 2009). The Balkan case is again instructive in illustrating the role of international intermediaries. Although European integration has been a common political project for all member countries in the region, and the business sectors in all countries have tangible interests in regional integration in the Balkans, often it is the international organizations and other institutional intermediaries that "activate" the interests among the stakeholders by giving them a voice within the national as well as European political process (Minić interview 2012).

Another argument about the centrality of state versus nonstate actors is an organizational one. Hwang (2006) maintains that devolution of authority within a state has already occurred, while the state as an organization has expanded dramatically. Public agencies have been disembedded from the state, as their links and contacts with professional epistemic communities around the world have expanded, the argument goes. This phenomenon is particularly pronounced at the regional level in both the industrialized and developing worlds. In the latter, the international community is represented by a dense network of organizations that often advance their regional strategies in foreign aid disbursement. Related to this, a qualitatively new organizational develop-ment—"regulatory regionalism" (Jayasuriya 2008)—has been contributing to this process of disembedding public agencies. Regulatory regionalism is a process in which "domestic regulatory agencies develop connections with their foreign counterparts as well as with transnational regulatory bodies, thereby taking on a 'global' function" (ibid.). Such regulatory regionalism also chal-lenges the simple dichotomy of state versus nonstate actors, calling for mul-tifaceted understanding of governance, particularly in the politically divided developing world.

Finally, whether or not the state is central to regional politics is treated dif-ferently by old and new regionalism. In contrast to old regionalism, new re-gionalism, being multidimensional, treats regions as more than political se-curity systems; it also highlights their economic and social dimensions (Kelly 2007; Fawcett 1995; Farrell 2005). Such an expanded view allows for a multi-plicity of actors consequential for regional politics, ranging from NGOs and business associations to government agencies. It is the interstate, intersocietal shared interests that emerge as a driving force of greater regional cooperation (Weichert 2009). However, although such state and nonstate actors are thought to be important to new regionalism, the importance of the domestic context in activating such shared interests is not always considered in this scholarship.

Conflict or Cooperation as a Regional Marker

Regions, then, are defined around a variety of factors, most of which are quite complementary and overlapping. Some of these factors are constant, such as geography and cultural affinity; others are variable, such as levels of economic development, degree of interdependence, and level of democratiza-tion (Morgan 1997). One of the broadest delineations of regional borders is on the conflict-cooperation continuum: regions can be defined either as security complexes (Buzan and Wæver 2003; Morgan 1997) or as regional orders/se-curity regimes (Morgan 1997). Conflict and cooperation are the respective re-gional markers. Kelly notes that instead of downscaling international relations theories to the regional level, new theories of regional order and integration in response to the realities of violence and dislocation in the "postoverlay Third World" need to be introduced (Kelly 2007). At most, the developing countries are poorly consolidated democracies, which makes conflict and instability a part of daily life (Mansfield and Snyder 1995), but that does not preclude all the prospects of regional cooperation (Minić interview 2012). Therefore, regional theories developed for the postoverlay Third World need to explain the ways in which conflict and cooperation interact in forming and consolidating regions in the developing world.

Whether states see their regional neighborhoods in cooperative or conflictual terms is largely a function of their domestic politics, including political institutions, political culture, strength of civil society, freedoms in the economic sphere, to name a few. Two factors pertaining to domestic politics are consequential here. The first is the extent of state weakness and state strength (Ayoob 1992, 1999), which was discussed earlier in this chapter. This factor is often defined as the infrastructural power of a given state, with a focus on the strength of the institutions of governance. The World Bank, for example, identifies the following key governance measures: (1) voice and accountability; (2) political stability; (3) government effectiveness; (4) regulatory quality; (5) rule of law; and (6) control of corruption.[1]

The second factor has to do with whether a state is modern (Westphalian) or postmodern (post-Westphalian) (Buzan and Wæver 2003). The political treatment of its own sovereignty is the crucial characteristic of this dichotomy. For Westphalian states, the norms, values, and incentives of strengthening their state through transnationalism and ceding sovereignty to supranational institutions are still an unrealistic prospect. For post-Westphalian states, which constitute the industrialized democracies, transnational sovereignty bargains are the norm. According to Buzan and Wæver (2004), Westphalian (modern) states tend to produce more turbulent regional orders and post-Westphalian (postmodern) states more peaceful regional orders. Modern states are characterized by

> strong governmental control over society and restrictive attitudes towards openness. They see themselves as independent and self-reliant entities, having distinctive national cultures and development policies. . . . [T]heir borders mark real lines of closure against outside economic, political, and cultural influences, and their sovereignty is sacrosanct. (Ibid., 22–23)

The authors point to China, North and South Korea, Iran, India, Burma, Iraq, Saudi Arabia, Turkey, and Brazil as contemporary examples of modern states. Postmodern, industrialized democratic states have a more open attitude toward cultural, economic, and political interaction, and firmly believe that opening their economies, societies, and polities to a wide range of interactions

TABLE 1.1. Types of States in Terms of Governance Effectiveness, Westphalian and Post-Westphalian

	Westphalian	Post-Westphalian
Strong	India, China, Brazil, South Africa, Turkey, Georgia, Armenia	Industrialized democracies
Weak	Russia, Kazakhstan, Pakistan, Azerbaijan	Bosnia and Herzegovina, Albania, Romania

Source: Kaufmann, D., A. Kraay, and M. Mastruzzi. 2010. *The Worldwide Governance Indicators: Methodology and Analytical Issues.* Policy Research Working Paper no. 5430 (Washington, DC: World Bank Development Research Group)

TABLE 1.2. Types of States in Terms of Control of Corruption, Westphalian and Post-Westphalian

	Westphalian	Post-Westphalian
Strong	Brazil, South Africa, Turkey, Georgia,	Industrialized democracies, Bosnia and Herzegovina, Romania
Weak	Russia, Kazakhstan, China, Pakistan, Azerbaijan, Armenia, India	Albania

Source: See Table 1.1.

TABLE 1.3. Types of States in Terms of Rule of Law, Westphalian and Post-Westphalian

	Westphalian	Post-Westphalian
Strong	Brazil, South Africa, Turkey, Georgia, India	Industrialized democracies, Romania
Weak	Russia, Kazakhstan, China, Pakistan, Azerbaijan, Armenia	Albania, Bosnia and Herzegovina

Source: See Table 1.1.

is good for the economic prosperity and the physical security of their states (Buzan and Wæver 2003).

There is certain variation between the two factors: stronger states over time become post-Westphalian, and weaker states are usually Westphalian. However, not all administratively strong states are post-Westphalian. There are three institutional and political categories of such states, with the fourth one—weak post-Westphalian states—currently emerging as a significant category in the developing world (see Table 1.1 for the institutional possibilities). The three governance indicators selected from the World Bank database and reported in Tables 1.1–1.3 are the most indicative of governmental capacities for greater regional cooperation and regionalization. Not reported here are voice and accountability, internal political stability, and regulatory quality. Countries with high government effectiveness are in the 50th to 100th percentile, and the ones with low government effectiveness are between 0 and the 50th percentile (Kaufmann, Kraay, and Mastruzzi 2010).

States with weak governance but a post-Westphalian posture can be found in conflict regions with a dense international institutional presence. The degree of density of international organizations in a country is indicative of a strong international regulatory environment, combined with the norms of openness and cooperation that such an environment tends to transmit. The European Union has been advancing outward into its immediate neighborhood by blanketing such regions with deep regulatory mechanisms, while pushing for greater regional cooperation (anonymous interview with a senior EU delegation official in Bosnia and Herzegovina 2012; anonymous interview with a senior EU delegation official in Armenia 2012). In such politically divided areas, there seems to be an institutional jump, as represented in all three tables by the lower-right quadrant. The states in conflict in such areas tend to have weak administrative capacities of governance, and they are largely modern Westphalian states looking inward and guarding their political sovereignty. At the same time, these states are usually hosts of dense networks of international organizations, bilateral and multilateral agencies, and transnational NGOs, which are carriers of post-Westphalian values, championing open borders and greater interaction among states, societies, and individuals.

As the empirical cases will reveal, these international actors are assisting such states in the region with administrative support and technical assistance, and the governance practices and values they transfer into these states are post-Westphalian and postmodern. In short, states in politically divided conflict areas are more open to the transfer of international governance processes. As a result, they often experience a level of institutional jump—that is, having to embrace post-Westphalian values in governance without necessarily going through the required political transformations domestically. As a result, a certain degree of fragmentation is evident in administrative practices and value orientations among the government officials. To put it differently, modern states in PDAs are taken under the postmodern umbrella, with varying degrees of success from region to region. The inherently weak Westphalian states are treated with deeply postmodern, post-Westphalian policy tools as introduced by the international community.

Indeed, the international community seeks to transform the regional conflict dynamics into cooperative ones, although the bulk of their conflict management instruments remain focused at the national level. None of the representatives of international organizations interviewed for this study put forth a regional approach to conflict management processes. Indeed, analysts note that the conflict management capacities of the international community are in flux, and, although the links between local, national, and global security challenges are recognized (Crocker 2011a, b), no major reform or revision of global conflict management processes around those links has been carried out. As a result, the transformation of conflict regions from security complexes to regional order (Morgan 1997) by the international community remains a politically limited initiative because the national governments in politically divided regions continue to see their neighborhoods in threatening terms as opposed to registering the opportunities that greater regional integration can bring.

Autonomy of Regions

Assuming that a region exhibits some level of autonomy, the extent of it has been one of the major debates driving comparative regional studies. Neorealist analysis has put forth a rather skeptical assessment of the extent of regional autonomy, arguing that tensions and competition between great powers will replicate in various regions that will likely become platforms for U.S. primacy (Kelly 2007; Katzenstein, Keohane, and Krasner 1998), and this constitutes the bulk of the neorealist critique. Neorealists maintain that the regional level of analysis adds little value to the contemporary studies of international relations because regional politics is just another arena in which the great power interests are projected and play out.

Alternative perspectives have pointed out that the decline in superpower rivalry reduced the penetration of great power interests into the rest of the world (Katzenstein, Keohane, and Krasner 1998; Beeson 2003). The end of the Cold War opened up a new space of political action at the regional level, where the great power influences are not projected as deeply and extensively as during the Cold War. Moreover, some even maintain that the regions evolved into political entities much earlier, after the decolonization processes (Katzenstein, Keohane, and Krasner 1998; Buzan and Wæver 2003). Within such frameworks, regionalism and regionalization are viewed as associated with state-building processes and national self-determination struggles in the aftermath of World War II.

In the contemporary context of greater economic, political, and social globalization, the great powers are dealing with a developing world that is now more mobilized (Kelly 2007), which increases the costs of interventions for superpowers and makes the intervention politically unpalatable domestically and internationally (Falk 1999; Fawcett 2003; Väyrynen 1984)—and which, some argue, is a measure of the autonomy of the regional level of analysis, at least within the security area (Buzan and Wæver 2003; Morgan 1997). Even if great powers intervene, evidence suggests that local actors use external powers to advance their own goals relative to those of their opponents (Kelly 2007; Acharya and Johnston 2008; Hemmer and Katzenstein 2002; Lemke 2002). Others go even further and point out instances of "reactionary regionalism," as arguably observed in East Asia. Beeson (2003) claims that in reaction to the U.S. intervention in East Asia, the region has been characterized by a form of reactionary regionalism in which "regional initiatives have frequently been both a response to external events and designed to mediate and moderate their impact" (252).

The literature on policy diffusion also lends support to the autonomy of the regional level of analysis. Some within this literature argue that in their policy-making and reform initiatives states are influenced primarily by geographically proximate states (Berry and Berry 2007), and that each region often possesses a pioneer, which then sets the trend within a given region. Finally, economic regionalism is on the rise,[2] and an increasingly dense economic fabric supporting regionalism will generate a demand for regional-level governance institutions.

Also pertinent to this discussion of regional autonomy are the regions with weak or failed states that have become a persistent source of regional and global instability (Smith and Weiss 1997; Miller 2005; Ayoob 1992, 1999). Weakness and failure make states vulnerable to humanitarian interventions, some of which are driven by the interests of great powers in a region. In a way, one could argue that state weakness is a factor reducing regional autonomy. Weak states are open and porous, and the great powers find them easier to penetrate, so the argument goes (Katzenstein, Keohane, and Krasner 1998). At the same time, such regional instability places pressures on the great powers to intervene, but such interventions are increasingly costly politically and financially. The deterioration of Syria in the wake of the Arab Spring and the resistance of the international community to intervention are illustrative of how great powers do not take advantage of the vulnerability of Syria for penetration or overlay. This is particularly striking when the rise of ISIS is considered: even with this new threat and increasing instability it created in Iraq and Syria, direct forms of intervention from the West, in addition to supplying arms to Kurdish fighters and Iraqi army, have not been forthcoming. In a way, the great powers find regions with weak or failed states characterized by deep security externalities, violence, and institutional deterioration harder to control. The eruption of the civil war in Iraq in the aftermath of the U.S. intervention is a good case of "malignant autonomy" rapidly reducing the agency of the great powers.

Regions with weak or failed states transcend a simple dichotomy of autonomy versus dependence. Instead, the dense organizational presence of the international community or a particular great power in a weak or failed state fails to guarantee them complete control over the domestic politics in a given weak or failed state. As a result, although the multilateral and bilateral agencies may be pushing in one direction—such as the Balkans toward Europe—local actors may be pushing in another direction—such as Republika Srpska toward neighboring Serbia or independence. Even though the Balkans may be advancing free markets and open societies, the local elites may be sticking to the status quo of nepotism and ethnically protected markets, such as in Bosnia and Herzegovina (Kumar and Haye 2012; Jarstad and Belloni 2012). As a result, the state exhibits political autonomy of a destructive kind in one area of society and the economy, and dependence in other areas, such as security and social development.

In understanding the extent and nature of regional autonomy in the politically divided developing world, it is useful to distinguish among the political, economic, institutional-administrative, and social dimensions of the power and autonomy of these states. Realists often conceptualize the dependence of regions on great powers through penetration and overlay, which is further described purely in political-military terms. Opening up the "black box" of states in the developing world reveals that great powers as well as regional ones are connected with developing countries in complex ways that easily transcend the political-security axis.

Finally, the growing research in regional studies calls for greater differentiation among regional powers. Prys (2010) notes that the presence of a materially preponderant power does not always lead to hegemonic behavior on its part. The differentiation among regional powers and their behaviors, in turn, highlights the limits of the argument that a given regional hegemon has direct influence over a given developing country.

Conclusion

The regional dynamics in politically divided areas challenges the dominant regional theories and main debates within the international relations field, illustrating the limits of their downscaling to explain regional politics in PDAs.

Each dominant theoretical tradition has been able to explain one aspect of regional politics. Neorealism effectively affirms the importance of territory and geopolitics in regional dynamics. It also has been useful in understanding the politico-security relationships in PDAs. However, it has been silent in cases in which the great powers have been struggling hard to push a conflict state in a particular direction in a reform process or a negotiating position. Neoliberalism illustrates the importance of domestic politics, highlighting the way non-state actors shape regional dynamics or how the nonmilitary issue areas can generate a push or pull in regional dynamics in a given direction. Constructivism exposes the role of identity politics as an important regional marker, maintaining that regions are "imagined communities." However, even combined, these theoretical traditions fail to produce a complete picture of regional politics, leaving a range of questions unanswered and major aspects of regional politics unexplained.

The most glaring gap in regional studies is the lack of understanding of how integrative and fragmenting forces interact in PDAs and what tips the balance. Neorealism makes the case for great power overlay and penetration, but it says little about how domestic corruption and the weakness of administrative structures can create powerful pressures against hegemonic influence. Although some PDAs may be able to resist great power overlay, they also remain incapable of forging regional ties on their own. There also seems to be a lack of understanding of how regional actors as sources of instability (criminality, environmental degradation, informal trade) interface with national and regional structures of governance. What is the institutional makeup supporting this duality?

As I argue in Chapter 2, the network approach is a framework in which the existing duality of political fragmentation versus economic integration, the co-existing structures of conflict and cooperation, and state versus nonstate actors can be analyzed. Most important, this framework is useful in explaining the politics of layered governance in PDAs—that is, imported governance structures that are outward-oriented with national structures that are inward-oriented. Cases in which countries tie their political lot of security with one power and their economic one with another also can be addressed more effectively through the network approach of regionalism. For effective and even radical changes in the global and regional infrastructure of conflict management, it is necessary to understand these dualities of regional dynamics in PDAs.

2   Ties that Bind ... or Bond? Network Theory of Regionalism in PDAs

When asked about the feasibility of greater regional integration in South Caucasus, an Armenian analyst, reflecting on the lack of political will in South Caucasus for greater regional integration, pointed out that "you can't build regionalism on *khinkali* [a Georgian traditional dish]"—in other words, there are few economic complementarities among Armenia, Azerbaijan, and Georgia. By contrast, a senior European Union official, when asked about the prospects of economic regionalism in South Caucasus, said it is self-evident that each country would benefit from greater regional integration. When asked about the lack of complementarity among the three economies, he brought up the case of the now enlarged European Union. There are lots of tomatoes being sold in Europe, he noted, but that does not mean that Romanian tomatoes are unwelcome. "They are not just tomatoes. They are Romanian tomatoes," this official commented lightheartedly. And then there was the representative of the Regional Cooperation Council (RCC) in the Balkans. When asked about the feasibility of greater regional integration in politically divided conflict regions, she said that "it is not a question of *whether*, it is a question of *how*. Conflict is in the air we are breathing. On a daily basis we are figuring out how to cooperate and manage our relations with one another without having settled our political disputes" (Minić interview 2012).

These conflicting perceptions constitute the current reality of regionalism and regionalization in South Caucasus as well as the Balkans. Indeed, greater regional integration is facing real political challenges. South Caucasus, for example, is completely fragmented from the still frozen conflicts between Armenia and Azerbaijan, Georgia and Abkhazia, Georgia and Ossetia, and Georgia and Russia. These conflicts have elevated the politics of relations between states at the expense of the economic dimension of their engagement. The people there have not been able to benefit from the peace dividend that can come from greater regional integration. In parallel, and despite massive political roadblocks, there have been solid gains toward greater regional integration in both South Caucasus and the Balkans, largely driven by the business sector. In between these two realities are the policy entrepreneurs who see regionalism as a potential pathway toward conflict management and who are actively working to that end, particularly in the Balkans.

These layered realities and the strange coexistence of integrative and fragmenting forces in PDAs require novel and flexible theoretical toolkits to study them. This chapter presents one theoretical possibility, the network theory, as a framework for comprehending the uncultivated Caucasian complexity of interdependence. It is also a framework for understanding and learning from the bourgeoning Balkan regionalism, despite the persistent political division in this region. I argue that the network theory, as a theoretical framework, is superior to the dominant theories in international relations for capturing the dualities and complexities of regional politics in PDAs. Indeed, the oft-cited American hegemonic decline as well as the greater regional empowerment have not resulted in systematic processes of regional governance and concerted efforts at regionalization of conflict management. Power vacuums in regions are filled unevenly. The network theory provides the tools for capturing the multiple pathways of power and authority channeling through various PDAs. Understanding such processes at the lowest level is a key added value of the network approach to regional studies in PDAs.

This chapter begins by discussing the rationale for the network approach to studying regionalism in PDAs. It then calls for a distinction between networks and networked governance at the regional level, identifying the theoretical and policy implications stemming from that delineation. The distinction between networks and networked governance are then taken a step further by posing the question, What institutional attributes of networks matter for conflict management processes and outcomes? Although Chapter 3 tackles that question more systematically, the section here on network attributes builds the case for the theoretical and policy value of those institutional attributes for the theory and practice of regionalism in PDAs. The chapter concludes by applying the network attributes to some of the dominant types of regional forms as presented in the literature. In this respect, the discussion of various regional forms and their respective network compositions connects with the varied perceptions of regionalism so prevalent in PDAs.

Network Approach for the Study of Regionalism in PDAs

Comparative regional studies literature has been explicit in cautioning against simply downscaling dominant theories in International Relations (IR) to explain regional politics. On the one hand, such downscaling has been helpful in capturing particular dimensions of regional politics. For instance, in theoretical terms, neorealism adds great value in explaining some regional and intrastate conflicts. Downscaling neoliberalist IR theories also is valuable because these theories illuminate the role of international organizations in regional politics. However, each of these theoretical strands deals with only one dimension of regional politics, leaving many questions unanswered. Therefore, the instinct to downscale IR theories to explain regional politics is unwarranted. For example, simply by downscaling IR theories it is unclear under what conditions international organizations are more effective in forging cooperation between states. How do states in PDAs challenge the processes of cooperation, even after nominally agreeing to them? How should one go about studying the latent clash between international organizations and domestic players in this area? When are external powers capable of directing regional dynamics in a given PDA? How do domestic and international politics interact in the processes of conflict management, if at all? Perhaps the most important question is, How do multiple pathways and channels of power in a multistakeholder environment interact with one another, and what are the ultimate policy and political outcomes in PDAs?

Network theory is a powerful theoretical alternative for addressing some of these questions and capturing the complexity of regional dynamics in PDAs. In particular, it offers a more flexible theoretical toolkit for use in exploring the ways in which international actors interact with domestic players. Understanding the institutional interface between domestic and external actors helps uncover the effects of institutions in such networked environments on the behavior of all actors in the network, as well as the outcomes generated through such interactions. The Regional Cooperation Council in the Balkans is instructive in this case. As an institutional intermediary, the RCC has developed a range of strategies intended not only to generate the political will for cooperation among otherwise unwilling partners and former foes from the Balkan war but also to translate tentative agreements into solid implementation processes on the ground. The network mode of operation of the RCC has been a key factor in the process of region building in the Balkans (ibid.).

The rationale for the inclusion of network theory in the study of regionalism in PDAs is multifold. First, exploration of the regional level of analysis requires study of the different ways in which regional arrangements can be institutionally structured (Acharya and Johnston 2008). The practitioners and policy-makers promoting regionalism in PDAs such as the Balkans point out that "regions have been more and more shaped as networks of networks," and networks are emerging as the key mode of operation for the new regionalism (Minić 2009, 15). The study of networks as institutional arrangements helps to show how deep into the society of a state a given regional arrangement can reach. It can also reveal the breadth of policy issues it covers. Regional networks can vary from shallow and narrowly focused to broad and deeply integrated into the societies of states in a given region. Understanding the network structure will emerge as a key variable in regional studies, thereby broadening the debate on regional governance (Ohanyan 2008, 2009; Benner, Reinicke, and Witte 2005).

Second, conventional views on regional governance cast regionalism as "ceding of state sovereignty and national decision-making authority to supranational institutions" (Hettne and Soderbaum 2006, 15). The tension between state autonomy and regionalism is characteristic of this line of scholarship. The network approach to regional theories makes possible a more nuanced understanding of the interface between state structures and regional governance. In particular, network theory allows investigators to examine a growing number of cases and issue areas in which regional governance is instantiated within the national state, as opposed to being above it (Jayasuriya 2008). The study of network composition, its density, the direction of links, and network centrality will reveal the ways in which the regional layer of governance becomes incorporated within the political space of the state (ibid.). Indeed, the network approach itself provides the toolkit needed to examine how "the rise of the regional scale is deeply intertwined with the restructuring of the state" (Harrison 2006, 42).

Third, network theory is an effective framework for understanding the processes of transgovernmental network formation and their impact on national-level policy-making (Slaughter 2004). Regional theories can borrow the tools and analytical frameworks of international relations in order to understand how professional transgovernmental networks develop, but their local application is still important. Here the network approach can be helpful in revealing how the domestic political context can shape and be affected by regional network governance that is increasingly embedded in state structures themselves.

Fourth, the network approach to regional studies offers vast policy insights. The study of the network composition of regional arrangements will allow for their more strategic management for enhanced effect in conflict management processes in PDAs. As in global governance, in regional governance issue-based policy networks also connect professional and technical communities that can help to depoliticize the relationships between countries in politically divided areas. In this respect, network management and the development of network governance at the regional level help to capture the potential of strategically cultivating processes of region building. This dimension of regional politics is distinct from the more spontaneous region formation.

Perhaps the most important theoretical potential of the network approach to regionalism is its ability to recognize the emergence of a new institutional space of political action at the regional level, intermediating between the state and global structures. It also uncovers the regionalization of the nation-state by pointing out processes such as "regulatory regionalism" (Jayasuriya 2008) and "transgovernmental networking" (Slaughter 2004). Moreover, some researchers show that states networked across functional lines and issue linkages reflect a growing disjuncture between democratic political authority and political practice—that is, there is a gap between the increasingly institutionalized and politically supported functional linkages between states that may or may not add up to national interests (Goetschel 2000).

Networks and Regional Governance in PDAs

A small strand within the literature on regional studies focuses on the network approach to regional integration. It defines region building as a form of interorganizational networking: "the interplay between different layers of networks, of which some are more and some are less institutionalized, some are more and some are less formal. . . . In this context, 'region' is understood not as a territory, but as a flexible concept of common interests" (Weichert 2009, 5). Indeed, in PDAs, fully institutionalized regional governance structures are quite sparse, although issue-based functional network structures are quite tangible. One example of an issue-based functional network structure is the Disaster Preparedness and Prevention Initiative (DPPI) as developed by the Regional Cooperation Council in Sarajevo. The initiative brings together relevant functional agencies from Albania, Bosnia and Herzegovina, Bulgaria, Croatia, the Former Yugoslav Republic of Macedonia, Moldova, Montenegro, Romania,

Slovenia, Serbia, and Turkey. Developing a regional strategy for disaster preparedness and prevention has been the key goal of DPPI. This network brought together donor countries and national and international NGOs and governmental organizations in its efforts to coordinate ongoing and future activities for improved national disaster management.

Global networks are patterned sets of relationships among actors of various types (Jönsson 1993). In PDAs, they can also be institutional arrangements developed by default or by design, connecting bilateral and multilateral agencies and state and nonstate actors within the PDAs. Often, such networks can be created strategically and in an effort to develop local and transnational partnerships and forge cooperative structures, largely along technical and often nonpolitical issue lines. These networks allow the international actors to advance their global policy goals and to increase their individual impacts on the ground; to secure access to levels of local, regional, and global governance; and to satisfy multiple stakeholders (Ohanyan 2008).

Network governance in PDAs is a form of institutional intermediation between international organizations, on the one hand, and government authorities, on the other. Such networks link government authorities with international structures, thereby creating new spaces for the governments to project power, while at the same time being constrained by the international structures. Although governments remain important actors in the provision of governance, a large number of governance functions are currently exercised through a variety of institutional forms, including networks (Held and Koenig-Archibugi 2005; Duffield 2006). Indeed, some of the problems facing nation-states are global or regional, and states are largely unable to handle them on their own (Crocker, Hampson, and Aall 2011). States have "the capacity to disable decisionmaking and policy implementation by global bodies like the UN, but they generally lack the vision and will to empower and enable global problem solving on issues such as environmental degradation, human trafficking, terrorism, and nuclear weapons" (Thakur and Langenhove 2006, 233).

Another perspective on the relationship between the nation-state and regional governance highlights the continued political importance of the nation-state, although noting its highly conditional nature (Harrison 2006). For the nation-state to maintain political relevance against the rise of the regional scale, its traditional institutional hierarchy must be modified, so the argument goes. "The change at the bottom is no longer expected to come about through change at the top; change at the top is called for to consolidate and develop the achievements at the bottom" (ibid., 422). It appears from the research produced to date that networks, as instruments of governance, are key to the successful modification of the hierarchical state. The research task at this stage becomes (1) to describe and explain the way in which the interface and cooperation between states and regional networks can produce governance; and (2) to identify the institutional and political conditions in various regions that are conducive to a more effective interface between the state and networked governance.

Both the quality and quantity of regional networks are important in discussing the way networks connect to governmental agencies and international organizations. Regional arrangements may be supported by disconnected networks or driven by a more comprehensive networked governance. The distinction between the two types of regional arrangements reveals the degree to which a particular region "hangs together." It also captures the diversity in institutional forms that various networked regional arrangements can take

The network literature makes this distinction (Parker 2007); networks are mere aggregations of social relations and ties, whereas networked governance also has steering and coordinating functions. Networks able to produce governance outcomes have particular structures that allow them to "order action such that the behavior of participants is altered" from their actions as individual players (ibid., 118). Building on the network literature, Parker further specifies that networks must have particular structural features—density, breadth of issues covered, and values of trust, reciprocity, and common identity—in order to produce governance outcomes. Regions supported by networks of lower density and limited scope, with poorly evolved values of trust and reciprocity, fail to produce systemic governance processes. By contrast, cases of regional governance tend to be supported by networks of high density and broad scope, with high levels of trust and reciprocity. Duffield claims that governance does not reside in a single powerful institution with a clear international mandate, bureaucratic competence, and recognized regulatory authority. Instead, as Duffield maintains, it comes from processes of decentralization and burden sharing (Duffield 2001, 44).

Networked governance at the regional level is an important institutional development in world politics. Multilateralism is often behind such networked governance. Larger states and great powers see multilateralism as a policy tool and an effective instrument for forging global cooperation, particularly because the developing world is highly sensitive to hegemonic initiatives stemming from their former colonizers. For smaller states in the developing world, multilateralism is a tool for avoiding exclusion and uneven bilateralism (Vucetic 2001), thereby elevating their voices at the regional and global levels. Network formation at the regional level reflects regionalism as a project "whereby states and nonstate actors cooperate and coordinate strategy ... [in order] to create an interlocking web of regional governance structures such as those already found in Europe" (Fawcett 2004, 24). Network governance, usually associated with global levels of governance, has emerged as a distinct pattern of authority.

Börzel notes that, particularly in the context of the European Union and its relationships with the rest of the world, regionalism has evolved beyond its use as a mere instrument of promoting free trade under the World Trade Organization. Instead, the EU as well as the other great players are increasingly regarding regionalism as a new building block of a world order (Börzel and Risse 2009; Katzenstein, Keohane, and Krasner 1998). Whereas the United States tends to pursue the more limited trade- and investment-focused "hub-and-spoke" models of uneven regionalism, the EU favors regionalism as a set of political, socioeconomic reforms and a bundle of region-building institutions and integrative schemes (Grugel 2004; Börzel and Risse 2009). The types of regionalism favored by the great powers can be differentiated in their institutional fabric. Regions that are strongly integrated tend to have network arrangements that are dense and diverse in their membership.

In studying network governance at the regional level, theorists tend to downscale IR theories to the regional level by utilizing the same analytical machinery for both international/global politics and regional politics (Kelly 2007; Prys 2010). And yet the politics of networked governance at a regional level indicates that the traditional IR theories fall short of capturing the simultaneous patterns of tension and cooperation among the great powers, which often operate through developing region-level policy networks. For example, both the EU and Russia, having a deep strategic partnership, are also emerging at the very least as unintentional competitors in South Caucasus. The EU has extended the Eastern Partnership to the Caucasus, and is also deploying its Deep and Comprehensive Free Trade Agreement (DCFTA), which seek expansive governance reforms in each country. It is also creating a free trade zone with the South Caucasus states. Meanwhile, Russia has been talking about the Eurasian Customs Union (which will become the Eurasian Union in 2015). A senior official from the EU delegation indicated that the union is quite contradictory to the specificities of the DCFTA. The senior official also asserted that the EU is not imposing its regionalist model on the countries in South Caucasus, and that they should choose between the DCFTA and Eurasian Union, which is their sovereign right. Regardless of the intentions of the great powers in this case, their global ambitions are unfolding through institutional outlets, in parallel to their own deep partnerships with one another. The EU presence in the Caucasus seems to be more networked and formalized than the integration models championed by Russia. Because the traditional IR theories of great power rivalry and hegemony add little to the debate, new variables are needed here to explain how the EU and Russia interact through networks, and whether the network structure can eventually translate into political power.

Regional governance is often advocated by both academics and policy-makers alike. Regional-level governance is supported on the grounds of practicality. By strengthening structures at the regional level of governance, countries can avoid the unnecessary and often infeasible centralization of decision-making and policy authority at the global level such as in the UN family of international organizations. Such a pathway calls for

> an optimal partnership between state, regional, and global levels of actors and between state, intergovernmental, and nongovernmental categories of actors. Structured, systematized frameworks for collective action at the regional level can offer an escape from the bind between unilateralism at the state level versus multilateralism at the global level. (Thakur and Langenhove 2006, 34)

In PDAs, a more realistic assessment of regional governance is needed. In particular, the domestic democratic institutions are weak, if in place at all, and in such settings the civil society sector is poorly developed. In South Caucasus, the civil society connections across conflict divides are few, although the existing initiatives can have a qualitatively powerful impact in altering intercommunal relationships across conflict divides. The case of the Union of Wives of Invalids and Lost Warriors, a Tbilisi-based NGO, is instructive here. This NGO has been working across conflict lines surrounding the Abkhazia and South Ossetia breakaway region on confidence-building programs, ranging from socioeconomic and legal to medical assistance provisions for affected communities (Mebuke interview 2012).

Despite the domestic constraints to enhanced regional cooperation in PDAs, the need for regional governance in conflict areas is particularly acute. There is growing support for strengthening the regional levels of governance in conflict management processes, which highlights the need for collaborative initiatives between the local, national, regional, and global levels of governance instead of relying on one country or institution. Nurturing networks of formal and informal institutional arrangements across national subregional and regional boundaries is a strategy for shaping contemporary conflict management strategies (Crocker, Hampson, and Aall 2011). The regional network approach allows the mobilization of the diverse tools, insights, and socialized capabilities that single institutional actors often lack (ibid.).

Describing the Networked Regional Forms

Der Derian (2011) has rightfully pointed out that "the rise of networks can change not only how war is fought and peace is made, but also make it ever more difficult to maintain the very distinction of war and peace." A descriptive account of the networked texture of regional engagement in a PDA is a necessary first step toward understanding the specific pathways through which network governance at a regional level interacts with and influences conflict management processes in PDAs. This section provides an overview of the existing literature on the nature of regional integration, while developing the network approach to reveal the limits and opportunities for conflict management and resolution that various types of regional arrangements possess.

Attributes That Matter

There many different definitions of networks and numerous frameworks describing those network attributes that matter (Ruiz-Dana et al. 2009; Benner, Reinicke, and Witte 2005; Rhodes 1990, 1996; Robinson 2006; Ohanyan 2008, 2009, 2010). Citing Kriesi, Adam, and Jochum (2006), Rhodes (1990), and Scharpf (1997), Blanco, Lowndes, and Pratchett note that networks are assessed in terms of their "openness/closeness, the number of actors, the degree of diversity/symmetry among actors, the power structures or the degree of consensus/conflict" (2011, 300). They further recall one of the most commonly used distinctions in the network literature—large, diverse, unequal, fluctuating issue networks and smaller, cohesive, equilibrated, stable policy communities (Ruiz-Dana et al. 2009; Rhodes 1990). Perhaps a more pragmatic way of thinking about those network attributes that matter is to evaluate them in terms of their ability to solve complex social problems (Robinson 2006; Koppenjan and Klijn 2004). In this respect, identifying the attributes that matter in networks unavoidably becomes a functional and normative exercise. The goal of the research, then, is predominantly whether networks are, for example, assessed in terms of their democratic credentials or effectiveness, or their ability to mobilize resources or access the grassroots efficiently. In the context of this research, the ability of networks to forge and consolidate the kind of regional governance that can add up to systematic, collective conflict management processes in PDA is the underlying concern.

Glaser and Strauss (1967) developed the method of grounded theory, which enables researchers to identify variables during data collection, thereby grounding theory building in the empirical stage of the research. Both the empirical literature on regionalism in PDAs and the data collection in the Balkans have played an important role in distilling the network attributes that matter for region building in PDAs. Because social experimentation with region building is a relatively recent phenomenon, the data points for this study are limited. Nevertheless, there is enough empirical evidence and there are enough cases of successful regionalism in PDAs to enable detection of patterns of region building and network attributes.

In looking at specific cases in which regionalism or regional organizations play a constructive role in conflict management, with an emphasis on their network attributes, the case of ASEAN is instructive. According to Ahmed, the end of the interstate conflict in Southeast Asia has been "both marked and consolidated by the strengthening of the Association of Southeast Asian Nations (ASEAN), its enlargement to such countries as Cambodia, Laos, Myanmar and Vietnam" (Ahmed and Bhatnagar 2008). Similarly, the establishment of a Growth Triangle in the Mekong River area by creating the Mekong River Commission in 1995 was guided primarily by security considerations (Dosch and Hensengerth 2005; Browder 2000): Thailand and Vietnam were driven to build relations in the aftermath of the Cold War in order to contain the conflict over water resources. The Mekong case is frequently cited as an example of using a resource regime to foster greater political security and stability in a PDA (Makim 2002).

Similarly, in Latin America Mercosur is credited with facilitating the management of interstate political rivalries and with creating a dense institutional framework in which to address and prevent future tensions and political divisions (Hurrell 1998). Overall, there is a growing consensus that in the post–Cold War period regional conflict management needs to be taken seriously because it appears to be the main promising instrument of security provision (ibid.; Tavares 2008; Crocker, Hampson, and Aall 2011).

Success stories in which greater regional engagement has improved security dynamics and enhanced conflict management processes seem to have several commonalities. First, in all PDAs, regionalism does not seem to be an arrangement that has evolved organically, driven by business interests and people (Andreev 2009). Instead, the political cultivation of regional arrangements either by states or through international actors is a necessary condition for region building. The political will of Argentina and Brazil played a role in forging greater integration between them and replacing the divisive geopolitical narratives that dominated the region. At other times, such political will is cultivated by external actors, either by great powers or by international organizations. The efforts of the European Union to forge regional cooperation in the Balkans through the Regional Cooperation Council is a good case in point. In addition, the countries in South Caucasus are currently negotiating Eastern Partnership agreements with the European Union. The partnership stipulates regional cooperation among the member-states in the region, in addition to bilateral ties with the EU. In short, *the pattern of regional mobilization—bottom-up or ground-up—is an important feature of regionalist projects and a key network attribute.*

Second, in addition to being top-down affairs, region building in PDAs requires that the international organizations engaged in region building be embedded in the civil society. It really matters who drives a regionalism project in a PDA. Although top-down, state-led initiatives may be characterized by greater political capital, they also tend to be supported by closed, highly politicized networks. By contrast, the links to and embeddedness in civil society of the processes of regionalism are important for strengthening the societal base of a regional project, thereby adding to its prospects for sustainability. Hurrell (1998) acknowledges that markets and private trade are the most powerful engines of regionalism. But he also adds that "another important element is societal and transnational; increasing flows of people, the development of multiple channels and complex social networks by which ideas, political attitudes and ways of thinking spread from one area to another, leading to the creation of a transnational regional civil society" (538). Similarly, Dosch and Hensengerth note that the very limited societal involvement in intraregional affairs around the Greater Mekong subregion has been one of the stumbling blocks for region building in that area (Dosch and Hensengerth 2005). Furthermore, they highlight two conditions necessary for the Greater Mekong subregion to integrate further: "the willingness of state actors to develop a wider set of integrative formal and informal institutions" and "a more prominent participation from societal actors, ranging from the private sector to NGOs" (285). In short, the *extent of institutional density in the networks supporting given regional projects, in addition to the extent of their multisectoral nature, can have a measurable impact on the prospects of regionalism as well as its conflict management capacities.*

Third, successful regionalism in PDAs tends to follow certain patterns of resource mobilization. Regionalism efforts predominantly led by civil society with limited resources, such as in South Caucasus, tend to be marginalized, with few prospects for scaling up their initiatives. Regional networks that are multisectoral and multilevel in their patterns of resource mobilization tend to be better endowed with financial and political resources, and therefore tend to possess better prospects for sustainability and scaling up. In short, *the extent to which networks are multisectoral and multilevel (local, national, and global)* can be consequential for their success and can shape their conflict management capacities. Perhaps a more succinct characterization of the multisectoral and multilevel nature of networks is *heteropolarity,* which is a concept borrowed from Der Derian (2011) but slightly modified to reflect the research needs of this study. Der Derian applies the concept of heteropolarity to the changing security environment in the world, directly referring to the network patterns of war and peace. "The world is not divided between opposing poles or among various state actors, but through complex networks of differentiated, unorthodox and distinct international actors. . . . Heteropolarity broadens the scope of diplomacy to include non-governmental organizations, multi-national corporations, high-powered individuals, and other actors" (ibid.). In this research, heteropolarity is applied to a narrower context of network politics—that is, those networks composed of actors from various sectors (public, private, and the civil society) and those that connect individuals and groups from the local, national, international, and transnational levels of governance.

Fourth, regional arrangements also tend to differ in the extent to which the "regional project" is driven by one or two specific actors or a larger number of players. In the first case, specific regional champions can support regional projects through variety of resources, such as political, organizational, or financial support to foster greater regionalism. In the latter case, no specific champions may be present, leaving regionalization to take place in a more organic manner, driven by a variety of actors. The first case is supported by networks with one or two power centers, whereas in the latter case the power base within the networks is broad-based. The first type of arrangement also tends to be driven by networks that are developed by design, whereas the latter is advanced

TABLE 2.1. Network Attributes, Regionalism in PDAs

Network attributes that matter	
Patterns of regional mobilization	Bottom-up Top-down
Extent of institutional density	High Low
Degree of power concentration	High Low
Heteropolarty	High Low

through networks developed by default and spontaneity. While the first types of regional networks are centered in terms of their power base, the latter types of networks can be described as "stretched" and "loose." Each has unique opportunities and challenges for conflict management purposes, as discussed in Chapter 3. Table 2.1 presents the network attributes reviewed in this section.

Types of Regional Forms

This section, building on the key debates in regional studies covered in the previous chapter, applies the network approach to three most dominant regional forms as discussed in the regional studies literature. The application of the network approach of regionalism, developed earlier, allows assessing each of the regional forms within a single prism of network governance. In policy terms, this is important because understanding the network composition supporting each regional form will help to evaluate the effectiveness of each regional form in conflict management for a given PDA.

Soft and Hard Regionalism

One of the most frequently cited distinctions of regionalism is that between soft and hard regionalism, which are strikingly different in the composition of their support networks (Fawcett 2004). Soft regionalism is characterized by the involvement of civil society and regional integration at the level of civil society actors, with economic and political integration playing only a marginal role (Harrison 2006). By contrast, hard regionalism is characterized by interstate and intergovernmental agreements of regional integration, which, by extension, span projects of economic cooperation. The distinction between soft and hard regionalism has been supported by institutional economics and economic sociology (ibid.), which maintain that soft regionalism embeds the global processes in place, and the institutional capital they produce becomes the prerequisite for the long-term success of economic/hard regionalism (ibid.).

The networks supporting soft and hard regionalism differ in their patterns of mobilization (Ohanyan 2003). The networks supporting soft regionalism tend to have more grassroots origins and bottom-up patterns of mobilization; civil society groups are the primary actors. By contrast, the networks supporting hard regionalism are hierarchic and top-down, supported by state-led initiatives and intergovernmental agreements (Fawcett 2004). Interestingly, studies in regionalism recognize that "a network of weak ties could theoretically be more dynamic than those dominated by strong ties of enforced loyalty and contract-based relations" (Harrison 2006, 38).

Often, the soft regionalism networks are developed more quickly and effectively if they are supported by government circles. Moreover, government initiatives can catalyze soft regionalism. An example is the European Union initiatives in the Balkans, where the Stability Pact for South Eastern Europe later became the Regional Cooperation Council. Similarly, the European Union has begun to have a more proactive role in the political and economic development in South Caucasus. Because the countries in South Caucasus are in the process of negotiating the Eastern Partnership, the stipulation for regional integration in the agreement needs to be considered seriously by all parties. At this point, it is too early to tell whether the EU initiative of hard regionalism can catalyze the more expansive and institutionally thicker soft regionalism in South Caucasus.

It would be misleading to claim that soft regionalism is characterized by higher levels of institutional density than hard regionalism; rather, high and low levels of institutional density are found in each. Hard regionalism, which refers to state-to-state agreements forged between government officials, can be associated with high levels of density, which in PDAs would indicate scenarios of great power involvement or regional initiatives in largely undemocratic settings, where civil society is weak or nonexistent. Similarly, hard regionalism may be advanced on the grounds of "national interests" through states and the regional organizations in which they participate (Carroll and Sovacool 2010). In such cases, the societal contacts between countries across conflict lines remain marginal. Such a scenario tends to occur when conflict lines are heavily consolidated and conflict structures institutionalized, which is the current situation between Armenia and Azerbaijan over Nagorno-Karabakh. Similarly, high levels of institutional density in soft regionalism may indicate regional mobilization patterns that are highly sporadic and led by civil society actors or the business sector because the government structures are fragile or collapsed. Such scenarios may also capture instances of regional criminalization, and should not be excluded from definitional discussions. Overall, the trend in hard regionalism is that it is usually advanced through state-led initiatives and rarely coordinated with soft regionalism, which is driven by more spontaneous and less orchestrated processes of regionalization. The patterns of hard regionalism are most reflective of Southeast Asia, with the formation of ASEAN. Many researchers highlight the state-led nature of regionalism in that region, pointing to its less institutionalized and less bureaucratic nature (Acharya and Johnston 2008).

Whether a regional network is dominated by one, two, or a larger number of players also produces institutional variation in regional arrangements. Centered networks (one or two dominant players) can be observed within both soft and hard regional arrangements. Similarly, stretched networks (no single dominant player) can also be observed within soft and hard regional arrangements. Centered networks with a high degree of power concentration in cases of soft regionalism indicate scenarios in which one or two NGOs are advancing regional projects, that, however, tend to be poorly integrated with other sectors. Similarly, a high degree of power concentration in centered networks in the context of hard regionalism reflects a state-led effort in which one or two government agencies or international organizations are plowing through the regional effort, which often creates problems of long-term sustainability for such regional projects. All of these scenarios have concrete implications for the conflict management processes and outcomes in PDAs, as examined in Chapter 3.

The distinction between centered and stretched networks is also related to the neoliberal perspective on regionalism—in particular, functionalism, which assumes that cooperation on a single issue will spill over to others. However, this perspective, of which the EU is the best encapsulation, is based on the assumption that regions have active civil societies, organized interest groups, and states whose administrative structures are sophisticated (Ohanyan 2007). The assertion that functionalist approaches to regionalism are difficult to apply in developing countries (Acharya and Johnston 2008) is explained in part by dramatically different network composition supporting such regionalisms. These tend to be primarily centered networks and hard regionalism, which are poorly conducive to spillovers from one issue area to the next.

Soft and hard regionalism also tend to differ in terms of the extent to which actors from various sectors of society (state, market, and civil) are represented, and whether such networks are effectively connecting the local with the national, regional, and transnational spheres of economic and political action. Earlier in this chapter, the multistakeholder networks connecting local, national, and regional levels were described as heteropolar. As noted, in broad strokes soft regionalism tends to be driven by a variety of state and nonstate actors, and hard regionalism is purely a state-led initiative. Soft regionalism is supported by relatively more horizontal networks, and hard regionalism is led by predominantly hierarchic and state-centered ones. The types of networks supporting soft regionalism are also multisectoral, drawing from civil society, government, and the private sector. Still, not all cases of soft regionalism are heteropolar; some initiatives are led primarily by either civil society or the business sector.

Hard regional networks, composed mainly of government agencies or international government organizations, tend to be more political and also closed to society. As political creatures, these types of networks are able to maintain more control over the policy processes inside the network, albeit the global trends show it is increasingly difficult to do so. Like soft regional networks, hard regional networks are also vulnerable to power differentials among their members. Even though sectorally such networks are more uniform, because they all primarily represent the states, the geopolitical factors can be in favor of some members of the networks and not others. In short, these networks, like soft regional networks, can be highly imbalanced in political terms and differ in the levels of their heteropolarity.

Security Complexes and Regional Orders

Building on Buzan's work, Morgan developed a typology of regional security orders that describes the dominant patterns of security management utilized in a given regional security complex. Lake and Morgan (1997) describe regional security orders as the mode of conflict management within the regional security complex. The theory presented in their study articulates a clear link between regional security complexes and regional security orders, explicitly stating the importance of region-building initiatives: "[T]he discussion that follows treats security orders as rungs on a ladder up which regional security complexes may climb as they pursue security management" (Morgan 1997, 33). To this end, Morgan identifies (1) power restraining power; (2) great power concert; (3) collective security; (4) pluralistic security community; and (5) integration, as models of regional security orders.

The "power restraining power" regional scenario refers to situations in which calculations of the balance of power among great powers and their regional client states are the dominant tool of security provision. Morgan (ibid.) further clarifies that "since we are talking about regional orders deliberately chosen and implemented, this means treating the distribution of power as consciously pursued, not as something that automatically or unconsciously emerges" (33). "Great power concert" refers to regional orders in which security becomes the collective responsibility of the most powerful states in that complex that provides hegemonic stability in the region as a public good. "Collective security" describes cases in which members of the regional security complex organize themselves as a collective to manage security in a given region. In a "pluralistic security community," violence is not even considered by members to be a tool for managing relations with one another. Members retain national autonomy because there is no organized collective effort to manage the security relations among the members. Finally, "integration" refers to regional arrangements that are pluralistic security communities, but with higher levels of institutionalization of their relationships. A transnational institution is usually created to manage relations among the members, with the European Union as the most visible case.

The strong theoretical rationale for the application of the network approach to the study of the ideal types of regional orders developed by Morgan is effectively articulated by Lake (1997), who maintains that "rather than build institutions into the definition of a regional system, it is preferable to treat the degree of institutionalization as a dimension of possible variation for further analysis" (47). Although the call to examine the institutional texture in regional orders is valuable, that call alludes to the higher levels of institutionalization within pluralistic and integrative communities as opposed to the lower levels of regional security orders. Application of the network approach to the study of regional orders produces a different conceptualization. Specifically, it shows that, although the institutional density from one regional order to the next may change, with integrative models being the most institutionalized, one should not assume that orders that rest purely on power politics are devoid of an institutional core. The current regional developments in South Caucasus are a good case in point, with Armenia facing a choice between the EU's Eastern Partnership and DCFTA and the Eurasian Union/Customs Union. At the time of this

TABLE 2.2. Network Approach to Regional Orders

	Patterns of regional mobilization		Extent of institutional density		Degree of power concentration		Heteropolarity	
	Bottom-up	Top-down	High	Low	High	Low	High	Low
Power restraining power		Mostly top-down networks	Can vary and can be characterized by both high and low levels of institutional density		Mostly with a high degree of power concentration		Tends to rank low on heteropolarity, unless civil society and the business sector are deployed for geopolitical reasons, producing so-called mercantilist networks	
Great-power concert		Mostly top-down networks	Tends to have low levels of institutionalization			Relatively lower levels of power concentration	Tends to rank low on heteropolarity	
Collective security		Mostly top-down networks	Higher levels of institutionalization			Relatively lower levels of power concentration	Tends to rank low on heteropolarity	
Pluralistic security community	Top-down and bottom-up		Higher levels of institutionalization			Relatively lower levels of power concentration	Higher levels of heteropolarity	
Integration	Top-down and bottom-up		High levels of institutionalization			Lower levels of power concentration	Higher levels of heteropolarity	

writing, Armenia is in the process of negotiating the DCFTA with the EU, and is expected to sign it by the end of 2013. At the same time, in a sudden albeit somewhat predictable move, the Armenian government has also stated its support for the Customs Union, which will be signed in early 2013. The senior EU delegation official in Armenia stated in an interview that it is Armenia's sovereign right to decide whether to move ahead with the Eastern Partnership/ DCFTA or Eurasian Union/Customs Union, but he also clarified that some aspects of DCFTA will conflict with and are not compatible with the Customs Union (anonymous interview with a senior EU diplomat 2012). What transpires from the current state of regional politics in South Caucasus is that the relationships between greater powers are moving into the institutional domain: the dueling models of regionalism in South Caucasus reflect that development. The clash of geopolitical interests seems to have an institutional flavor, at least in South Caucasus.

At the risk of oversimplification, the application of the network attributes to the typology of regional orders (Morgan 1997, 33) is presented in Table 2.2.

Nested Regionalism

Another model of regionalism—the nested model—has been developed by Sakwa (2011), especially for the conflict-ridden South Caucasus, and its conceptual framework is well suited to capture regional dynamics in other PDAs. This model identifies four dimensions of regionalism in conflict areas: microregions, mesoregions, macroregions, and megaregions. *Microregion* refers to the relations between the subnational units, such as intrastate ethnic groups, and their relations to external state actors. Abkhazia's and South Ossetia's relations with Russia and Nagorno-Karabakh's relations with Armenia are cited as examples. *Mesoregion* applies to the Caucasus, with an emphasis on relations between states and protostates. *Macroregion* captures the relationship between "the putative and actual regional hegemons with their potential suzerains" (Sakwa 2011, 467). And *megaregion* describes the involvement of external great powers, which in the case of the Caucasus entails the Commonwealth of Independent States (CIS), the Caspian and Black Sea littoral states, the European Union, and the United States (Sakwa 2011).

The typology of nested regionalisms is useful because it draws attention to the organizational complexity of regionalisms in PDAs, enabling understanding of the role of external powers as well as local dynamics at the lowest level. In terms of the patterns of regional network mobilization at the microlevel, the initiative of engagement between the substate unit and the external capital can exhibit both top-down and bottom-up patterns, depending on the sources and the manifestation of a given conflict. Often, the relationship is driven by both mechanisms, particularly if there is ethnic homogeneity between the substate unit and the country supporting it, such as in Nagorno-Karabakh. The same is true of the extent of institutional density: whether regional arrangements at this level will be supported by many highly integrated networks or by a few isolated ones will vary. In Nagorno-Karabakh, there is significant institutional density in regionalism, with highly organized investments occurring in Nagorno-Karabakh, some of which are being supported even by Armenian diasporic communities around the world. The degree of power concentrated in such networks will be low relative to the other types of nested regionalisms: usually in such cases there is greater societal involvement, and there are no power rivalries among political actors. The level of heteropolarity in such networks will also be low because such arrangements are simply isolated from macro- and megalevel regionalisms and are not integrated into global structures.

Mesoregions, if they are even formed, are perhaps the least evolved institutional layer of regionalism in PDAs. Cease-fires and temporary peace agreements are forged between the governments, and even after cease-fire arrangements have been made, the conflict tends to be consolidated around the governments as the central loci. If there are any regional agreements signed between the parties in conflict, as well as the neighboring states that are not directly involved in a conflict, such arrangements are usually top-down, with very little involvement from the communities. The extent of institutional density tends to be low, because such arrangements, if ever formed, are sporadic and uneven. The degree of power concentration is relatively high because such arrangements are usually orchestrated and managed by the government agencies, and the networks that are formed are usually closed and very tight. As a result, the level of heteropolarity tends to be low because such arrangements, which are supported by closed and unevenly formed networks, also fail to reach out to various levels of governance and do not include actors from different sectors. In this model of layered and nested regionalisms, mesoregions are perhaps the weakest link in the chain of regional governance.

Macro- and megaregions apply to the involvement of regional and great powers, respectively, in a PDA. Because there is often ambiguity in classifying particular powers as either regional or global, as it is particularly true of Russia, treating macro- and megaregions together is more sensible. Both layers of regionalism signify the politics of overlay and penetration, and PDAs are usually quite vulnerable to such influences. Usually driven by geopolitical calculations, such arrangements are mostly top-down, although regional as well as global powers will often pursue political arrangements after making an economic footprint in a given region. Russia's involvement in Armenia is instructive. Russia has made major investments in Armenia and has acquired key strategic sectors, ranging from energy to telecommunications (anonymous interview with a senior diplomat from the Russian embassy 2012). Only after such investments is Russia now advocating for Armenia's involvement in the Eurasian Union— a regional arrangement that includes Belarus, Kazakhstan, and Russia (ibid.). The extent of institutional density in networks supporting such arrangements tends to be high: both regional and great powers are increasingly consolidating their power and influence in a region by forging and institutionalizing regional ties with their clients. As noted earlier, in the context of an increasingly globalizing world, the great power rivalry is moving into institutionalized forums. The rise of "institutional hegemony"—a network composition in which a single international organization or a government agency acquires a superior

TABLE 2.3. A Network Approach to Nested Regionalism Model

	Patterns of regional mobilization		Extent of institutional density		Degree of power concentration		Heteropolarity	
	Bottom-up	Top-down	High	Low	High	Low	High	Low
Microregion	Could be both, but predominantly top-down		Could be both		Relatively low		Low; global and regional structures are poorly integrated into the networks	
Mesoregion	Top-down		Relatively low		Relatively high		Relatively low	
Macroregion	Top-down		Relatively high		Relatively low		Relatively high	
Megaregion	Could be both		Relatively high		Relatively high		Relatively high	

institutional position to advance its goals via the network, often to the detriment of the other network members—is a steadily developing phenomenon.

As reflected in Table 2.3, in terms of the degree of power concentration, the macroregions are more likely to be controlled by a single (regional) power, and therefore such networks are more likely to have higher degrees of power concentration. By contrast, megaregions are more institutionalized, and the degree of power concentration tends to be much lower relative to that of macroregions. Similarly, megaregions are more heteropolar than macroregions because they have greater capacities to connect various sectors and stakeholders across conflict lines.

Conclusion

This chapter highlights networks as an analytical method for studying regionalism and as distinct institutional structures, with concrete policy implications in terms of conflict management processes in PDAs. As an analytical approach, network studies applied in the context of regional analysis allows investigation of the organizational complexity of interstate and transnational relations at the regional level. The variety of conflicting perceptions of regionalism in PDAs is indeed the reality in such regions. Study of the variety in regional forms is one way to reconcile seemingly contradictory perceptions of the practice of regionalism, as articulated by some of the respondents in this study. Chapter 3 focuses on the relationship between the structure and institutional texture of a give regional network arrangement and the conflict management processes and outcomes in a PDA.

3   Networking Peaceful Regions

In Armenia, the frozen conflict in Nagorno-Karabakh (NK) is in the news daily, as are the strained relations with Turkey. Recently, the word "enemy" seems to have quietly entered my children's vocabularies while visiting Armenia.[1] Still, I was pleasantly surprised when my seven-year-old daughter, Isabelle, began ruminating about peace in an unprompted manner: "Peace is when all the garbage in the world is collected from the streets, and Armenia and Turkey are friends." Whether peace should be understood in broad terms (that is, strong governance, including garbage collection, as my daughter insisted), or limited terms (that is, cessation of hostilities) is a question that has stimulated much research and produced policy frameworks in conflict areas. The discussions of the meaning of peace are particularly crucial in the post–Cold War environment, in which there is a marked proliferation of conflict actors as well as third-party interveners. The stability of the cold peace of the Cold War gave way to a more complex security environment, as well as a multilayered conflict management infrastructure.

There is a broad consensus within academic and policy circles on the need to reform and revamp the global and regional conflict management infrastructures. However, as this chapter reveals, most of the proposals are directed at the organizational level, and primarily the question of the extent to which the capacities of regional or international organizations should be enhanced to effectively address the persistent frozen and active conflicts. Slowly the realization is building of the need to reform not only the internal organizational capacities of regional and international organizations but also their external links with one another. Even though the research on subcontracting and task sharing is growing, there is a glaring gap in the literature on the nature of the effects of such links and relationships between organizations and the nature of the peace and security they seek to establish.

This chapter examines the existing proposals to reform the current global infrastructure of conflict management, most of which center on international organizations (IOs). Then, drawing on institutional analysis, it situates international organizations as third-party actors in the context of multidisciplinary studies in conflict management and peace and conflict studies. In examining the issue of "IO effectiveness," the chapter develops a framework for identifying "successful interventions." These interventions are examined in terms of the kinds of peace created by a particular intervention, as well as the institutional depth and extent of intervention in a given conflict area. The second half of the chapter investigates how the regional network attributes developed in Chapter 2 condition the impact of interventions in terms of the types of peace achieved as well as the extent of intervention in a society.

Reform Politics in Global Conflict Management Infrastructure

Figure 3.1 illustrates the three levels of reform initiatives directed at enhancing the global conflict management infrastructure. Advocated by academics and practitioners, they are renovating, rebuilding, and rewiring/restructuring. "Renovating" perhaps encapsulates the most cosmetic changes among the three main areas, while "rewiring" necessitates the most structural changes needed to strengthen the global and regional infrastructures of conflict management in PDAs. These levels are discussed in the sections that follow.

Renovating: International Organizations as Actors in
Conflict Management

The end of bipolarity in the post–Cold War period is associated with a rapidly shifting security environment worldwide. The bipolar stability in world order gave way to an increase in the number of intrastate conflicts, accompanied by the major powers' reduced appetites for becoming involved in various regions. The changing, and increasingly regional, nature of contemporary conflicts and the inability of state borders to contain them have also fueled a push for regional solutions (Haacke and Williams 2011; Fawcett 2004). Perhaps the most significant change in the global conflict management infrastructure in the second half of the twentieth century was the replacement of states and coalitions of states as third-party intermediaries with more multilateral management, led largely by international organizations (Frazier and Dixon 2006).

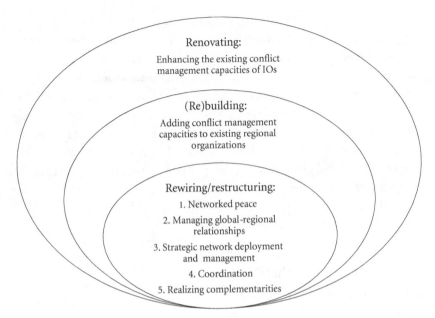

Fig. 3.1. Reform Spheres in Global Conflict Management Infrastructure: Networked Peace

Greater centralization of cooperation among states is a key characteristic of this particular transformation.

Considering the significance of the changes in the security environment in the post–Cold War period, such ad hoc adjustments in actors as third-party intermediaries were inconsequential. Adequate responses in the form of institutional innovations in the structures of global governance failed to materialize (Crocker, Hampson, and Aall 2011a, b; Tanner 2010).

There is a broad-based consensus that the current infrastructure of conflict management is poorly equipped to contain and manage recurring as well as new sources of insecurity (Smith and Weiss 1997). The menu of choices to date has entailed a consideration of several areas of reform. Enhancing the conflict management capacities of existing international organizations has been central among them. For the purposes of this research this area is described as "renovation" because it entails reforming the existing set of international organizations and maintaining their continued centrality in conflict management.

Academics and policy-makers alike disagree on the effectiveness of international organizations in conflict management capacities. Comparing international organizations to states and coalitions of states, some studies show that international organizations have been the most effective in conflict management as third-party intermediaries (Frazier and Dixon 2006). Abbott and Snidal (1998) attribute the IO effectiveness in conflict management to their organizational independence and centralization of decision-making. Specifically, some organizational independence allows an international organization to achieve a certain level of neutrality, which is an important asset for a third-party intermediary. Centralization of decision-making helps an international organization to engage in developing norms within a given region, as well as in the context of a given conflict, which allows that organization to transform the overall conflict environment.

Others claim that in the post–Cold War period international organizations such as NATO and the UN have been less effective in addressing the rapidly changing security environment around the world (Deudney 2011; Hampson and Heinbecker 2011). Some scholars have called for specifying the conditions under which international organizations can be effective as third-party intermediaries, arguing that not all such organizations are created equal in this respect. To this end, there is growing research, with a specific emphasis on the attributes of international organizations that purportedly make them better conflict managers. For example, it is argued that a higher level of institutionalization and a membership with homogeneous preferences and composed of more established democracies enhance the conflict management capacities of international organizations (Hansen, McLaughlin MItchell, and Nemeth 2008). Similarly, level of institutionalization, cohesion among members, and IO security mandates are also found to enhance IO conflict management capacities (Gartzke, Li, and Boehmer 2001). In a review of international organizations and their conflict management capacities, Fausett and Volgy (2010) point out that international organizations are able to reduce uncertainty by providing information and helping to integrate states into regional and global norms (Russett, Oneal, and Davis 1998), providing organizational mechanisms for states to advance their objectives at global forums (Katzenstein, Keohane, and Krasner 1998), and socializing states into the modern international system (Thomas et al. 1987; Finnemore 1996; Schimmelfennig 2005; Fausett and Volgy 2010, 81). But in their research, Fausett and Volgy (2010) claim that the membership in international organizations can also fuel low-intensity conflicts, thereby contributing to the formation of higher-intensity conflicts.

Although the literature agrees on the need for particular types of international organizations for effective conflict management, the growing demand for such interventions highlights the shortage of such organizations that are effective (Nguyen 2002; Alagappa 1995) and possess the strong capacities needed to intervene in a large number of conflicts. Creating new international organizations specifically equipped for conflict management has been dismissed so far because of a lack of political will within both advanced and developing countries.

Rebuilding: Regional Organizations as Actors in Conflict Management

Building the conflict management capacities of regional organizations has been another reform area advocated by academics and policy-makers alike. It should be understood as a two-pronged initiative. First, and at a minimum, it entails strengthening the capacities of regional organizations in conflict management by changing their mandate, adding specialized departments in conflict management, tailoring their projects in conflict regions, channeling greater resources, and, in general, achieving greater institutionalization in conflict management within them. In this study, this effort is described as "rebuilding": it considers the existing embryonic conflict management capacities in regional organizations, but also recognizes the need for massive construction and adding competencies of conflict management to these organizations. Second, this study argues that such efforts are likely to bear fruit if paired with higher levels of regional integration in a PDA, which only then can culminate in stronger regional organizations as axles of regional cooperation (Alagappa 1993; Ruiz-Dana et al. 2009; Lake and Morgan 1997; Hettne and Soderbaum 2006). In this study, this second reform path is referred to as "rewiring," which is described in the next section.

Although the expansion of regional spaces for conflict management has been a prominent development in the post–Cold War period (Nguyen 2002; Diehl and Cho 2005; Kelly 2007; Lake and Morgan 1997; Frazier and Dixon 2006), there has been no transfer of responsibilities from international organizations and superpowers to regional organizations (Diehl and Cho 2005). Indeed, Diehl and Cho (ibid.) show how the increased involvement of regional organizations in conflict regions has been mirroring the growth of IO involvement in conflict management (defined as mediation and peacekeeping) in the post–Cold War period. The growing demand for interventions, international or regional, highlights the magnitude of the gap between the supply and demand for conflict management interventions worldwide.

The lack of theoretically informed studies in regional approaches to conflict management has been a broadly shared concern within the academic and policy-making community (Haacke and Williams 2011; Acharya and Johnston 2008; Duffield 2006). A consistent research agenda on the topic, and the resultant policy implications that it can produce, have been slow to develop. Still, scholars have already outlined areas of future research, and the variance in institutional arrangements has been one of the chief among them. The study by Acharya and Johnston (2008) has been noteworthy in that it seeks to explain how and why different regions produce institutional regional arrangements that vary in their design and efficacy. Specifically, they highlight the variations among regional organizations in membership rules, scope of issues tackled, level of centralization of tasks, rules for controlling the institution, and level of flexibility of arrangements. Haacke and Williams (2011) maintain that the sources of variation among regional organizations rest in the exercise of political power in the region, domestic political variables, ideational factors, and their collective capacities.

The problem with the varied capacities of regional organizations is also echoed in their security operations (Hettne and Soderbaum 2006), which also influences their ability to remain neutral in conflict situations. The shortage in resources can make regional organizations vulnerable to great power influence, which can take the form of disproportional funding flows into the organization, thereby undermining the neutrality and organizational autonomy of the regional organization. Indeed, the feared dominance of a regional hegemon has been a major factor undermining the greater involvement of regional organizations in conflict management in PDAs. The Economic Community of West African States (ECOWAS) and Organization of the Black Sea Economic Cooperation (BSEC) are some examples.

Also critical for the conflict management capacities of a regional organization is the question of whether the organization specifically identifies conflict management as one of its political objectives (Haacke and Williams 2011). Most regional organizations are created to foster greater regional cooperation among their member states, and their involvement in conflict management is often a secondary, or an indirect, initiative. The conflict management tools that such organizations have in their possession are limited, as are their mandates. For anyone evaluating effectiveness in conflict management, identifying the regional organization mandate for conflict management is a necessary first step; essentially, it is an issue of institutional commitment to conflict management. The latter is associated with enhanced institutional capacity, resource availability, legitimacy, and credibility as determinants of the effectiveness of regional organizations in conflict management (Alagappa 1995).

Analysts also mention that the proximity of a regional organization to a conflict will add greatly to its commitment to addressing it. The political appetites of the great powers or distant international organizations can wax and wane, depending on the political moods of the former and the resource availability in the latter, whereas regional organizations and their members have to live with the consequences of unsolved conflicts. Thus they have a strong interest and commitment to managing a conflict, so the argument goes (Hettne and Soderbaum 2006).

Similarly, Alagappa (1995) observes that, by virtue of being rooted in regionalism, regional organizations are capable of facilitating communications and socialization, sharing information, increasing consensual knowledge, and increasing their power through pooling resources and collective action. By extension, these assets translate into direct and indirect processes of conflict management, such as norm setting; assurance in increasing transparency and reducing uncertainty; community building in eliminating the role of force as an option in resolving political disputes; deterrence in preventing aggressive behavior by member and nonmember states; isolation in the sense of containing a conflict and preventing its spillover and widening through the involvement of other parties; and direct intervention through directing political, economic, and military resources toward containing or terminating a conflict.

Rewiring: Regionalism and Conflict Management

Practicing regionalism as a conflict management strategy is an alternative to strengthening the conflict management capacities of regional organizations alone. In this framework, the conflict management capacities of regional organizations are strengthened in tandem with fostering deeper and more expansive regional integration between governments and societies, which necessitates "rewiring" links and connections between regional organizations and other stakeholders in the peace processes. Indeed, this approach to peace building essentially tackles the agency of the regional organization together with the broader context of regionalism, which is a dramatic departure from the existing reform initiatives for enhanced regional or international engagement in conflict management. Importantly, the overview of the conflict management capacities of regional and international organizations presented earlier is characterized by a sole focus on the organizations themselves, with little consideration of their institutional embeddedness in their geopolitical and socioeconomic contexts.

Several theoretical directions in regional studies speak to the "peace building as region building" approach to conflict management. The critical theories of regionalism are perhaps the most explicit in this regard: they explicitly call for supporting regions as order-building projects as opposed to focusing and debating the regions as analytical concepts and emerging socioeconomic and political units in post-Cold War world order. Such calls for regions as deliberate tools of creating order and stability usually culminate in a regional organization (Kelly 2007). Both the regional security orders theory (Lake 1997), and the regional security complex theory (Buzan and Wæver 2003) consider regions to be instruments of security provision, while also recognizing regions as sources of instability. Another theoretical approach that is looking for security solutions at the regional level is the concept of a regional cluster introduced by Tavares (2008): this is an analytical framework in which to examine a region in terms of its agents of peace and security, its instruments of peace and security used, the security and conflict patterns it exhibits, as well as the level of regional integration.

The treatment of regional organizations and regions as security-producing constructs ultimately calls for a theoretical investigation of regional governance and regional multilateralism. This will make possible a greater understanding of the ways regional organizations are connected to various actors within conflict societies, ranging from civil society to the business sector. Equally important, understanding regional governance and regional multilateralism will illuminate the global-regional interface (Crocker, Hampson, and Aall 2011), such as the balance of the operative capacities of regional organizations deployed in conflict regions, as well as the nature of the cooperation and complementarities with global actors, and the implications for policy-making power this entails on the ground.

As revealed in the overview of regional studies in Chapter 1, there are a variety of understandings and definitions of regionalism, and this variety also applies to the analysis of regional governance infrastructure. A key marker among the variety of understandings of regional governance is the organizational and political center attributed to regional-level structures of governance. Most often regional governance is analyzed in light of global structures such as the UN system. Enhanced regional multilateralism in this framework entails improved links and relationships with the global structures of conflict management, and the global-regional relationship is always hierarchical, with the global structures steering the security boat—that is, the UN model in which the global organization delegates tasks to the subordinate regional organization is perhaps the most common understanding of the global-regional relationship (Hettne and Soderbaum 2006).

The UN Charter incorporates a clear hierarchy in which the UN maintains primacy and dominance over the enforcement actions of regional institutions in the area of international peace and security (Smith and Weiss 1997). In this framework, regional governance is a set of state-centric legal tools and agreements directed at various issue areas, ranging from drug trafficking to environmental degradation. A certain division of labor among regional and global structures is occurring, "sometimes consensual, sometimes contested" (Fawcett 2004, 430), but, even so, global institutions and great powers are in the driver's seat, and the process of interaction between them is still considered managed and predesigned.

On the other hand, regional studies have registered a "picture of growing regional empowerment" (Fawcett 2004), in which the growing autonomy of regions from the influence of great powers and multilateral institutions is the main development. New regionalism as a theoretical approach has bestowed regions with a newfound autonomy and independence from great power influence. In this approach, regional multilateralism means a much deeper engagement of regional organizations in conflict areas, with the great powers playing limited roles in containing and managing conflicts in PDAs (Smith and Weiss 1997). Still, even if the hierarchy of the UN is challenged by regional organizations and regional arrangements in general, a certain degree of ad hoc or concerted division of labor is still taking place. The question is, who is in the driver's seat in determining the processes and tools of conflict management and design of projects deployed in PDAs?

There is an inherent tension between the two approaches to the global-regional relationships just discussed. Some even argue that the global/UN and regional layers of governance are based on competing structures: "The UN model is based on a Westphalian nation-state logic, whereas the regional approach, at least in the longer term, is more consistent with a post-Westphalian world order" (Hettne and Soderbaum 2006, 227). The growing political and institutional maturity of regions has resulted in more complex relationships between regions and the UN.

Indeed, Hettne and Soderbaum (2006) maintain that the policy and academic debates tend to miss this emergent organizational and political complexity of the global-regional interface. They argue that the emerging regional arrangements have acquired a degree of legitimacy and organizational independence that the traditional regional agencies lack. Therefore, regional organizations are ceasing to be the pillars of "orthodox multilateralism," centered on the UN with nation-states as the basic units. Instead, the authors claim, the ultimate outcome may be a "regional multilateralism" that is built around regional organizations, such as ECOWAS, South African Development Community (SADC), and the EU (ibid.). This approach seems to assume that regional integration occurs organically, from the bottom up, eventually resulting in the higher institutionalization of a regional organization.

Yet in the postcommunist space, organic regionalism has been slow to develop. Here top-down international organizations have usually led the way, at times interlocking with bottom-up forces, and at times operating in parallel to them. Understanding the network structure underpinning regional arrangements is an important task when seeking to explain the impact of regional integration on conflict management and peace building.

Both perspectives of regional governance—as subordinate or as empowered and primary—recognize the existence and significance of collaboration and cooperation and subcontracting and task sharing among the UN, regional organizations, civil society, and business sector actors (ibid.; Smith and Weiss 1997; Alagappa 1995; Crocker, Hampson, and Aall 2011a, b; Ohanyan 2009). However, there has been scant research on how such actors connect with one another, and whether the nature of such links can have an impact on peacebuilding processes and outcomes. Investigation of peace building as region building calls for understanding how these actors come together and the institutional texture of the interorganizational arrangements formed among them through task sharing and subcontracting and coordination and collaboration in collective conflict management.

Rewiring: Regions as Actors and Structures of Conflict Management

A networked peace paradigm can be described as a policy framework to reorganize and restructure the existing conflict management machinery that is deployed by the international community in PDAs. At the regional level it is in accord with the existing scholarship, which calls for a more enhanced role for regional and international organizations in conflict management and security provision. However, a networked peace paradigm calls for significantly deeper engagement at a regional level beyond merely strengthening regional organizations. Specifically, it underscores the importance of the broader institutional environment in which regional organizations are embedded in PDAs. To that end, it focuses attention on the relationships and interactions among various conflict management actors (local, national, regional, and global) and invites careful research on the multiple ways in which these actors come together and get assembled into complex systems of conflict management in various PDAs worldwide.

When inviting an examination of relationships and interactions between conflict management actors, the networked peace paradigm introduces an important new variable that has been largely neglected in the field of conflict management: institutional preconditions for effective interventions. Issues of coordination between various conflict management initiatives (Crocker, Hampson, and Aall 2011b) and challenges surrounding the transfer from a project to the larger community have deep institutional dynamics, because they are highly dependent on the way each initiative is linked to others in organizational and institutional terms. The network approach makes possible exposure of the relationships between various initiatives and tracks (Bohmelt 2010), as well as the ways in which such initiatives link with the broader political environment in a conflict region.

To explore these issues systematically, the networked peace paradigm at a regional level necessitates a conversation between institutional theories and conflict management scholarship. With this objective in mind, this section provides a short detour, in an attempt to situate the theory and practice of conflict management within institutional theory. To stimulate a comprehensive discussion on restructuring the conflict management machinery at a regional level, an understanding of the way structures and actors come together toward jumpstarting stalled or nonexistent peace processes is an imperative.

Institutions are understood to be formal and informal rules that create incentives or constrain behavior (Thelen 1999). They cannot undertake overt enforcement because "they are created and sustained through societal legitimation and are enhanced by repetitive social behaviors and strong normative systems" (Ohanyan 2012, 367). A variety of institutional understandings of peace and conflict are possible, but the tension between rational choice approaches and historical institutionalism is most relevant and consequential for the theory and practice of conflict management and resolution in PDAs. In particular, both institutionalist approaches emphasize the importance of actors versus structures as possible sources of change and stability, and this reverberates within the conflict management discourse.

Many theories of conflict analysis and resolution are actor-centric, seeing an individual, a grassroots group, or an elite as the primary target for change, and a first step toward conflict management. For example, theories of shifts in consciousness maintain that if key actors or enough individuals undergo constructive shifts in their consciousness, they will have the capacity for and the commitment to addressing conflicts peacefully. Meeting this goal requires advocating consciousness-raising workshops or processes, meditative activities and educational programs, and identity-based training (Nan, Mulvihill, and Salinas 2010). Another example of an actor-centric theory is advanced by community-based peace-building approaches. Here the assumption is that if belligerent groups in a community have an opportunity to interact with one another, conflicts within the community will have a better chance of peaceful resolution (ibid.). Contact hypothesis is a theoretical approach that shares the same assumptions about bringing people from conflict societies together as a way to transform conflict-ridden societies (Ohanyan and Lewis 2005).

When it comes to understanding sources of conflict, perhaps the historical institutionalist approach to conflict management may be more helpful. Criticized for rigidity in explaining change (Peters, Pierre, and King 2005), historical institutionalism has focused on revealing how institutional legacies shape concrete historical processes (Thelen 1999). Within this perspective, many processes are largely rooted in formal and informal institutions (Pierson 1996; Skocpol 1992), and political behavior is explained by the opportunities and limits created and imposed by the institutions.

Meanwhile, Thelen maintains that rational choice and historical institutionalism do not necessarily contradict each other (1999). Citing Zysman (1994), Thelen claims that "naked" institutions emerging from a state of nature, as argued by rational choice, and from "socially embedded" institutions, as advanced by historical institutionalism, are two sides of the same coin. Each highlights a different process within a common story, so the argument goes. This position seems to be supported by the main families of conflict analysis and resolution theories. The field recognizes the effects of institutions on political behavior, and some studies look at the institutional sources of a conflict. Perhaps the most recognizable institutional argument on peace and conflict studies is the vast research on democratic peace theory, which maintains that, for variety of institutional reasons, democracies do not fight one another. The overview of a U.S. Agency for International Development (USAID) study points out that theories on the culture of peace aim to craft institutions for peaceful change through instruments such as peace education, advocacy campaigns, and enhanced peace media capacity. Even in such frameworks, though, the primacy still rests with a particular actor, be it a donor or a nongovernmental organization (NGO), that undertakes the challenging task in any of the related activities. The most direct treatment of institutions as tools for change is provided by the "Functioning Institutions" theories within the USAID study, which highlight that properly functioning economic, political, security/judicial/human rights, and social service delivery institutions would make possible more harmonious relationships within and between societies.

The tensions between historical institutionalism and rational choice theories are highly relevant to revealing the role that a particular conflict management infrastructure can play. Rational choice theories, when explaining social change, tend to place the emphasis on individual actors. Applied in the context of conflict analysis and resolution, programs and interventions should ultimately target individuals, groups, and communities, and actor-centric theories advocate doing just that. At the same time, historical institutionalism, while less effective in explaining social change (Peters 1999; Peters, Pierre, and King 2005) places the emphasis on historically developed structures as sources of conflict and stability. In this respect, historical institutionalism is a structural, as opposed to actor-centric, approach because it conceives of institutions as sustained systems of values, norms, and practices in society (Peters, Pierre, and King 2005). Thus the social change in conflict management within this framework starts with modifying broader institutions and structures within the society. Theories advocating building a culture of peace and strengthening media capacities and security and justice institutions are some examples of targeting the institutional environment in conflict regions.

The networked peace approach to regional conflict management recognizes the value of both agency and structure in cultivating effective conflict management processes in a region. In this respect, it rests on the assertion by Thelen (1999) that institutions and broad processes also have microfoundations (Zysman 1994) and are affected by individual actors and groups. Within the networked peace approach, the microfoundations represent the individual initiatives, but their institutionalization becomes as important as starting such individual initiatives in the first place. The actor-centric rational choice approach does not go far enough in explaining the problem of isolated projects within the field of conflict management. When and under what conditions do such isolated conflict management initiatives begin to yield results and have enough of an institutional value to be a game changer?

The theoretical core of the networked peace approach is that the immediate institutional environment of individual conflict management initiatives is as important as the initiatives themselves. Interorganizational networks feeding and supporting a particular conflict management initiative can be understood as organizational fields, which is a concept developed within sociological institutionalism (Bruszt and Vedres 2008; Wooten and Hoffman 2008). In this theoretical context, networks can be understood as organizational fields, because they represent a community of organizations "that share a meaning system and that interact more frequently with one another than with the outside world" (Ohanyan 2012, 372). Networks as structures intermediating between an actor and the institution need to be analyzed comparatively in order to delineate the attributes of those networks that yield better institutional value for conflict management infrastructure in a region.

The networked peace approach to regionalization of collective conflict management recognizes the importance of agency—that is, specific actors and their role as social change agents. But it also stresses the importance of the institutional environment surrounding the actors, which can be consequential for the effectiveness of an actor as a conflict management player. Understanding the structural fabric of a network that is feeding a particular conflict management initiative will make it clearer whether a particular initiative is well suited for future institutionalization, or whether it is vulnerable to the problem of isolated interventions that plagues the field of conflict management.

Another area of significance in the distinction between actors and structures is the breadth and depth of third-party interventions in conflict areas. Actor-centric theories tend to prescribe limited interventions, in addition to evaluation interventions. The literature on regional and international organizations in conflict management capacities reflects this tendency. The review provided earlier of the role of regional and international organizations in conflict management is quite illustrative of this point: these actors are predominantly evaluated in terms of their "capacities," remaining focused at the organizational level,

TABLE 3.1. Actors and Structures in the Study of Peace and Conflict

Actor-centric		Networked peace paradigm	Structure-focused
Extent of intervention prescribed	Limited engagement	Networked peace paradigm	Societal transformation
			Regional governance
			Global governance
	IO studies		Lederach and Galtung tradition on conflict transformation
Theoretical approach utilized	Conflict management literature		Peace and conflict studies
Type of peace	Cold to normal		Normal to warm

and their impact on the broader conflict environment is rarely assessed. This is in sharp contrast to the focus adopted by peace and conflict studies, which have been calling for broader societal transformation as an ultimate measure of success in third-party interventions. Studies of regional and international organizations are supported by actor-centric theories, whereas peace and conflict studies tend to move toward broader institutions and institutional change. Table 3.1 presents the basic institutional distinctions between actor-centric and structure-focused approaches to the provision of peace and stability in conflict areas.

Because the actor-structure debate within institutionalist theories touches directly on the extent of interventions in conflict management initiatives as well as the breadth of outcomes envisioned by such interventions, the next section focuses on these two dimensions. The extent of intervention and the type of peace achieved constitute two broad areas of assessing "successful" initiatives within the networked peace paradigm.

Successful Interventions within the Networked Peace Paradigm

Most of the efforts within the scholarly literature to understand peace have focused on exploring conditions of war—its types and manifestations. Peace has usually been associated with the absence of war (Hoglund and Kovacs 2010; Barash and Weber 2008). Understanding the conditions of peace, its parameters, and its types and manifestations, is a relatively recent research avenue both in peace and conflict studies and in international relations scholarship. This emergent literature can be broadly divided into two research directions:

(1) conditions and types of peace, and (2) the extent and depth of intervention by third parties in a conflict region. It is worthwhile to highlight that the distinction between actors and structures as targets of interventions in conflict management, as just discussed, is very useful when seeking to understand how interventions differ in terms of their extent and depth in a given conflict region: whether an intervention targets particular communities and groups, or whether it is the broader structural transformation in a conflict society that is at the center of an intervention. That distinction directly follows from the institutionalist analysis, and serves as the primary "dependent variable" in this study.

Regarding the first research direction, conditions and types of peace, the emerging scholarship is calling for more precise analytical differentiations in the quality of peace arrangements other than describing peace as the absence of violence. Miller's differentiation among cold, normal, and warm peace is one example (Miller 2005). In a cold peace, the main issues in a conflict are mitigated, but they remain unresolved. In a normal peace, the main issues are resolved. And in a warm peace, they are transcended or rendered irrelevant. Channels of communication are limited to those between governments in a cold peace. By contrast, in a normal peace, the intergovernmental contacts are supplemented by transnational ties, which in a warm peace are fully developed and institutionalized. The level of sustainability of peace is the main marker in the three levels of peace identified by Miller (ibid.).

This framework on types of peace echoes much earlier research carried out by Galtung (1996), which distinguishes between negative and positive peace. Negative peace is associated with the absence of war, which, to Galtung, masks the structural inequalities and structural violence that continue to exist within a society or between two societies (ibid.). Related research has shown that the inability of peace agreements to address such structural inequalities, reflecting conditions of a negative peace, usually result in the resumption of the conflict (Mac Ginty 2010; Hoglund and Kovacs 2010). Positive peace refers to the absence of war, as well as the elimination of structural inequalities between individuals, communities, and states (Hoglund and Kovacs 2010; Galtung 1996).

The second research direction refers to the extent and depth of third-party interventions in conflict areas. Here also an analytical split has emerged, with peace and conflict studies calling for more comprehensive societal transformations as the ultimate goal of interventions, in contrast to conflict analysis and resolution, which is primarily concerned with managing the existing conflicts in a constructive manner. The research direction on the depth of intervention is distinct from, but also related to, the types and conditions of peace. Specifically, cold peace signifies mere management of conflict and violence without affecting the institutions and structures in a society. The deeper engagements possess a transformative quality and are associated with a more sustainable warm or positive peace. Research by Lederach (1997) is significant in this respect, with its emphasis on conflict transformation as opposed to conflict management. Conflict transformation in his scholarship is described as a coordinated action among the grassroots, the middle level, and the governmental levels of society (ibid.; Gawerc 2006). In a way, conflict transformation requires structural reordering of the society in order for peace to take hold (Hoglund and Kovacs 2010; Lederach 1997), which may translate into changing the existing power structures internally or externally within a conflict society or a region.

Hoglund and Kovacs (2010) point out that despite the scholarly emphasis on the limited goals of war termination and conflict management, the policy-oriented scholarship and the peace-building practice in war zones have been advancing a rather extensive intervention package and a particular type of peace—a liberal peace (Paris 2004). This kind of peace rests on a massive restructuring of the conflict society, thereby manifesting transformative capacities. Liberal peace building entails deep engagement of the international community in a state to assist with the transition from war to peace, as well as to a market economy and a democratic political system (Ohanyan 2002). These are considered the main elements in the liberal peace-building tripod leading to peace consolidation. The proponents of liberal peace building argue that because it calls for institutional transformations and the introduction of market structures, the inequalities and injustice within a society can potentially be addressed. Indeed, in a way this paradigm is geared toward achieving conflict transformation (Hoglund and Kovacs 2010). Yet others highlight that liberal peace building creates new socioeconomic and political cleavages and new sources of conflict (Paris 2004), and that institution building in settings with poor governance needs to happen before economic and political liberalization. Although liberal peace building mirrors the structural changes required by the conflict transformation paradigm, it falls short of creating the much sought after reconciliation, which seems to be the Holy Grail of the field of conflict resolution and peace and conflict studies.

Research on type of peace and extent of intervention as two broad assessment areas for third-party interventions would challenge the predominant as-

sumption within the peace and conflict studies literature that conflict transformation, which assumes extensive institutional intervention, is the only
outcome associated with warm/positive peace—that is, the type of peace. At
the regional level, where some conflicts are interstate, characterized by geographical separation of conflicting societies, the deep and meaningful reconciliation processes brought about by conflict transformation are hardly possible, or, I would argue, even a necessary condition for sustainable peace to
take hold. Elsewhere, in the much smaller context of peace education programs
for Abkhaz and Georgian youth, for example, the causality between attitudinal
changes (conflict transformation and reconciliation) and conflict management
has apparently not taken hold (Ohanyan and Lewis 2005). The more than five
hundred program participants surveyed indicated a willingness to engage in
joint projects and business initiatives across conflict lines, even though significant attitudinal changes (that is, reconciliation) across ethnic lines did not take
place. At a minimum, this finding challenges the value attached to reconciliation as an ultimate goal for the sustainability of peace. Instead, it reverses the
assumption that attitudinal changes are prerequisites for behavioral ones. This
study reveals that it is more realistic to expect behavioral changes (such as a
willingness to engage across conflict lines) as a first link in a chain of social
change leading to lasting attitudinal changes (that is, sustainability of peace
and ultimately reconciliation).

Against this backdrop, the regional networked peace paradigm developed
here recognizes the limits of intergroup reconciliation or attitudinal changes as
a prerequisite for broader social change. Because of the geographical isolation
of conflict societies, close contact between critical masses of individuals across
those societies is untenable. Instead, it is the interface between certain professional communities (business groups, civil society clusters, political gatherings,
professional networks) that could serve as a building block in greater intersocietal engagement. Therefore, the regional networked peace paradigm assesses
the impact of an intervention by its ability to create a cold or normal peace
(that is, not necessarily a warm peace). Some would argue that such a bench-
mark lowers the threshold for successful interventions. However, at the regional level, where geographical separation places a premium on targeted and
strategically developed cross-conflict contacts, it is a more tangible outcome
and realistic expectation than intersocietal reconciliation, which may not take
hold for decades.

In terms of the extent of intervention, the effectiveness of regional net-

TABLE 3.2. Evaluating the Effectiveness of Interventions in Conflict Areas

Nature and extent of intervention	Type of peace	
	Cold	Warm
Limited, cosmetic intervention, conflict management	Unsustainable outcomes, lack of institutionalization, high likelihood of resumption in hostilities, danger of accidental war	According to peace and conflict studies, this is not a possible outcome. Perhaps attainable in smaller scale conflicts.
Extensive, structural intervention, conflict transformation	The ultimate measure of effective interventions in this study; creation of peace-building systems; high level of institutionalization prospects	The ultimate goal of effective interventions, according to peace and conflict studies. In this research on regional peace building, it is considered unattainable.

works in conflict management can be assessed by the depth of their penetration across conflict societies. Here, conflict transformation as a reordering of societies at the regional level is a realistic expectation, but one that has not been pursued seriously by the policy-making and practitioner communities. Instead, it is the expectation that even deep intervention and transformation of conflict structures in PDAs can result in reconciliation and a warm peace that may be unrealistic. Table 3.2 clarifies the parameters of types of peace and the depth of interventions as two indicators of effective conflict management.

What is significant about the table and the conceptualization of successful outcomes in interventions in this study is the fact that the lower-right quadrant is not considered the ultimate measure of success, as would follow from the existing literature. Instead, in the regional networked peace paradigm, the lower-middle quadrant is considered to be a tangible success case for interventions in PDAs. Although the lower-right quadrant places a premium on intergroup/intersocietal reconciliation, in the proposed framework the creation of institutionalized peace-building systems that can function on a long-term basis is considered a desirable outcome.

The rationale for this framework of evaluation and its emphasis on developing network-based peace-building systems in PDAs is the persistence of conflicts and disputes between neighboring countries, even if the current conflict is addressed (Minić interview 2012). Therefore, creating permanent structures of conflict management and diversified systems of interstate and intersocietal interface makes it possible to absorb tensions and disputes through institutionalized channels (Ohanyan 1999), as opposed to addressing just the current conflict.

The rest of this chapter investigates how each regional network attribute shapes the prospects of conflict management initiatives in terms of the type of peace produced and the extent of the intervention created, because both of these dimensions characterize the nature of peace systems created by regional network governance in PDAs.

Regions as Networks and Long-term Prospects for Peace

The four attributes of regional networks identified in Chapter 2 directly challenge the actor-structure debate that divided historical institutionalism from rational choice analysis. The networked peace approach highlights the complementarity of microinterventions, as well as macrolevel changes within structures of national and regional governance. Microinterventions are the microfoundations of institutional changes, as articulated within the institutionalist literature. However, their role is highly conditional on the network structures supporting such interventions: whether a given smaller-scale project can catalyze a broader change is dependent how that project is positioned within the overall machinery of conflict management deployed in a given region. Some network structures can elevate and magnify even the minor impact of smaller-scale initiatives, while others can simply muffle and mute them. Depending on a structure of the network in which a particular initiative is embedded, the broader institutional impact of a given microintervention will vary. This section describes the specific network conditions feeding individual initiatives.

Patterns of Regional Mobilization

Patterns of regional mobilization, the first network attribute highlighted as consequential for conflict management, is actor-specific, focusing on the agency within a conflict management initiative. The literature in conflict management and political science has treated the top-down versus bottom-up patterns of conflict management and peace process designs extensively. Top-down approaches to conflict management processes are primarily driven by negotiating elites, which, if achieving an agreement, are then tasked to sell it to their respective publics (Hancock 2008). The core assumption in this approach to conflict management is that the elites are motivated to achieve, and capable of achieving, an agreement, and that peace is always in their interests (ibid.).

In reality, the broader institutional environment in which elites operate is highly consequential for the outcomes of a peace process. In particular, the regime type matters greatly in whether elites are genuinely seeking peace and compromise, or whether the peace process is captured by narrow political and economic interests. To that end, the literature in political science and international relations has produced significant scholarship that can be translated into the field of conflict management. In particular, the institutional analysis of top-down processes quickly reveals their shortcomings for producing and consolidating negotiated agreements over protracted conflicts, as discussed next.

First, top-down, elite-driven peace processes are vulnerable to the institutional design in political systems supporting each conflict side: if the conflict is unfolding in poorly consolidated democratic or hybrid/authoritarian settings, then the dynamics of top-down peace processes are dramatically different from those in consolidated democracies. The weakness of democratic institutions and the lack of their consolidation in transitioning countries are known to elevate the use of the "ethnic card" by politicians in order to mobilize people around them in contested political environments (Mansfield and Snyder 1995; Rabushka and Shepsle 1972; Horowitz 1985; Mitchell 1995).

In addition, the role of elites in conflict areas has been captured directly by the diversionary war theory, albeit with mixed results. Some analysts have maintained that leaders are more likely to initiate or prolong conflicts when their chances of losing their office are high (Bueno de Mesquita et al. 1999; Bueno de Mesquita and Siverson 1995; Goemans 2000; Siverson 1996; Reiter and Stam 2002; Chiozza and Goemans 2003). This scapegoat hypothesis maintains that an external conflict allows leaders to point to a foreign enemy for their failed policies (Morgan and Bickers 1992). Others claim that an external conflict allows leaders to solidify their bases in domestic politics as people rally around the flag. By contrast, Chiozza and Goemans (2003) find that a heightened risk of losing office makes leaders less likely to initiate a crisis, as the chances are higher that they may lose office. Regardless of one's position in this debate, it is evident that the elite-driven conflict management and peace processes are more likely to be politicized, which adds significantly to the complexity of conflict management processes.

Second, top-down models are also problematic because they lack the public legitimacy needed to support the long-term sustainability of negotiated outcomes (Pearson 2001; Hancock 2008; Lipschutz 1998). The literature in conflict management and peace studies seems to have arrived at a broad consensus on the limits of relying only on top-down, elite-driven peace processes. The research in this area, drawing primarily from single or comparative case studies, has shown that top-down approaches, if unattached to grassroots initiatives, tend to accomplish little. Elites, who claim to speak for the masses, are often out of touch and out of tune when it comes to representing the needs and interests of the people at the negotiating table (Pearson 2001; Hancock 2008; Lipschutz 1998; Ross 2000; Lederach 1997, 2002).

One specific problem with top-down approaches to conflict management is that elite involvement usually translates into principled negotiations, and in such cases leaders may block any conflict resolution efforts between communities (Ross 2000). Principled negotiations limit the possibilities of understanding the needs and interests of communities—understanding what is needed to generate creative solutions to a conflict, as advocated by the human needs theory (Burton 1990).

Third, a set of factors revealing the impact of broader institutional conditions on top-down networks in conflict regions rests with the problem of war economies; a business sector, formal or informal, may be benefiting from closed borders and the unresolved status of a conflict. Many Armenians participating in this study pointed out that because of the economic blockade imposed by Turkey and Azerbaijan on Armenia, only a few, usually politically connected, oligarchs are able to import any goods into Armenia (Iskandaryan interview 2012). Conflict resolution would entail liberalization of the borders, which would create better conditions for more equitable and accessible economic transactions in the region. In such cases, the elites are captured by narrow business elites, and civil society is poorly organized and so unable to exert any meaningful pressure on the government to advance the needs of the people in policy-making.

Fourth, a set of institutional factors that negatively elevate the shortcomings of top-down networks have to do with the weak administrative capacities of poorly consolidated democratic or hybrid regimes. Combined with weak civil societies, such governments are plagued by poor infrastructural power (Ohanyan 2007), which is manifested in their inability to reach out to the larger segments of the society. In such cases, the elites are also out of touch with the broader society. During the course of this study, a senior government official in Armenia dismissed the arguments that certain segments of Armenian society, particularly those in border areas, may be hurt by the closed borders with Turkey. He argued that Armenia is focusing on developing its information technology sector and does not need Turkey as an economic partner.[2] His viewpoint would be of little consolation to a shoemaker in the border area who has to travel to Yerevan to purchase leather from an intermediary instead of crossing the border easily to obtain it himself.

Fifth, top-down models of conflict management are associated with closed foreign policy development processes, and so are vulnerable to influences from other regional or great powers. Under such conditions, national security as perceived by leaders dominates the discourse, with little attention paid to human security. The latter may include issues such as human trafficking, environmental problems, migration, and immigration, to name a few. Human security is not only a source of problems and conflicts to be addressed between communities, but also a platform and an opportunity to forge compromises.

The existing research tends to associate the provision of human security in conflict areas with bottom-up, as opposed to top-down, processes of conflict management. To address human security is to forge sustainable relationships with local communities and to consider them as legitimate "targets" of programmatic interventions for peace-building processes. It is often through the bottom-up approaches of working through NGOs and their networks that human security becomes institutionalized in conflict zones (Richmond 2005). Principled negotiations and closed diplomacy carried out from the top down have rarely been conducive to community needs, particularly in poorly consolidated democratic or (semi)-authoritarian contexts.

In part because top-down conflict management processes are driven by government actors and political elites, any regional networks that may emerge from such forums are also top-down, characterized by the dominance of state actors and state-centric intergovernmental organizations. They are also purely political as opposed to developmental (Diaz 2001). The programmatic coverage stemming from such networks is quite thin in terms of content and format. Most of the top-down conflict management processes in a PDA tend to be built around individual conflicts, regardless of the regional implications of that conflict for other states or the impact of other crises on the conflict. The role of the Organization for Security and Co-operation in Europe (OSCE) in the Nagorno-Karabakh conflict is a good case in point. To date, it has succeeded in diffusing the tensions between the two countries, but it has failed to produce a settlement of the conflict:

> During the war itself, the mediation effort of the Minsk Group was poorly coordinated, and Russian and Western diplomats began to act in rivalry with one another.

Russia's envoy Vladimir Kazimirov increasingly acted on his own and mediated the ceasefire agreement of May 1994 almost single-handedly. The Minsk Group also suffered from lack of resources. The Balkans peace processes benefited from a much stronger mediation effort and the promise of peacekeepers to back them up. By contrast, no full-fledged Western peacekeepers were sent to any of the Caucasian conflict zones. (De Waal 2010, 124)

Viewed as a network, the OSCE Minsk Group, discussed in greater detail in Chapter 5, stands out with its top-down structure, which favors a closed negotiation process and lacks links and relationships to the broader societies on both sides of the conflict. Some critics argue that the negotiations have even been "derailed by the conflicting motivations of regional/global partners that for various reasons are reluctant to see any variation from the status quo" (Crocker, Hampson, and Aall 2011, 53). As a collective conflict management effort and a step toward managing disputes in a post–Cold War period, the OSCE case illustrates the need for strategic network cultivation for better results. Although top-down networks are not always detrimental to conflict management processes, a greater understanding is needed of the complementary tools that will enable conflict managers to capitalize on the added value of top-down conflict management processes.

Another example of a regional, collective top-down network is the Dubai Process. Although it was launched as a top-down network of regional governance, the Dubai Process quickly developed ties with local communities. The initiative was facilitated by Canada, following up on the Potsdam Statement and the Pakistan-Afghanistan Joint Peace Jirga. This tool enabled Pakistan and Afghanistan to meet in regular working-level workshops to discuss cross-border management issues. The five working areas were customs, counternarcotics, managing the movement of people, law enforcement in border areas, and connecting governments to people through social and economic development (Crocker, Hampson, and Aall 2011).

Top-down networks that foster top-down conflict management processes also lack the tools to address the "mass-based emotive" component of the conflict through such means as dialogue (Pearson 2001). Engaged primarily in focused and principled bargaining processes, such top-down networks fail to provide more extensive identity-based tools for and approaches to collective conflict management (ibid.). It is against this backdrop that practitioners and scholars of conflict management highlight the need to supplement even successful top-down processes with bottom-up approaches, as advocated most extensively by Lederach (1997, 2002). Yet such scenarios are possible only if the appropriate adjustments are made to the respective institutional environments: bottom-up networks need to be linked and integrated with top-down networks in order to provide the most value for collective conflict management processes.

In summary, top-down networks create and reflect an institutional environment that (1) produces limited tools for conflict management built mainly around focused, principled negotiations; (2) creates a highly politicized conflict management process, completely decoupled from developmental issues, thereby reducing the scope of conflict outcomes; (3) favors closed negotiation processes, which are highly undemocratic because they reflect the national interests as they are perceived by leaders as opposed to the public's needs and interests; (4) lacks the tools to reach out to the public, thereby raising legitimacy concerns about negotiated outcomes; and (5) makes the bargaining process susceptible to capture by the interests of the great/regional powers that are not the primary parties to the conflict.

These hypotheses have the most implications for the type of peace created and the extent of interventions. Principled negotiations produced by top-down patterns of regionalization will not produce expansive, multilayered, multi-stakeholder peace systems. Highly politicized conflict management processes will fail to connect with a variety of sectors in conflict societies in a region. Institutionalized peace systems, associated with a normal-warm peace and extensive interventions, also depend on negotiation processes that are perceived as legitimate by the public: closed negotiation processes will fail to produce such level of legitimacy.

Extent of Institutional Density (High/Low)

The importance of network density is also emerging as a key factor in the literature on reforming the global infrastructure of conflict management. There is a consensus that greater complementarities and task sharing, as discussed earlier in this chapter, are essential for the international community to address the increasingly complex and numerous conflicts in various regions. The notion of collective conflict management directly raises the issue of density, which reflects the multiactor operations, but also calls for more cooperation, coordination, coherence, and integration (Tanner 2010). Although researchers and practitioners agree on the need for more efficient and effective multi-stakeholder collective conflict management processes to support peace (ibid.), there is little understanding of the institutional parameters and mechanisms to generate and sustain the kind of coordination and coherence highlighted by reformers.

In addition, understanding the politics of deploying institutionally dense networks is also supported by the need to modernize the relationships between regional organizations and the UN system. Even though the density of links and relationships between them is paramount, it is still necessary to understand the quality of such task sharing (Smith and Weiss 1997) and subcontracting (Richmond 2005; Mertus and Sajjad 2005; Duffield 2006).

Institutional density refers to the quantity of the links and relationships between network members (Bohmelt 2009). Parker (2007) argues that density is one of the main institutional conditions that differentiate between networks and networked governance. Higher-density networks signal a dramatic qualitative change in patterns of governance at the regional level. Higher levels of density among network members also indicate higher levels of institutionalization of the relationship among them, which produces predictability and reinforcement of norms and values as advanced by the network.

In the context of regional studies, the presence of higher-density networks signals a transition from government to governance (ibid.). The literature on regional studies echoes such an analysis, reflecting a convergence with network analysis literature. Fawcett maintains that a successful regionalist project today presupposes ties and linkages between state and nonstate actors, which ultimately produce an interlocking network of regional governance structures (Fawcett 2004). Researchers of new regionalism also point out that contemporary regions shift away from territorially bounded structures to open systems, which makes them more multidimensional, complex, and fluid (Solioz and Stubbs 2009). New regionalism from this perspective is first of all a regionalism of networks and network power (ibid.), and density is a crucial ingredient of institutionalization of the network power. Density makes a difference as to whether a network is merely an aggregation of few interconnected nodes, or whether there are enough network ties to create a critical mass for making an institutional impact on the policy outputs as delivered by the network.

Regional network density has the most direct implications for conflict management processes in PDAs. First, the problem of isolated interventions discussed earlier is partly a result of a low-density network environment. Individual conflict management interventions, primarily among civil society groups across conflict lines at the regional level, are usually poorly connected. Indeed, an official from Georgia's Ministry of Foreign Affairs said that the Georgian government does not attach much importance to civil society initiatives on conflict management (Mebuke interview 2012). Higher-density networks of regional conflict management would add to the legitimacy of such initiatives, making them a force to be reckoned with by government officials. Isolated interventions supported by low-density networks fail to create the much-needed momentum for the peaceful resolution of conflicts and, most important, do not add up to any significant institutionalization that could transform the conflict environment in PDAs.

Second, higher-density networks change the institutional fabric of the conflict area by providing multiple access points to the society. Higher-density networks may be concentrated within the civil society or among government officials. Both scenarios of high-density networks are associated with different models of regional integration. The first is bottom-up, and probably largely informal, regionalism; the latter is top-down regionalism, controlled and driven largely by government officials. It is within this context that actor membership in the network (that is, the level of heteropolarity in networks) has also been identified as a network attribute that matters for understanding regionalism in PDAs. This attribute is discussed later in this chapter.

Third, higher-density networks create better institutional conditions for integration, coordination (Schnabel 2002; Crocker, Hampson, and Aall 2011), and transfer effects among various conflict management initiatives. Dense networks of cross-cutting ties are said to reduce the fallout from disagreements and can even serve preventative functions by creating an atmosphere more supportive of peace agreements, thereby enhancing the political will needed to achieve a resolution (Gawerc 2006).

The outcomes from the transfer of a single initiative to the broader society, another perpetual challenge for conflict management, are also better addressed through high-density networks. One example is the Georgian-Abkhaz peace education program developed by USAID in 1998–2002: the participants were given the tools to integrate the peace education into their respective communities. Many of them established youth houses in their communities, thereby capitalizing and multiplying the original effects from a single peace education initiative (Ohanyan and Lewis, 2005). In similar cases, such networks provide better chances of transferring the outcomes of microinterventions to the more tangible institutional foundations of peace. In fact, they increase the "peace pressure points" throughout society, generating capacities to integrate interventions at the grassroots level. The availability of multiple access and peace pressure points throughout the society also creates a snowball effect and a momentum for one initiative to serve as a foundation for the next, thereby slowly and incrementally altering the broader institutional environment for conflict management processes to take hold. Der Derian (2011) calls such network effects "force multipliers" that can also produce unintended consequences.

Fourth, a related implication of high-density networks for conflict management processes is that indirect links between two states via one or more third parties can determine whether a given conflict will be mediated (Bohmelt 2009). Direct ties are important because they reflect mutual interests and shared preferences, but Bohmelt says that these outcomes will be eliminated once the ties are severed by a conflict. The indirect links, however, create a social network that involves "outside parties in the dispute process, and indirect ties increase the exchange of information between belligerent and potential mediators and the chances that third parties will have a vital interest in intervention" (ibid., 298).

Finally, the key implication from the research on network density for conflict management is the challenge to the rationale on problem-solving meetings, such as track II diplomacy workshops (Ohanyan 2012). Such workshops are usually held to improve the relationships between the parties to a conflict. The underlying assumption and hope are that the participants will become aware of each other's interests and needs, which ultimately will spill over into the governmental track of conflict management. Elsewhere, I have discussed the limits and opportunities of the transfer-up/track II mode of conflict management (Ohanyan and Lewis 2005). At this point, it is the value of broader dense and indirect ties for conflict management processes that merits examination. As Bohmelt rightfully points out, the research on network density illustrates the limits of track II approaches in generating mediation efforts (Bohmelt 2009). Moreover, it appears from the research on network density that indirect and dense networks, with both state-centric and nonstate memberships, diversify the frontlines of conflict management in terms of possible third-party mediators, as well as intensifying the links of interdependence between the actors.

In summary, Institutional density in regional networks is associated with enhanced information flow among the disputants, which conflict management researchers and practitioners maintain to be an important, albeit not a determinant, tool of conflict management. The enhanced information flow supports the prospects for the creation and consolidation of peace systems. In particular, by creating multiple pressure points and enhancing information flow, denser networks permit the achievement of a critical mass of stakeholders for peace, built around organically developed ties between issue networks across conflict lines. Such ties are more promising for normal to warm peace and for the sustainability of peace arrangements in general. Dense networks also provide tangible institutionalized ties around which extensive third-party interventions can be built. Combined with high levels of heteropolarity, the subject of the next section, dense regional networks create the foundations for establishing institutionalized peace systems in PDAs.

Heteropolarity

Another network attribute of collective conflict management, beyond the institutional density of networks supporting such arrangements, is heteropolarity. This refers to the extent to which regional networks are pulled together by actors from a variety of sectors, state and nonstate. The concept of heteropolarity in this study is borrowed from the security literature, which has highlighted the rise of actors from a variety of sectors as an emergent condition of the rapidly changing security environment. Der Derian notes that in a

> heteropolar world, [a] diverse range of different actors are able to produce profound global effects through interconnectivity. Varying in identity, interests, and strength, ranging from fundamentalist terrorists to peace activists, new global actors gain advantage through the broad bandwidth of information technology rather than through the narrow stovepipe of territorially-based sovereign governments. (Der Derian 2011, 11)

Der Derian further observes that heteropolarity transformed the traditional forms of diplomacy and statecraft, as well as the conditions and parameters of conflict management.

The network literature describes such networks as multisectoral, and highlights the added value that such networks bring to governance processes (Benner, Reinicke, and Witte 2005; Ohanyan 2003; Reinicke et al. 2000). In fact, the rise of networks in governance has been celebrated by their proponents precisely for their ability to create institutional spaces for various types of actors, who bring unique resources to the table. As a result, it has been argued that the multisectoral nature of networks adds novel and innovative problem-solving capacities to the infrastructure of global governance, also addressing the operational and participatory deficits within those structures (Benner, Reinicke, and Witte 2005).

At the same time, there is a dark side to heteropolarity, as recognized by the conflict management literature. Jarstad and Belloni (2012) describe the condition of hybrid peace governance, maintaining that international efforts to promote liberal peace (Paris 2004) often clash with the views of many other actors who do not share the liberal vision of peace and the values it promotes. They specifically highlight realities in which the international peace infrastructure clashes with, accommodates, or coexists with illiberal actors, institutions, and norms in conflict areas, ranging from warlords and clientelistic and patrimonial networks to (semi)authoritarian states. The unpredictability in world politics as created by heteropolarity is a concern also shared by Der Derian when he ponders whether "the potential risk posed by negative synergy, cascading effects, and unintended consequences [outweighs] the actual benefits of networks" in the context of a heteropolar world in which global issues are no longer reducible to a single actor (Der Derian 2011).

In terms of conflict management processes, heteropolarity in regional networks is mostly an asset. By connecting actors across public and private divides, heteropolar regional networks craft new negotiation opportunities and complementarities in efforts. Lederach (1997), for example, conceptualizes conflict transformation as processes occurring at the top (policy) level, mid-level (community), and grassroots level. He further elaborates that strategic peace building entails coordination across all three levels (ibid.). Top-down and bottom-up approaches to conflict management, while at times supported by rather segmented literature, together recognize the importance of a diverse range of actors and the much-needed coordination among them. Practitioners in the field place a great premium on heteropolarity, arguing that it reflects inclusive networks and inclusive coalitions to generate collective political will for reform (Kumar and Haye 2012).

Perhaps the most important implication of heteropolar regional networks is their ability to address the problem of isolated interventions. Heteropolarity in interventions provides practitioners with access points to various sectors in society, thereby diversifying the pressure points for peace. The problem of isolated interventions is largely a manifestation of fragmented initiatives: it refers to outcomes when one initiative remains confined within a community, preventing any transfer and spillover into the broader society or the negotiation process. Heteropolar networks help to link such varied interventions by providing multiple access points and pathways, thereby strategically increasing and diversifying the pressure points for peace in a conflict region.

Heteropolarity in regional networks also exposes the "time difference between economic and political globalization" (Goetschel 2000, 262). It can potentially address the existing disjuncture between territorially confined democratic political authority and the globalized practice of economic power (Goetschel 2000). In particular, heteropolarity is at least a manifestation of, and potentially a remedy for, addressing the gap between the "functional linkages and motivations for political action based on particular national interests" (ibid., 262). By bringing together actors from various sectors in politics and economy, heteropolar regional networks create new institutional forums and forms of engagement at the regional level. These spaces offer unique opportunities for regionalized conflict management initiatives.

However, heteropolarity also presents practitioners and policy-makers with a range of problems and limits. First among them is the issue of accountability (Forman and Segaar 2006; Benner, Reinicke, and Witte 2005; Zurn 2005), which is one of the main criticisms faced by heteropolar/multisectoral networks within the literature on global governance. Papadopoulos (2007) concurs with the literature on the democratic deficit in network governance and provides various explanations for it. Some of his concerns are the weaker visibility of such networks, their selective composition and the weak presence of citizen representatives in networks, and the prevalence of peer over public forms of accountability. This is in contrast to more optimistic accounts of network effects on states and societies, which claim that such heteropolar networks simply transform, as opposed to erode, democratic accountability. Heteropolarity in networks is viewed as a postdemocratic form of governance that relies on credibility building through mobilizing coalitions with multiple stakeholders, as opposed to universalistic mechanisms of representation (Carlarne and Carlarne 2006). By building networks with other actors from other sectors, each organization builds credibility, thereby gaining legitimacy in the eyes of the public (ibid.).

But to what extent do accountability and democratic deficit in the context of network governance matter in conflict management processes? Diplomacy and foreign policy are usually considered the purview of governments, and the elite bargaining model is the traditional route to conflict management. According to the conflict management literature, more inclusive peace-building systems on the ground are more likely to produce sustainable and legitimate outcomes than any negotiated settlements between government elites. There is growing support for mutlitrack and multiactor conflict management processes, and this scholarship considers grassroots ties a major asset for successful peace-building outcomes (Racioppi and O'Sullivan See 2007; Rotfeld 1997).

Saunders (2000), Lederach (1997), and Galtung (1996) are perhaps the most recognizable advocates for inclusive conflict management processes. Saunders (2000), in strong support for heteropolarity, has noted that "the concept of the peace process will not be complete until the potential contribution of citizens outside government is recognized and included. It will not be brought into play with full power unless it is seen at the highest levels as operating at both the official and the unofficial or public levels" (ibid., 10). Elsewhere, I have argued that track II initiatives have a sovereignty bias, in addition to being somewhat apolitical. The track II initiative, particularly when applied in undemocratic settings with curtailed freedom of speech and a state-imposed narrative of a conflict, faces an uphill battle in achieving successful outcomes because of the absence of civil society actors at the negotiating table (Ohanyan 2012). The sovereignty bias of the track II paradigm is reflected in the assumption that political communities are territorially confined, which underestimates the role of diasporic communities in peace-building efforts (ibid.). This is particularly relevant to regional conflict management processes.

Another strong endorsement of the rationale for heteropolar, open, democratic peace-building processes emerged from the conflict in Northern Ireland. Byrne points out that for almost thirty years Great Britain relied on the elite bargaining model in its efforts to manage the conflict in Northern Ireland. Only later, in a new phase of the peace process as the United States helped to broker the Good Friday Agreement, was there recognition of the need to coordinate and integrate the elite bargaining system with the middle-tier elites and grassroots participants in an effort to create a participatory peace-building system (Byrne 2001).

That being said, building open and heteropolar peace-building systems could perpetuate interethnic cleavages between communities. Opening up peace-building processes to such nonstate actors as church leaders and grassroots organizers could also intensify the existing conflict lines, because such actors are not necessarily neutral. Indeed, taking such a step requires recognition of both the potentials and the risks associated with heteropolar networks in peace-building processes (Racioppi and O'Sullivan See 2007, 364). For example, Varshney (2001) sees an integral link between the structure of civil life in a multiethnic society and the presence or absence of ethnic violence. Interethnic networks build bridges and manage tensions, which makes them effective agents of peace. By contrast, intraethnic links with poor interethnic connections tend to enable ethnic violence in multiethnic societies (ibid.).

Regional networks with high levels of heteropolarity produce peace systems with enhanced democratic credentials. By engaging individuals and diverse communities in conflict societies, such networks nurture conflict management processes that are dramatically different from the traditional state-centric and grassroots diplomacy. Heteropolar networks lead to extensive intervention strategies that touch on various sectors in a society. They span open, inclusive, and participatory conflict management processes and structures. Recognizing the value of heteropolarity as an added value to conflict management processes can then enable the management of such networks to maximize the potential benefits. The strategic cultivation and management of such networks entail enhancing coordination and complementarities between initiatives, which is a necessary step toward building sustainable and institutionalized regional peace systems in PDAs. An important variable in greater network management is the distribution of power resources within regional networks, which is discussed in the next section.

Degree of Power Concentration and Power Centers

One of the main criticisms facing network governance in the international relations literature is the lack of coordination among the members and the propensities of networks to create fragmented policy outcomes (Ohanyan 2009)—the problems with accountability were discussed in an earlier section. Often such criticisms are based on the assumption that networks are largely horizontal structures in which no single actor drives their operation and functioning. However, recent research has pointed out the great diversity in network arrangements, particularly in power arrangements. Parallel to horizontal networks, largely composed of transnational civil society actors (Keck and Sikkink 1998), are vertical networks with a rather varied composition: some have a clear power center, with one or two network members driving the network politics; others lack any such direction and management.

As discussed in Chapter 2, there are two main types of regional networks in terms of their power distribution: centered and stretched. Centered networks, which have a clear power center, tend to be mobilized by design, with a clear strategy and predetermined expectations and goals in a PDA. By contrast, networks without nerve centers are mobilized by default, largely lacking a strategy for mobilization and being driven at times by uncoordinated efforts and initiatives from civil society actors or state-centric institutions.

In PDAs, centered networks are usually built around a single international or regional organization. The Regional Cooperation Council in the Balkans is one example. However, not all regional or international organizations are created equal in terms of their abilities to drive the network. Specific conditions tend to shape their abilities to evolve into power centers in the network and to become institutional hegemons. The ability of a regional or international organization to transform itself into an institutional hegemon in the network and to drive the network operation is contingent on two dimensions of network power. For any regional or international organization to evolve into an institutional hegemon in the network, at a minimum the organization must possess a favorable network position, centrality: it is a network characteristic borrowed from social network literature to describe cases in which an organization has the largest number of connections to other members of the network. *Higher centrality* is a term applied to an organization that is a central node in the network. *Low centrality* is applied to organizations that are connected to only a few network members.

For an institutional hegemon to capitalize fully on its superior structural power of centrality within the network, it also needs to possess the requisite resources—political, financial, and organizational (Ohanyan 2008). Therefore, it is only in such network conditions of structural superiority that an organization can translate that power into institutional might, thereby becoming an institutional hegemon within the network. Similarly, it also follows from resource dependency theory that organizations will evolve into institutional hegemons if they provide incentives to other network members. Specifically, by being a key supplier of financial, institutional, or political resources (Ohanyan 2009), international organizations can control the resource allocation within the network. Their exit from a network can seriously undermine the performance of implementing actors such as NGOs (Pfeffer and Salancik 1978).

Any discussion of the regionalization of conflict management usually centers on building the conflict management capacities of regional organizations, without paying attention to their broader network environments. Instead, in the research direction proposed here, international organizations are treated as constituent parts of internally differentiated interorganizational systems and structures (Ness and Brechin 1988), built around interorganizational bargaining, conflict, and cooperation (Ohanyan 2008). Within organization theory, the network approach signifies a shift away from treating organizations as closed systems to treating them as open and interacting with their environments.

Against this backdrop, acknowledging the organizational embeddedness of regional or international organizations in their respective institutional environments allows one to delineate between networks with a clear power center and those characterized by a power vacuum. In the case of centered networks, the role of individual organizations, mostly international or regional, is important for this distinction. In cases of regionalism in PDAs, it is the international or regional organizations that usually support and center regional networks as they champion and advance greater regionalization in a PDA. In stretched networks without a clear nerve center, no such organization drives regionalism, which has limits as well as opportunities for conflict management processes.

In conflict management processes, the distinction is dramatic between centered networks mobilized by design and strategic planning and stretched networks with default and spontaneous mobilization patterns. The centered networks with institutional hegemons are better positioned to address coordination problems (Crocker, Hampson, and Aall 2011; Schnabel 2002), which has been one of the main criticisms directed at the network mode of global governance (Ohanyan 2009, 2008). The institutional hegemon in a network, because of its centrality, possesses the tools to reduce duplicated efforts and provide continuities among various conflict management initiatives. Occupying a position of institutional hegemony, such organizations can thus transfer effects up and down the society, thereby diversifying and enhancing the peace pressure points within a PDA. For anyone thinking about networks as peace-building systems, the institutional hegemons emerge as critical nodes in balancing the opportunities for conflict management created by regional networked governance. Therefore, such networks are best equipped to address the problem of isolated initiatives.

An often ignored implication of networked governance that is pertinent to this study is the ability of some networks, particularly the ones with an institutional hegemon, to create an institutionalized environment, thereby filtering some of the political pressures from the states. In particular, institutional hegemons enjoy superior network power, which allows them to professionalize their authority through issue-based networks and technocratic tools, thereby creating strong buffers against the political pressures and influences coming from the states. In conflict management processes, this plays out in terms of the ability of institutional hegemons to create and facilitate issue-based networks at the regional level that have a strong technocratic/professional flavor. Such networks are usually able to depoliticize and facilitate cross-conflict communication between the communities. When such links are dense, the institutional space for conflict management increases. As a result, political influences of the states, which tend to advance narrowly defined national security issues, weaken. The Regional Cooperation Council is one such example, to be discussed in Chapter 5.

Although the institutional hegemons in centered networks are able to produce coordination and cooperation among network members, the peace process they foster is still top-down. This chapter has already examined the ramifications of top-down peace processes. Unless the institutional hegemon is able to enhance the heteropolarity within the network by involving stakeholders from various sectors, the centered networks will most likely produce a cold peace as opposed to a normal to warm peace, which tends to develop in a more organic manner. Similarly, stretched networks without a clear nerve center are vulnerable to duplicated efforts by third parties and to the problems caused by isolated interventions. However, by their design such networks are well positioned to activate more organic peace processes by connecting with a variety of actors and stakeholders from all sides of the conflict.

When it comes to the extent of intervention and the prospects for building institutionalized peace systems, the centered networks with institutional hegemons provide the basic infrastructure on which more extensive interventions can be built and institutionalized for long-term purposes. Although the stretched networks do not have the organizational advantages for coordination provided by institutional hegemons in centered networks, they are superior in terms of their closeness to the public and the grassroots in terms of the sheer quantity of peace pressure points they possess.

Conclusion

In contrast to simply enhancing the conflict management capacities of international or regional organizations, the networked peace paradigm introduced in this chapter calls for restructuring the relationships among the international organizations, regional organizations, NGOs, state actors, and the private sectors active in PDAs. The theoretical framework of the network peace paradigm developed in this chapter illustrates that the type of peace sought and the extent of interventions applied are highly sensitive to the structural composition of the networks active at the regional level in PDAs. Effective network governance in PDAs is assessed in terms of its ability to create institutionalized peace systems that can function on a long-term basis, even after the existing conflict has been mitigated or transformed. The type of peace established by third parties and the extent of their interventions in the conflict society are said to be important ingredients in building institutionalized peace systems in PDAs. The empirical chapters that follow will apply the framework of the networked peace paradigm in conflict cases in Northern Ireland, the Balkans, and South Caucasus.

4   Three Regional Approaches to Conflict Management

The use of regional approaches and regional integration as a conflict manage-ment strategy frequently elicits skepticism from policy analysts in South Cauca-sus. Since presenting the early findings of this research, I have grown accustomed to the comment, "Nice idea, but where else has it worked?" Customarily, I point to the European Union, and then engage in a discussion about whether the EU experience in Northern Ireland is relevant to regionalism and security provision in the developing world. As in other politically divided areas (PDAs), in South Caucasus geopolitical, power-based policy approaches are dominant, and geog-raphy and history are viewed as destiny. It is with this backdrop in mind that I have set out to explore other PDAs where regionalism has been cultivated despite ongoing interstate or intrastate conflicts, or where regional approaches to con-flict management have been sought. The lack of research on such areas, which I call the "high N problem" for studies in conflict management, has been a sig-nificant roadblock to taking more creative and innovative approaches to conflict management interventions in PDAs in the developing world.

This chapter is an overview of the ways in which the regional cooperative structures have developed over the years in PDAs other than Balkans and West Europe (Tannam 2012). Within that overview, the chapter seeks to fulfill three specific objectives. The first is to take a small step toward addressing the "high N problem" by asking, "Where else has it worked?" The short answer is "Every-where." Indeed, instances of deploying regional structures to cultivate coop-eration and ensure regional stability are numerous. For example, Mercosur, a regional organization created to reduce tensions between Argentina and Brazil, began as a free-trade zone in 1991, with the ultimate goal of full South Ameri-can economic integration.[1] The organization is currently debating whether to add political cooperation to its organizational structures. Another example is the South African Development Community (SADC). Even though SADC did not receive its current organizational form until 1992, the political underpinnings of its formation date back to the 1960s, when the leaders in several newly decolonized countries with majority black governments in southern Africa joined forces to push for an end to white minority rule in other countries in the region, best exemplified by the apartheid regime in South Africa.

And yet another example is the South Asian Association for Regional Cooperation (SAARC). Formed in 1983, it brought together rivals in one of the most protracted conflicts in the world: India's and Pakistan's dispute over Kashmir. Interestingly, the regionwide discussions among the regional elites to form such an organization date back to 1950s. Like many regional organizations in the developing world, SAARC began by building cooperation around socioeconomic structures, but it is now signaling a move to political and security issues as well. The Association of Southeast Asian Nations (ASEAN) and the System of Central American Integration (SICA) are also examples of regional organizations in the developing world that were created in regions with serious security fault lines. They are analyzed in greater detail in the rest of this chapter.

The second objective of this chapter is to acknowledge and appreciate the diversity of regions and institutionalized forms of cooperation they sustain. Understanding how regions vary as well as the various kinds of institutionalized forms of cooperation they can have is necessary to craft regional approaches to conflict management and more efficiently use regional integration as a conflict management strategy. Developing this understanding calls for novel research avenues both within political economy and comparative regional studies and in the field of conflict analysis and resolution. Institutional forms of regional cooperation vary in the extent to which they specifically focus on political security or start from nonpolitical issues with the intention of moving into security issues down the road. The network approach developed in this study is one way in which to understand and analyze such diversity in regional forms, looking specifically at their prospects for conflict management in the region. It is also a way to determine the centrality of a regional organization—the pivot—for crafting, maintaining, and managing regional governance processes. A network analysis enables an assessment of how deep a regional organization reaches into each society. Knowing the extent to which it is embedded in the political and social fabric of member states helps to determine the extent to which the regional organization can be a reliable axis for building conflict management infrastructure in the region.

In parallel, as often pointed out by skeptics of the use of regionalism as a conflict management strategy, regions also differ in their vulnerabilities to external powers or the extent to which an interstate or intrastate conflict is central or peripheral to a region. It is often argued that regions differ in their predisposition to successful regional conflict management applications. As one moves toward addressing the "high N problem," the institutional scenarios around the world in which regional tensions were tamed through regional organizations and regionally formed structures of cooperation are revealed. In short, regionalism offers a way to reduce the political space of a conflict, thereby limiting its centrality in a region.

The third objective of this chapter is to apply the regional theory for conflict areas developed in Chapter 1 to Central America and Southeast Asia. The regions covered in this chapter are analyzed in terms of (1) their abilities to assert autonomy from external powers in the region; (2) the extent to which shared regional problems, as opposed to geographical proximity, have been driving regional cooperation; and (3) the ways in which nonstate actors have played a role in pushing or hindering greater regional cooperation in a PDA. Network analysis is then applied to the regional organizations central to each region—SICA in Central America and ASEAN in Southeast Asia—as well as the EU's involvement in the Northern Ireland conflict. Note, however, that the chapter applies the network approach to understanding the politics of regional cooperation in PDAs without necessarily testing causal claims about greater regional cooperation and conflict management outcomes in each case.

This chapter thus describes three regions and their corresponding "regional pivots." Because of the vast literature on the European Union, the chapter focuses mainly on the specific role it has played in addressing the conflict in Northern Ireland. The chapter concludes with a discussion of how each regional organization and its conflict management capacities compare with the current general reform initiatives of the global conflict management infrastructure.

European Union and Northern Ireland

The Context

The European Union is perhaps the most recognizable model of regionalism, but that recognition often obscures the rich diversity of institutional possibilities for supporting regional integration in developing countries. Although the scholarly literature is slowly moving toward understanding the conditions, contexts, and types of regional integration in the developing world, national policy-makers in such regions are still generally skeptical about the prospects for integration. In such contexts, the EU is not considered applicable to developing countries. Indeed, Diez and Hayward (2008) maintain that Northern Ireland was one of the few lingering conflicts related to a border within the fifteen member states of the EU before the 2004 accession. Although the EU has been a successful regional initiative in transcending borders between its member states, its impact is significantly more nuanced when applied to conflict cases in which a border is a signifier of a conflict (ibid.).

The key rationale for including the EU and Northern Ireland in this study is the ability of the EU to "network the peace" in Northern Ireland. The EU approach to addressing the Northern Ireland conflict is most representative of the regionally networked peace paradigm. Although a complete transfer of regional integration models from the EU to developing countries may be challenging, the specific techniques and strategies of "networking peace" through regional governance are quite applicable and relevant to conflict regions in the developing world. Indeed, both Central America and Southeast Asia have significantly evolved regional structures, but their ability to network the peace and build a networked-based infrastructure of conflict management has been lagging behind that of Europe. The comparative network analysis of the regional pivots in Central America and Southeast Asia relative to the EU and Northern Ireland will reveal the reasons behind such a gap.

The complex relationship between regionalism and conflict management in Northern Ireland can be described in terms of its systemic and organizational dimensions. In its systemic dimension, the emphasis is on greater regional integration as promoted by the EU and the rather indirect effect that it had on making the 1998 Good Friday Agreement possible. In the relationship's organizational dimension, the EU has altered the organizational contours of political action in the conflict area, thereby enabling and building cooperation on the ground between elites as well as within the grassroots community.

The systemic effects of greater regional integration in Europe on conflict management in Northern Ireland are broadly recognized. First, according to Laffan and O'Mahony (2008), "[T]he EU system offered a far more benign external environment for small states, including Ireland, than traditional balance of power systems or empire (199)." They maintain that EU membership produced a formal equality between Ireland and Great Britain, thereby moderating and taming the asymmetrical relationship between them. This equality, the argument goes, played a key role in improving relations between the two countries and the signing of the Anglo-Irish Agreement in 1985, which preceded successful negotiation of the Good Friday Agreement in 1998 (ibid.).

The second set of systemic effects of regionalism on the dynamics of conflict and its management on the ground relates to global forces (Ruane and Todd 2002). Globalization introduced new political possibilities by creating fresh economic incentives for cooperation between elites and grassroots communities. Globalization does not guarantee the continued success of the agreement, but it creates new space for radical political initiatives for peaceful coexistence, while also enabling tendencies that challenge their success (ibid.). Therefore, the observers of this conflict highlight the continuing need to nurture and expand the political achievements from the 1990s in the new and highly uncertain environment created by globalization.

Global forces can also interact with domestic political settings and economies to heighten income inequalities and other conflict fault lines. However, Northern Ireland was largely shielded from such pressures by the British state as well as the European Union (ibid.). This was accomplished by subsidies and politically motivated investments that prevented cuts in the public sector and stimulated demand, such as for tourism in the border area. The EU funding for developing cross-border areas and local microeconomies is one example of such an investment (McCall 1999).

A third set of systemic effects includes the dimensions of globalization that made it possible for the Good Friday Agreement to disaggregate the various dimensions of statehood—sovereignty, decision-making, cultural presence, administrative integration, citizenship rights—"and to redistribute them more evenly between the sovereign British state, regional Northern Ireland institutions, the Irish state, and new North-South institutions" (Ruane and Todd 2002, 121). In this respect, global forces allowed for policy interventions in softening borders and reconfiguring the institutional boundaries of the statehood by enhancing the role of Ireland in exercising certain dimensions of sovereignty, such as cultural presence and emergent new layers of administrative integration between the Republic of Ireland and Northern Ireland. The EU as a model of regionalism offered the normative frames, institutional tools, and economic incentives needed to make all of this possible.

The EU and the Networked Peace in Northern Ireland

In terms of its direct organizational impact on conflict management efforts in Northern Ireland, the EU offers many lessons for conflict management practitioners and diplomats in developing countries. The most commonly cited aspect of the "European dimension" of conflict management in Northern Ireland is the allocation of funds, such as the Structural Adjustment Funds, Interref II, and the EU Special Support Programme for Peace and Reconciliation in Northern Ireland and Border Counties of the Republic of Ireland (Ruane and Todd 2002). It is estimated that the EU contributed more than 1 billion to resolving the conflict (Racioppi and O'Sullivan 2007). The organizational underpinnings of this funding were also crucial to successful conflict management in Northern Ireland. The financial assistance allocated to the conflict was delivered through decentralized funding mechanisms, which complemented those by the British, Irish, and U.S. governments aimed at supporting highly targeted interventions in the conflict areas (ibid.).

Indeed, layers of new organizations were created to address the conflict within the EU framework. The Northern Ireland Centre in Brussels, set up in 1991, became a focal point for integrating business groups and political parties from the area into European structures. The Council of Europe, through the European Convention on Human Rights and the European Court of Human Rights, was critical, allowing individuals to take up cases against the British state. These new organizations created new layers of supranational governance and new models of politics, thereby weakening the power of the traditional governance structures centered around sovereign and territorially confined states. The Peace Programme was carried out in two phases (1995 to 1999 and 2000 to 2006), supporting more than seventeen thousand projects by 2003. The sheer scale of such an intervention is particularly valuable for engaging civil society across conflict lines, thereby grounding interventions in the grassroots and generating much needed public legitimacy for negotiated outcomes (Byrne 2001; Hancock 2008).

The added value of financial support and politically motivated investments, along with institution building within the EU aimed at Northern Ireland, rests with the networks that emerge across various levels of governance, connecting a variety of groups and communities across conflict lines. Many of the EU programs and initiatives required multilevel governance mechanisms and various types of partnerships across conflict lines. In terms of the regionally networked peace paradigm discussed in this study, EU programs have yielded a highly networked institutional environment across various levels of the conflict line. Although most of these initiatives had top-down patterns of development, upon implementation they required bottom-up partnerships for effective implementation (Laffan and Payne 2001). These networks are highly heteropolar, drawing from the civil society, private, and public (including local) sectors of the state (Diez and Hayward 2008; Racioppi and K. O'Sullivan See 2007; Hancock 2008). It is widely acknowledged within the academic and policy communities that the high capacity and institutional density of the networks created by EU funding in the Northern Ireland conflict have translated into a large number of community programs with intensive NGO and local governmental support (Hancock 2008).

The heteropolarity of these emergent networks has been further reinforced by their political links to EU Commission officials, which has created powerful feedback mechanisms between the grassroots and supranational governance structures of the EU. According to Diez and Hayward (2008), these networks have great capacity and have been strengthened by EU funding (Birrell and Hayes 2001). "Social partners and political actors at a regional level now have new roles, new responsibilities and new relationships—illustrated by the proliferation of partnership boards, regional networks and agencies in the past decade, many of which are cross-border and some of which have direct links with EU Commission officials" (Diez and Hayward 2008, 56). Such novel institutional features have allowed the initiation of innovative and risk-taking projects at the bottom level. Meanwhile, the highly networked peace systems deployed by the EU at the regional level have contributed to innovations within the practice of conflict management surrounding Northern Ireland:

> The EU is thus a blank canvas, for the most part, a pretty useful one. It can be stuffed into the gaps not met by mainstream funding, for instance, or thrown as a cover over politically sensitive projects (neither government would want to support publicly to many ex-paramilitary prisoner groups, for example). The EU's relative political anonymity is simultaneously one of the biggest opportunities for the EU in cross-border co-operation and one of its biggest impediments. In the absence of more-informed debate about the EU as a polity, this discourse, together with the required advertising of EU support for community projects and infrastructural development, creates the popular impression of the EU as a resource. Even those directly involved in PEACE-funded projects do not generally see the EU as a key player for conflict transformation, more as a facilitator for local actors to move towards that goal. (Ibid., 57).

The enthusiasts for the EU role in the management of the conflict in Northern Ireland clarify that the EU dimension did not by itself bring about constructive management of the conflict. Instead, the EU bolstered British-Irish cooperation and the peace process rather than directly fostering cooperation on the ground (Tannam 2012). The Anglo-Irish Agreement (AIA) increased bureaucratic cooperation and obliged government officials from both countries to meet at least twice a year. Such frequency of contact was embedded in layers of institutional engagement between both governments (ibid.), which directly contributed to the more consensual and less adversarial approach used by officials across the conflict line. The increase in formal and informal meetings played a crucial role in creating an institutionally dense mediation regime on the ground.

Perhaps the strongest endorsement to date of the network dimension of the conflict management infrastructure in Northern Ireland is that by Goddard (Goddard 2012), who has argued that the presence of brokers around the negotiating table was a factor in successful conflict resolution. The brokers were able to legitimate settlements by framing them in such a way that they were consistent with the principles and positions of multiple actors and coalitions. More specifically, Goddard clarifies that in highly polarized political settings (both between and inside conflict parties), brokers are crucial because they are links to a network's social and cultural resources. The network approach to understanding conflict management processes allows one to delineate the ways in which the societies on the two sides of a conflict connect with each other, ranging from polarized contacts between narrow political elites to more broad based and diverse exchanges between various segments of the societies across conflict lines.

In short, in terms of its conflict management capacities, the European region is an archetypical case of a networked peace system: it is characterized by both top-down and bottom-up patterns of regional initiatives, with extensive nonstate actor involvement, high levels of institutional density, and heteropolarity. These institutional attributes were instrumental in enabling a successful resolution and continued management and transformation of the conflict in Northern Ireland.

Central America

Regional Profile

The regional politics in Central America has shifted dramatically over the last three decades. Civil wars, their spillover effects, and interstate tensions have given way to drug trafficking and criminalization of the state. The transnational sources of contemporary security threats, of which drug trafficking is the most visible example, have solidified pressures for building regional structures and cultivating regional cooperation in order to produce an effective response to the emerging security threats. The regional politics surrounding the peace processes that ended the conflicts in Central America in the 1980s and 1990s is most directly related to the goals of this study, and those processes are the rationale for examining the regional politics in Central America during that period. This is not to minimize the urgency of the contemporary security threats in the region, nor to miss the great strides in strengthening the regional structures. Instead, the goal is to understand the institutional incentives and political forces that produced the regional responses to the multilayered conflict complexes dividing the region.

Indeed, throughout much of the Cold War, conflicts and wars, as opposed to cooperation, dominated Central America. In the 1980s alone, Central America was caught up in three civil wars—in Nicaragua, El Salvador, and Guatemala. These internal conflicts were intertwined with the East-West ideological confrontation (LeoGrande 1998). Meanwhile, instability persisted in a context of administratively weak states with poorly consolidated democratic institutions. Both the political and economic costs of the conflicts were enormous. Moreover, the military's role in providing internal social order simply emboldened that institution and further retarded the growth and development of civilian governance (Manaut and Macías 2011). The civil war in Guatemala (1960–96) resulted in 150,000 deaths, 50,000 missing, nearly 1 million people internally displaced, and 100,000 refugees. The Salvadoran conflict (1980–92) resulted in nearly 75,000 deaths (ibid.). The overall regional instability increased the risks associated with foreign direct investment, thereby creating a vicious circle of underdevelopment, poverty, and conflict.

Throughout much of the Cold War, the regional autonomy relative to the external powers, such as the United States and Soviet Union, was minimal. As a PDA, the region was highly vulnerable to external influences, especially that of the United States. Because of the geographical proximity and economic might of its neighbor, Central America experienced almost no regional autonomy for decades. Therefore, against this backdrop, the emergence of regional initiatives in conflict management, largely led by the countries in Central America (Solis 1995), was a qualitative break with the past and an instructive case for other PDAs that today are divided by conflict and caught up in great power rivalries. Indeed, Solis (ibid.) reminds us that dependency on external actors has been Central America's most enduring feature over the last 173 years. Similar to contemporary politics in South Caucasus (see Chapter 6), the region was dominated by zero-sum politics and driven by great power rivalries (ibid.). And yet the political will among governmental elites in the region to cooperate and take the peace and conflict dynamics into their own hands has played a key role in neutralizing the international variable that has traditionally fueled conflicts in Central America (ibid.).

Whether functional ties or geographic proximity is the primary regional marker as a regional profile attribute is rather complex in Central America. This region has a long history of regional cooperation and integration, and the depth of functional ties has waxed and waned over decades and even centuries. The history of regional integration in Central America goes back to its independence from Spain in 1824, when the Federal Republic of Central America (made up of the present-day states of Guatemala, Honduras, El Salvador, Costa Rica, and Nicaragua) was formed (Bull 1999). The Federal Republic collapsed in 1838, and subsequent regionalist initiatives enjoyed little success until the 1950s and 1960s, when the Central American Common Market was established. Unfortunately, the experimentation with regionalism was interrupted by the civil wars that demolished the region in the 1970s and 1980s. Interestingly, it was the regional efforts that played a key role in ending the civil conflicts and interethnic political tensions in the region.

Geographical proximity has been a major regional marker, manifested in conflict spillovers and the transnationalization of drug cartels in Central America (Manaut and Macías 2011). However, the long history of regional cooperation has contributed to the development of functional ties between the countries. Bull (1999) maintains that two regionalisms have competed for dominance of the official process. The first was related to the Esquipulas peace process, a regional initiative that ended the civil wars in three Central American countries. The second was largely a reaction to globalization and hemispheric economic integration. The latter, liberalizing regionalism, became dominant in the 1990s. Although the functional regional ties were formed in the economic sector, many businesses began to seek integration with the larger markets in North America, thereby making regionalism in Central America superfluous, according to Bull (ibid.).

Both types of regionalism, one driven by peace processes and one by global economic liberalization, positioned the region well to build functional networks at the regional level. The regionalism that evolved from the peace processes in the 1980s moved toward security sector reform in all countries. The key initiative in this area pursued by all the countries involved was based on demilitarization of their political systems. They reduced the size of their militaries and their budgets, and separated the defense and public security institutions while redefining the doctrines of the armed forces, slowly moving them away from providing public security (Manaut and Macías 2011). The regional dimension of these processes was centered in several highly specialized regional instruments, such as the Democratic Security Framework Treaty (1995), and some other instruments that have a more technical focus, such as the Treaty for Mutual Legal Assistance in Criminal Affairs (1993) and the Constitutive Agreement for the Central American Commission for the Eradication of Production, Traffic, Consumption and Illicit Use of Narcotics and Psychotropic Substances (1993).

Meanwhile, liberalizing regionalisms aimed at creating larger economic spaces in Central America so that countries could become more competitive in the global economy while building regional interstate ties and political agreements. In the 1990s, participants in the Central American summit meeting in Guatemala that kick-started this round of regionalism agreed on the Central American Economic Action Plan (Bull 1999). The action plan produced a new judicial framework for economic integration, a program for integration of infrastructure and trade, coordination of opening toward third countries, and policies to allow markets to play a larger role in domestic economies (ibid.). Another important regional agreement accompanied by a strong functional and highly specialized initiative was the Tegucigalpa Protocol, which was signed in 1991. It created the basis for the SICA. The Protocol of Guatemala, signed in 1993, modernized and reformed the Treaty of Economic Integration of 1962, resulting in the abandonment of protectionist policies at the regional level in favor of an "open regionalism" model (ibid.).

The functional dimension of Central American regionalism was further strengthened by the so-called institutional follow-up. The Tegucigalpa Protocol produced political institutions for a variety of issues. It was further embedded in the network of civil society actors who were committed to the regional integration in Central America and represented on the Consultative Council (ibid.). In this round of institution building, the Federation of Private Enterprises in Central America and Panama (FEDEPRICAP) was formed in 1993. In 1994 the Civil Initiative for Central American Integration was established (ibid.).

Yet another regional marker considered in this study is the extent of nonstate actor participation in a given regional integration initiative. Despite very vibrant institutional development at the regional level, largely driven by states and international organizations, commentators are more skeptical about the levels of civil society and nonstate actor support in regional integration initiatives in Central America. Overall, significant financial flows and intraregional trade are under way. Although historically the United Sates has been the main destination of Central American exports in agriculture, textiles, and manufactures, accounting for some 32 percent of total exports from the region, the intraregional trade also has been significant (World Bank 2013).[2] As of 2013, the Central American Common Market was the second largest trading partner of most countries in the region, with 26 percent of all exports (ibid.).[3] Moreover, these levels of intraregional export shares place Central America in fourth place among trading blocs, above Mercosur and the Andean Community of Nations (CAN) (ibid.). Such high levels of intraregional trade tend to be associated with dense networks among business associations and professional communities. At the same time, Bull (1999) maintains that the regional network of civil society organizations within the SICA process has been challenged by the bureaucratic procedures of the newly formed regional institutions. As of early 2000, there was little evidence of spontaneous regionalization and nonstate actor–led regional integration processes; formal regionalism was continually identified as the key pattern in Central American regional politics.

The Regional Pivot: SICA

The profile of Central America just presented indicates that the region does possess a solid infrastructure of regional governance, most of which was developed in the aftermath of the civil wars in the region. The parallel process of regionalism driven by economic liberalization reforms domestically and globally produced a momentum of regional institution building around free trade and the economic interface between societies.

The long experimentation with regional governance in Central America seems to have resulted in a formidable presence of regional-level institutions, which are important when thinking about regionally networked peace paradigms. Currently, active institution building is under way at the regional level in Central America, largely stimulated by the regional peace process initiatives, such as the Contadora Group, Esquipulas I, and Esquipulas II.

The regional institution building that has accompanied the inception of peace processes showcases Central America as a region in which the expanded regional cooperation is both an outcome of peace processes and a major facilitating/enabling factor in creating sustainable conditions for peace. In terms of the outcome of peace processes, regional cooperation is a force behind peace building: strengthening regionalism, whether driven by security sector reforms or economic liberalization, has been a way to enhance the problem-solving capacities of individual states to address domestic security challenges in drug trafficking, as well as to attempt to further economic development and close the income gap inside their respective societies. In terms of expanded regional cooperation as a major facilitating/enabling factor in creating sustainable conditions for peace, regional cooperation is an effect of peace building because it becomes possible after the cessation of conflicts, which makes it possible to open up borders. The Declaration of Esquipulas I, a key regional initiative in the peace process ending the civil wars in Central America, features the need to create institutional structures that can support and complement greater understanding of cooperation in the region. The agreement specifies that such regional institutions can "strengthen the dialogue, the common development, democracy and pluralism as fundamental elements for peace in the area and for the integration of Central America."[4] In addition, in Central America the end of conflicts also created openings for democratization because the rationale for military spending disappeared, and security sector reform limiting the role of the military to external protection of states as opposed to internal public security became possible.

In Central America, the network profile of regionalism, and the state of the networked peace that such regionalism conditions, can be characterized as "rebuilding," which is the middle tier in Figure 3.1, Networked Peace, in Chapter 3. Indeed, very early in the peace process in 1980s there was strong acknowledgment of the mutually reinforcing nature of peace, democracy, and economic development—the "holy trinity." Greater regional cooperation and rebuilding of regional governance structures were viewed as necessary in the midterm for its practical implementation. Although the civil wars interrupted the decades-long institutional experimentation with regionalism in Central America, the peace processes ushered in another round of regional institution building. These efforts can best be described as rebuilding the prior institutional machinery of regionalism in Central America, even though some of the regional institutions were just being created.

SICA, the System of Central American Integration, aptly reflects this period of regional institution building. It is an important regional organization in Central America in terms of promoting greater economic and political integration among its member countries. SICA was established on December 13, 1991, under the Tegucigalpa Protocol, which amended the Charter of ODECA (Organization of Central American States), signed on December 12, 1962. SICA began operations in 1993. Its founding members were Belize, Costa Rica, El Salvador, Guatemala, Honduras, Nicaragua, and Panama. Other countries around the world have extraregional observer status within the organization.

As the main institutional framework for regional integration in Central America, SICA is enjoying growing legitimacy, regionally and globally: Colombia, Ecuador, Haiti, and Uruguay are in the process of joining SICA as regional observers, and the United Kingdom is joining as an extraregional observer. As a pivotal network of regionalism in Central America and a networked organization itself, SICA has a clear top-down pattern of mobilization. The top-down pattern of mobilization is reflected in the strong UN support for the initiative in registering it and allowing SICA bodies and institutions to interact with the UN system.[5]

SICA as a network is highly institutionalized. It is structured around four tiers of governance that balance state interests with the increasingly vocal supranational institutions within the system, such as the Central American Parliament (PARLACEN). The first institutional tier includes the Meeting of Presidents, Council of Ministers, Executive Committee, and General Secretariat, all of which are centered around the interests and positions of member states as opposed to the broader supranational needs of the region. The first tier is supplemented with the Meeting of Vice Presidents, Central American Parliament, Central American Court of Justice, and Consultative Committee. The functional secretariats within SICA are numerous and include the Central American Secretariat for Economic Integration, Central American Secretariat for Social Integration, Executive Secretariat of the Central American Agricultural Council, Secretariat of Central American Tourism Integration, and General Secretariat of the Central American Educational and Cultural Coordination. The fourth tier of the SICA network is populated with highly specialized functional agencies, including the Central American Bank for Economic Integration, Coordination Center for Natural Disaster Prevention in Central America, and Foundation to Promote the Competitiveness of Micro and Small Enterprise in Central America. Twenty-five specialized institutions currently operate within the SICA network, all of which serve as mechanisms to strengthen regional contacts and regional policy coordination between the member countries within a given issue area of their operation. Their cumulative effect is to strengthen the regional dimension of governance processes within the member states, which is not a small undertaking considering the limited administrative capacities of the member states.

SICA's density of institutional links, which is best illustrated by the high number of interstate agencies within the SICA network, is matched by its high level of heteropolarity. The numerous agencies within the SICA network cover a broad range of issue areas, from higher education and small and medium enterprise (SME) development to fisheries and aquaculture. The effective operation of these agencies is highly contingent on their ability to reach out to the public and private sectors of the member states. The functional diversity of these institutions has positioned them effectively to penetrate multiple areas of societies, thereby generating new institutional spaces for resolving conflicts should they arise in various issue areas. Indeed, SICA lists forty-two "integration topics" that span the political, economic, and social areas of regional integration. Joining a mix of state-centric and regional/supranational institutions, SICA is also evolving into a network in which not a single state or organization has been able to concentrate political, financial, or institutional power, thereby dramatically affecting its operation. Geographically, the various agencies within the SICA network are spread over the region. Operating as a stretched, as opposed to a centered, network, the organization has been an effective tool for generating public support for regional initiatives, as evidenced by the high levels of regional trade, particularly when compared with other regions that are recovering from violent conflicts and wars.

Despite its top-down patterns of development, SICA has evolved into a network with deep grassroots ties and highly institutionalized supranational/ regional organizations. Its parliament, PARLACEN, is its most important institution. The value of SICA in terms of its conflict management capacities is significant. First, the internal networked structure of SICA has enabled the organization to develop functional ties with various levels of societies, ranging from grassroots to governments. Such institutional richness and heteropolarity has been effective in activating the stakeholders of regional integration in all member countries, thereby building and strengthening groups and communities that are direct beneficiaries of peace and stability in the region. Second, by strengthening its regional supranational dimension, SICA has created a forum for popular political participation, parallel to that shaped by the sovereignty of the nation-states. The expansion of regional supranational layers of governance transforms the relationship between the states and their people, providing the latter with new economic opportunities and instruments of political participation. The consolidation of regional supranational institutions offers numerous new spaces for institutionalized conflict management, thereby making SICA a powerful engine in absorbing socioeconomic and political conflicts of various sorts that may otherwise cripple its member states.

Southeast Asia

Regional Profile

Southeast Asia is an archetypal case of a politically divided area. It is a region of geographically proximate states with security and economic interdependencies. It is also a region characterized by relatively weak internal recognition but strong external recognition as a distinctive area. Southeast Asia lacks a coherent regional identity as a security community, and it is populated by countries with highly diverse political systems, religious traditions, and competitive (as opposed to complementary) economies (Emmerson 2008; Öjendal 2004; Rüland 2011). The autonomy of the region has evolved over the years. Even though states outside of the region, such as the United States, Russia, and the European Union, maintain an influence over it, making it vulnerable to externally induced geopolitical competition, the regional autonomy has evolved significantly over the last two decades, particularly with the strengthening of ASEAN as a regional organization in the post–Cold War environment. As a PDA, Southeast Asia is a region with uneven and embryonic functional ties and with national interests continually and strongly advocated by the political elites, often at the expense of regional values and regional interests.

The Regional Pivot: ASEAN

ASEAN has been central to Southeast Asia's story of regional integration. Even though in its institutional evolution Southeast Asia lacks the evolved structures of regional governance characteristic of the European Union, ASEAN, the organizational pivot of the region, is considered to be the most diplomatically advanced, politically successful, and comprehensively institutionalized attempt at regionalization outside Europe (Öjendal 2004; Acharya and Johnston 2008). As a result, the region is no longer defined by conflict and security crises. Territorial disputes and political disagreements are still numerous in the region, but interstate disputes have ceased to be a significant source of instability. Emmerson (2008) claims that since the birth of ASEAN in 1967, war has never broken out between any of its member states, indicating the capacity of this regional organization to cultivate order and security in the region (see also Acharya and Johnston 2008).

Cooperation, then, as opposed to conflict, is the main regional marker in Southeast Asia. The evolving role of ASEAN and the subsequent formation of the Asian Regional Forum (ARF) have produced "soft institutionalization," which has played a crucial role in the conflict management efforts of the organization (ibid.). The security threats have evolved from the traditional interstate political tensions and rivalries to nontraditional security threats such as maritime abuses of piracy and overfishing, transnational crimes of money laundering and human trafficking, illnesses from infectious diseases, violent internal conflicts, and societal deterioration (Emmerson 2008). Further institutional expansion of ASEAN and other organizations in the region has gained renewed importance in terms of facilitating issue-based linkages and professional communities in order to address the new and nontraditional security threats in a global era.

Although the geographical proximity of states is an important regional marker, issue-based functional ties have grown since ASEAN was conceived in 1967. ASEAN has evolved into an organizational engine for highly specialized network development around various issue areas. Such issue coverage includes transnational crime, financial transactions, agriculture and forestry, science and technology, tourism, culture and arts, education, and disaster management. ASEAN's structure includes regular and frequent ministerial meetings in these issue areas, thereby creating norms and setting agendas on these issues (Rüland 2011). In this capacity, ASEAN can be credited for creating multiple layers of regional governance in order to enhance member states' capacities to respond to increasingly regional and global problems. The establishment of such functional ties at the regional level is associated with increased institutional density at the regional level, resting on the assumption that such an institutional thickening can serve as a powerful antidote to power (ibid.).

Significant skepticism surrounds the institutional density of ASEAN. Some describe such institutionalization as shallow and pragmatic "hedging," as opposed to genuine multilateralism that can enhance the governance capacities of states by decoupling professional expertise from politics (ibid.). In its hedging, ASEAN has sought institutional balancing between its member states rather than striving for collective action–driven behavior and problem solving. This approach has been associated with "soft institutionalization," which is non-binding and nonprecise, and dispute settlement mechanisms do not infringe on state sovereignty. ASEAN has also been criticized for little investment in institutional deepening, and so it has continued to produce transaction costs as a result. Its reactive rather than proactive nature in agenda setting and its lack of strong early warning systems within the organization (ibid.) are considered indicators of shallow institutionalization and pragmatic hedging.

As for whether the Southeast Asian region has been largely cultivated by state initiatives or nonstate action, the picture is rather mixed. It rests on the extent to which ASEAN, the key regional organization in this PDA, is representative of broader processes of regionalism and regionalization. Emmerson (2008, 13) captures it well when he states:

> ASEAN is hardly synonymous with Southeast Asia. But it is practically impossible to think or write about regionalism there without referring to the Association. If the region as a region is to cope with new and complex challenges to security and democracy, action by ASEAN will be necessary.

The centrality of ASEAN to regionalism and regionalization in this PDA varies from one issue area to the next. In geopolitical security, ASEAN has been leading the way in establishing regional stability. Several treaties and legal documents, including the Bangkok Declaration and the Treaty on Amity and Cooperation, signed in Bali, Indonesia, in 1976, established the principles and practices of cooperation in the region, while also creating the foundation for the Asian Regional Forum, the key conflict management instrument developed by ASEAN (Öjendal 2004). In the sphere of economic integration, however, the centrality of ASEAN is more contested. As of 2005, an estimated 26 percent of all trade by ASEAN's member economies was carried out among themselves, whereas the same year, 53 percent of all trade by the ASEAN 10, plus China, Hong Kong, Japan, the Republic of Korea, and Taiwan took place among themselves. Even more revealing are the data surrounding the ASEAN Free Trade Agreement signed in 1992. It failed to turn Southeast Asia into a trading bloc because it did not enlarge the proportional extent of intraregional trade (Emmerson 2008). Since 1995, the levels of intraregional trade have stayed within the narrow range of 22 to 26 percent.

Although the levels of intraregional trade may not be as high as those of the European Union, they are significant when compared with those of other PDAs in the developing world. Nevertheless, they reveal the limits of a regional organization, and even a free trade area, to consolidate a PDA as a separate trading bloc.

On another issue—the extent to which regionalism in Southeast Asia has been led by state or nonstate actors—there seems to be a broad consensus. It appears that both state-led regionalism, spearheaded by ASEAN, and regionalism with strong nonstate actors are pronounced in this case. However, research indicates that throughout much of the Cold War the governments were in the driver's seat—a trend that continues. Emmerson (ibid.) argues that Southeast Asia has a pronounced nongovernmental character—private sector or civil society regionalism—but he questions whether these dimensions have added significantly to the regional agency of Southeast Asia. Others maintain that the region has not been regionalized enough (Rubin and Jones 2007). During the Cold War, the Westphalian model of regionalism was applied in the region. This model has been described as regional integration that is rooted in the sovereign values of nonintervention in a country's internal affairs by a regional organization (Öjendal 2004). This pattern of regionalism, marked with very little involvement of nonstate actors, has also been characterized as the "Asian Way" of regionalism, characterized as informal engagement by states and slow and cautious patterns of regional institution building. Regional observers credit the Asian Way of regionalism with pulling some rather disparate member states together, with their diverse political systems, cultural norms, and economic development (ibid.). At the same time, they note that this model of regional cooperation is becoming increasingly weak and unproductive in dealing with the contemporary problems of governance, most associated with growing regional roots and risks (Leifer 2000).

Moreover, the Asian Way of region building is associated with the realist approaches of "old regionalism," with its state-driven and top-down patterns. Researchers highlight instead the need to shift to bottom-up and open "new regionalism" (Öjendal 2004), which integrates nonstate actors into region-building processes. The calls for greater nonstate actor involvement recognize it as a more efficient way to address complex governance problems in the contemporary world. However, the weakness of nonstate actor involvement also highlights the lack of democracy in states as a key obstacle in the emergence of new regionalism as a pattern for region building (ibid.). Regionalism without integration—a key criticism of regionalism in the developing countries (Kelly 2007)—is also explained by the statist bias of regionalism in the developing world. Thus greater institutionalization of the nonstate dimension of regionalism is an important strategy for strengthening regions and building their autonomy in the developing world.

All these challenges notwithstanding, Southeast Asia is still credited with being the most evolved region outside of Europe, benefiting from integrated economic and increasingly institutionalized political security spaces. An equally important dimension of the regional maturity of Southeast Asia as a region rests with its growing autonomy and ability to withstand the outside pressures of geopolitical dominance. In particular, the ongoing organizational changes within ASEAN (discussed in the next section) have been associated with the growing autonomy and assertiveness of Southeast Asia as a region, particularly relative to the continued hegemonic ambitions by the United States and China in the region (Chye 2012).

The growing institutionalization of the region through the concentric circles of institutions that have formed around ASEAN is credited as a useful mechanism for maintaining the regional autonomy of Southeast Asia. In particular, adoption of the ASEAN Charter was an important move toward a more cohesive and rules-based organization, ultimately directed at realizing the ASEAN Community (ibid.). The regional autonomy of Southeast Asia has become especially relevant in the context of the Asian Regional Forum, which has emerged as an ASEAN-led initiative to create institutional space for addressing security in the region. Although it has enhanced the conflict management capacities of ASEAN, many contend that ARF has also become an instrument for balancing and managing the U.S.-China geopolitical rivalry in the region (Katsumata 2006). In a similar vein, Limaye (2007) has argued that broader regional developments in wider East Asia (Frankel 1997) (such as China's rising regional profile and the growth in transnational threats—particularly avian flu and terrorism), coupled with ASEAN's efforts to institutionalize itself further, have prompted the United States to take a more "regional" (rather than bilateral and global) approach. "The net effect of such developments has been to highlight the need for Washington to consider ways in which to strengthen its relations with ASEAN qua ASEAN" (Limaye 2007, 449).

In short, it is safe to argue that, like Latin America and Central America, Southeast Asia is pursuing greater regionalization as a strategy to containing broader hegemonic competition in the region. This strategy of joining region-building efforts has been particularly effective for small nations as a way to dilute large-power influence and leverage their individual positions more effectively through regional layers of governance.

ASEAN's "Networked Peace"

In terms of the conflict management infrastructure in Southeast Asia, ASEAN is credited with playing a pivotal role in maintaining stability and security in the region throughout much of the Cold War (Jetly 2003), particularly in the context of the global search for regional approaches to conflict management in the post–Cold War environment (Diehl and Cho 2005). The regional studies literature recognizes the centrality of ASEAN in processes of regional integration in Southeast Asia, but also asserts that it by no means incorporates the broader areas of regional integration led by nonstate actors and the regional civil society sector. Still, considering its pivotal role in regionalism in Southeast Asia, application of the network approach to its study helps to reveal its strengths and limits in conflict management within the contemporary and highly complex security environment in the region.

In terms of its patterns of mobilization, throughout much of the Cold War ASEAN operated as a top-down network, having been established and further consolidated through intergovernmental agreements such as the Bangkok Declaration and the Treaty of Amity and Cooperation (Rüland 2011). The norms and principles of conflict resolution were largely codified in such documents. The Treaty of Amity and Cooperation, for example, specified mutual respect for independence, sovereignty and equality, noninterference, settlement of disputes by peaceful means, renunciation of the threat or use of force, and cooperation (Jetly 2003).

As mentioned earlier, the top-down patterns of formation and organizational growth of ASEAN, while credited for maintaining regional stability throughout the Cold War, are increasingly insufficient for addressing new trends and patterns in the regional security environment. Indeed, as Emmerson (2008) cautions, its past notwithstanding, because of its government-led and top-down pattern of operation, ASEAN is increasingly challenged to address human security, such as protecting individuals and minorities from official predation, discrimination, and neglect; addressing environmental risks and other novel hazards that ignore national borders; and dealing with intrastate security, which is endangered by the rise and repression of movements against central authority.

Similarly, Askandar, Bercovitch, and Oishi (2002) maintain that during the Cold War ASEAN was central to resolving three out of seven interstate conflicts, but it has been less successful in solving "state formation" and "revolutionary" conflicts. The top-down pattern of organizational development has translated into the use of summit meetings, negotiations, and informal meetings between regional political elites as the key instruments of conflict management. They also maintain that such state-centric and government-led patterns of conflict management are increasingly insufficient for addressing the new security fault lines in the region.

As for the institutional density of ASEAN as a regional network, things are in a state of transition. In the post–Cold War environment, ASEAN moved toward greater "soft institutionalization" (Acharya and Johnston 2008). ASEAN is seeking to reform itself, and the signing of the ASEAN Charter in 2007 is one indication of that goal (Emmerson 2008). Within some circles, the charter was viewed as a sign of stronger regionalism, placing ASEAN on firmer institutional ground; considering the sovereignty emphasis in the Asian Way of regionalism, this, indeed, would have been a big departure from the norm (ibid.). Although the ASEAN Charter failed to dramatically transform the organization into a European-style economic and political security community, it produced a round of institutionalization, with the creation of biannual summits, diversified ministerial rounds, and a Coordinating Council, the Community Councils, and the Committee of Permanent Representatives (Rüland 2011). One important development is the sharp increase in the number of meetings under the auspices of ASEAN: 750 a year, which is a fourfold rise compared with the some 200 meetings over fifteen years ago (Collins 2008).

Another important development pertaining to ASEAN institutionalization was the formation of the Asian Regional Forum in 1994. Emmerson (2008) finds that ARF is increasingly confident about engaging outside powers in providing stability in the region without fear of being overtaken by their interests. Indeed, ARF is credited as an instrument of conflict management because it engages regional and great powers in the wider Asia-Pacific region. It is undisputed that the formation of ARF was a major institutional development and particularly consequential for the conflict management capacities of ASEAN. However, the key indicator for assessing the significance of such an institutional change for the organization has been the extent to which the formation of ARF made it possible for ASEAN to move from a model of limited security dialogue to a more institutionalized and comprehensive mechanism of preventive conflict management.

On this score, however, the record as well as the scholarship on the topic is more divided. On the one hand, some observers of the region have argued that because of the diversity of political outlooks and political systems of the member states, arriving at a shared understanding of a "preventive diplomacy" has been challenging (Ball and Acharya 1999; Haacke 2009). As a result, despite significant institutional changes, ASEAN and ARF continue to be criticized as "talking shops" rather than meaningful tools of conflict management. On the other hand, others have argued that ARF has been successful in socializing China (Haacke 2009), and that it has served as a "norm-brewery" (Katsumata 2006) and a normative framework for maintaining regional stability and security (Haacke 2009; Heller 2005). Overall, there is a broad-based consensus that, despite low levels of institutionalization under ASEAN, ARF failed to move the "cooperative security agenda to extend to concrete and practical security cooperation" (Haacke 2009, 428). The existing institutional advances in the region have yielded very little in the way of building a multilateral order there. Instead, they have been described as arrangements with "hedging utility" (Cheng-Chwee 2008; He 2008), which, simply translated, means using the emergent institutions to enhance the powers of the states inside the organization (Rüland 2011, 86).

In terms of the levels of political power concentration, ASEAN is more representative of a centered as opposed to a stretched network. The member states remain key power players within the organization, leaving the organization itself with little autonomy. As evidenced by "hedging" and the associated low levels of institutionalization inside and outside of the organization, ASEAN, while remaining a pivotal organization for Southeast Asia, has so far failed to serve as a significant power center of its own. And yet the organization has managed to contain regional powers such as Indonesia, thereby creating an institutional environment in which no single member state or organization controls the agenda.

Despite significant institutional developments in the region and within ASEAN, the state-centric nature of the Asian Way of regionalism remains predominant. Concurrently, the transformation of the security environment in the region to one with a more pronounced "human security dimension" seems to be placing this approach to regionalism under stress—so much so, in fact, that ASEAN has recognized the need for greater public engagement in the region. With the signing of the new charter, the organization specifically states its intention to become more "people-centered" (Emmerson 2008; Collins 2008). With the creation of the ASEAN Political-Security Community, ASEAN Economic Community, and ASEAN Socio-Cultural Community, ASEAN now spans numerous highly specialized and functional ministerial meetings, ranging from disaster management, education, health care, and rural development to agriculture, finance, and energy. In this respect, ASEAN has obtained multiple new institutional spaces for engaging with business associations and functional groups. However, the organization has failed to win over critics about the sincerity of its claims on "people-centered regionalism" in Southeast Asia. Emmerson (2008, 36) highlights the central challenge of building truly participatory patterns of regionalism by ASEAN: "To the extent that the Association does try to become more widely participatory, it may face a trade-off between regionalism as predictable cooperation managed by states and democracy as institutionalized uncertainty involving societies."

Civil society organizations remain ambivalent about the existing rhetoric on people-centered regionalism. Within the networked peace paradigm developed in this study, high levels of heteropolarity would entail deep and genuine engagement with the public and civil society organizations. The view of participatory regionalism for civil society organizations entails creating plurality in ASEAN decision-making structures that would allow "the people" to have a say in creating agendas and implementing policy (Collins 2008). High levels of heteropolarity would also enhance the conflict management infrastructure within the region by facilitating more contacts and connections across conflict fault lines in Southeast Asia and by enhancing the human security dimension of the organization. At this point, observers of the region maintain that ASEAN has created openings for engaging with civil society organizations, but that such opportunities remain controlled by state-centric and sovereignty-focused regional bodies such as ASEAN.

Conclusion

In this study, understanding the way regional integration affects conflict management processes in politically divided areas has been carried out by looking at two dimensions: (1) a regional profile of a given PDA, and (2) a network analysis of the regional organization pivoting the given region.

In terms of regional autonomy, the regional profiles of the EU, Central America, and Southeast Asia are much more comparable in the post–Cold War period: Central America and Southeast Asia have moved toward greater regional independence and built more capacity to resist "overlay" from great powers such as the United States and China. Shared among all three regions is the trend of building more functional ties, ranging from economic to security, which also accelerated in the post–Cold War period in Central America and Southeast Asia. The third regional attribute covered in the study—whether a region is defined by conflict or cooperation—has played out quite differently in the three regions. In the post–World War II period, the steadily growing institutionalization of regional politics in Western Europe contributed to its strong conflict management capacities inside the region, but Central America has exhibited more tumultuous patterns. Throughout much of the 1970s and 1980s, conflicts and security interdependencies between states in Central America were the trend. However, in the Cold War period this trend was reversed as regional approaches to addressing interstate and intrastate conflicts in Central America were devised and new security instruments to address regional criminality and associated security threats were sought. In parallel, the strengthening of regional governance structures in Central America in the post–Cold War period produced a region marked by cooperation rather than the conflict on view during the Cold War. In terms of this attribute, the Southeast Asia region behaved differently from Central America. As observers point out, ASEAN and the Asian Way of regionalism helped to provide relative stability in the region, although they failed to resolve or manage conflicts inside states. Overall, cooperation rather than conflict and conflict spillovers best describes the regional dynamics in Southeast Asia throughout much of the post–World War II period.

Yet another regional profile attribute relates to the extent to which nonstate actors shape regional developments in a given PDA. In this measure, the EU is quite distinct, signifying the embeddedness of its regionalism in the administrative structures of member states. Central America and Southeast Asia demonstrate similar dynamics. As state-led initiatives, both cases of regionalism are currently moving toward greater openness to nonstate actors. The opening up of state economies to their regional neighbors is a major driver in strengthening the input of nonstate actors to regionalism in each PDA. The existing research on regionalism in both cases seems to suggest, however, that regional civil society is more evolved in Southeast Asia than in Central America.

The network analyses of the EU, SICA, and ASEAN as the regional pivots for Europe, Central America, and Southeast Asia, respectively, point out that all three organizations are cases of top-down patterns of mobilization in the post–World War II period, albeit with different economic underpinnings to support such regional initiatives. In terms of institutional density, the EU continues to be the most evolved structure, but Central America and Southeast Asia are moving in a similar direction.

The power centers in all three regions are quite varied: the EU could be described as a stretched network with multiple sources of power at various levels of governance, whereas throughout much of the post–World War II period ASEAN was a centered network, with national governments fully in control of the regionalism processes in Southeast Asia. In both regions, the move toward greater nonstate actor involvement in regionalism will transform the regional pivots into stretched networks, opening up new possibilities for conflict management while also creating new risks. In terms of levels of heteropolarity, the growing institutionalization of regional cooperation in Central America as well as in Southeast Asia is preparing both regional organizations for heteropolar partnerships with business and civil society actors. In both cases, the heteropolarity of the organizations seems to be at a turning point, and the preliminary structures for engagement with multiple stakeholders have been established.

As for the implications for conflict management infrastructure in all three regions, the EU has managed to contain conflict through economic and political regionalism. Indeed, the EU is a model of networked peace, adding specialized conflict management organizations to its various institutions. In addition, the EU has created and maintained a free regional trading bloc, thereby motivating its stakeholders to seek peaceful resolution of any conflicts originating inside the bloc. The EU therefore has successfully "rewired" and "restructured" its security environment, which has been emulated with varying success in other parts of the world.

The case of Central America is particularly informative for PDAs in the developing world because, as in the case of other PDAs, this region lacked an overall and broad political umbrella and a normative regime to develop and sustain regionalism. Central America and the conflict management capacities of SICA are instructive for regions that have been vulnerable to great power overlay, such as South Caucasus, whose immediate neighbors are Russia and Turkey. Although SICA currently lacks specialized agencies in conflict management, it has been a main driver of region building, facilitating and initiating highly institutionalized and heteropolar networks around various issue areas. In this respect, SICA's agency in conflict management—while rather indirect and mediated through a complex web of professional networks and newly developing and rather nascent structures of regional governance—is highly consequential.

ASEAN, unlike SICA, is directed at "rebuilding" as the institutional pathway toward enhanced conflict management capacities. The Asian Regional Forum is serving as a tool to enhance the conflict management capacities of ASEAN without dramatically altering the Asian Way of regionalism practiced to date within the organization. Meanwhile, ASEAN is also moving down the "rewiring/restructuring" reform route. This entails greater regionalization of governance and genuine engagement with nonstate actors, even if it includes moving away from the Asian Way of regionalism given priority to date by the elites within the organization. It remains to be seen whether ASEAN may pursue a reform path in that direction.

In conclusion, this brief overview of Central America and Southeast Asia in relation to the European Union reveals several institutional pathways and possibilities for regional and networked conflict management infrastructure. The European experience, while extremely valuable for devising regional conflict management strategies around the world, should not, however, prevent consideration of other possibilities and reform pathways. A question to ask in addition to "Where else has regionalism as a conflict management strategy worked?" is "In what other ways has it worked?"

5   The Western Balkans: A Region on the Move

On my first flight to Bosnia and Herzegovina in 2001, when the wounds of war were still very fresh, the Bosnian passenger sitting next to me was unrelenting in her efforts to determine my religious and ethnic identity. She opened the small talk by asking, "What religion are you?" I was unsure how to answer the question in a way that would not land me on the "wrong" side of the fence. For a student studying the political implications of economic policies, the question was meaningful because it shattered my rather idealistic belief at the time in the power of economic ties to mitigate political conflicts.

Indeed, the Balkan case of regional cooperation in a politically divided area (PDA) offers an important implication: *types of ties matter for the patterns of peace*. In the Western Balkans, the nature of regional cooperation matters for the depth and durability of peace and stability in a region. Both the former Yugoslavia and former Soviet Union were integrative models that did not survive the test of time. As this chapter argues, the quality of regional ties—top-down versus bottom-up, heteropolar versus unipolar, high versus low institutional density, diffused versus concentrated power structures—has important political implications because they structure the political fabric of a society, thereby conditioning the chances of peace and security in a region.

When it comes to regionalism and calls for greater regional cooperation among the newly independent countries in the Western Balkans, many people in Sarajevo seem to think that history there is repeating itself. European support for greater regional cooperation, advanced through a complex web of bilateral and multilateral agreements, is met with suspicion by many locals, politicians, and citizens alike. "We spilled blood to separate. Are you trying to put Yugoslavia back together again?" is the common sentiment, as articulated by a respondent back in 2008. Against this backdrop, Bechev maintains, echoing Judah (Judah 2009), that the trade liberalization initiatives of the 2000s have bolstered the economic ties across the territory of the former Yugoslavia, "adding credibility to the contention that an informal Yugosphere is being recreated" (Bechev 2011, 94).

So was Yugoslavia, as an integrative project, ahead of its time, or did its top-down pattern fall short? Were the economic ties among the entities not strong enough to prevent the war, delivering a powerful blow to basic tenets of commercial pacifism, or were the interests versus identities a false dichotomy, as some observers maintain (ibid.)? Alternatively, is it the nature of ties that matters? Are qualitatively different kinds of integrative models needed in this region of vivid historical memories and strong ethnic identities? These questions will guide the rest of this chapter, but efforts to understand the kind of regionalism and its attributes in the Western Balkans will dominate. As I argued in Chapter 2, the network perspective to regional studies allows one to develop the kind of precision and nuance needed when explaining the impact of regional cooperation on peace and conflict dynamics in a PDA.

This chapter begins by revisiting the main theoretical divisions within the regional studies literature as discussed in Chapter 1, with an emphasis on how the case of the Western Balkans as a PDA supports, challenges, or enriches the existing theoretical debates. It then applies the network approach developed in Chapter 2 to the Balkan case of regionalism. This is followed by an in-depth investigation of the Regional Cooperation Council (RCC), which has been a key tool in building regional cooperation in the Western Balkans.

The Political Chemistry of Regionalism in PDAs

Building a theory of regionalism in PDAs for better conflict management based on a comparison of the Western Balkans with South Caucasus was questioned by some of the respondents in this study. Indeed, many may argue that, on the surface, the overt and violent conflict has ceased in the Western Balkans, indicating that the parties to the conflict negotiated political solutions (Gegeshidze interview 2012). In this respect, the existing skepticism toward comparing the Western Balkans to South Caucasus is based on the fact that in South Caucasus there have been no political solutions to any of the currently frozen conflicts.

However, the comparison is justified in terms of the persistent levels of political fragmentation in the Western Balkans, even after a political "solution" to most of the conflicts has been achieved. Analysts worry about the current state of highly divided political and societal realities on the ground, and some even argue that the conflict in Bosnia and Herzegovina (BiH) has been frozen (Perry 2009; Richmond and Franks 2009). In Bosnia and Herzegovina, the Dayton Agreement is credited with ending the violence, but also with creating a decentralized political system and a weak state authority that perpetually fuels instability and challenges the prospects of compromise among the country's three main ethnic groups (McMahon and Western 2009). The political elites in Republika Srpska continue to flirt with the idea of an entitywide referendum, repeatedly driving relations with Sarajevo to the brink (International Crisis Group 2011) and certain to trigger a military reaction from Bosnian Muslims should such initiatives come to fruition (Belloni 2009). In fact, many worry that Bosnia and Herzegovina is more divided today than before the war, as evidenced by the inability of politicians to cooperate effectively in the grinding work of governance, as well as by the de facto and often self-imposed segregation across ethnic lines within the country. In the latter case, a job posting in Sarajevo, specifically calling for a Serb applicant, often remains vacant because most Serbs refuse to move to Sarajevo, preferring to maintain a residence in Banja Luka (Anonymous Senior Official from OSCE, interview 2012). On the political level, although Bosnia and Herzegovina has been supportive of NATO membership, Republika Srpska has been quietly expressing reservations (ibid.). Such divisions and inability to achieve a compromise have been quite characteristic of the continued governance problems in the country (International Crisis Group 2011).

Kosovo's independence is still contested by some states, while in Macedonia the occasional outbreaks of localized violence signal a broader possibility of larger-scale instability (Belloni 2009). At the time of this writing, the EU-brokered deal between Belgrade and Pristina calling for Kosovo's northern Serb-populated areas to receive greater autonomy in exchange for the elimination there of Belgrade-based institutions was triggering angry protests by the Serb community.[1] The public upheaval in Serb-populated areas will surely complicate the implementation of the accord, at the very least.

These are only some examples of how shallow political stability is in the region, thus raising questions about the political value of negotiated political solutions by the governments and international organizations. The conflicts in the region are far from settled. Moreover, it would be overly optimistic to expect that a "final" solution to a politically protracted conflict can bring in a new area of peace and prosperity, devoid of any political tensions between states in the region. As a respondent from the Regional Cooperation Council pointed out, political conflicts between neighboring countries will not go away (Minić interview 2012), thereby calling for institutionalized and consolidated structures of regional conflict management for the long haul.

Theories of Regionalism for Western Balkans

Geographical Proximity or Functional Ties?

The Balkan case poses a formidable challenge to the orthodox theories of regionalism. This region defies theoretical divisions and dichotomous categories. The first division that dominated comparative regional studies, as discussed in Chapter 1, is whether regions are defined by the geographical proximity of the member states or the functional ties among them. In this respect, regional studies have been trying to specify whether the regions are territorial/geographic constructs, mental maps, or pragmatic aggregations of functional ties between governments and social groups. The political significance of territories and borders has been cast in contrast to the functional ties and economic interests. The Balkan case illustrates how both factors, the political dimension of space and territory, on the one hand, and the economic rationality of functional ties, on the other, are powerful enablers of region-building processes in PDAs.

The territorial dimension of Balkan regionalism is manifested in both economic and political terms (Bechev 2011). As in any other case, the economic dimension of geographical proximity in the Western Balkans matters because it creates the possibility of forming industrial districts (Becattini 1990) and economic clusters. A World Bank study has pointed out the need for deeper integration between countries across the Balkan territory as a way to increase inflows of foreign direct investment (FDI) and overcome disadvantages related to the small size of individual country markets (Kathuria 2008). This policy prescription is also echoed by the respondents in BiH (Kapetanovich interview 2012) as well as other observers of the region (Judah 2009). A respondent from the Ministry of Foreign Affairs in Bosnia and Herzegovina called attention to the case of the Croatian company Agrokor, which, he argued, was succeeding primarily by pursuing regional strategies of growth (Kapetanovich interview 2012). Blaženka Mišlović and Jelica Grujić of the Foreign Investment Promotion Agency (Mišlović and Grujić interview 2012) also described midsize furniture companies that have been crossing conflict divides and leveraging geographical proximity for their growth. In general, the trade liberalization initiatives in the 2000s, while mostly on a bilateral basis prior to the establishment of the Central European Free Trade Agreement in 2006, re-created the economic ties of the "Yugosphere" (Bechev 2011; Judah 2009). Economists talk about "regional competitiveness," highlighting the much-needed collective action at the regional level. The argument here is that regional competitiveness affects the performance of local firms (Boschma 2004).

Territory also matters at the political level. Many analysts point out that PDAs, including the Western Balkans, are politically constructed by politicians. Indeed, identification of the Western Balkans as a region is much more pronounced by external actors than the populations of the member countries. Andreev (2009) notes that international actors and instruments of regional integration are powerful forces of region building in the Western Balkans—examples are the Stability Pact for Southeastern Europe/Regional Cooperation Council and the South-East European Cooperation Process (SEECP). The external political tools forging regional cooperation treat the Balkan region on a territorial basis, but this does not weaken the argument that functional ties are an important part of the region-building processes. The same international organizations, while driven by geographical proximity of the countries in the region, also layer the region with a quilt of issue-based functional cooperative institutions and networks that function as yet another mechanism of region building. In short, space and functional ties as forces of region building are mutually reinforcing.

The dark side of the territorial argument for regional cooperation relates to the flourishing criminal networks in this postwar region (Politi 2001; Andreas 2005). Virgil Ivan-Cucu, a representative of the Regional Cooperation Council, maintained in 2012 that the criminal networks are either deeply penetrating the governmental structures in the region or are actively supporting them. One recent example of the ties between governments and criminal and drug trafficking networks was the arrest of Zivko Budimir, the president of the Bosniak-Croat Federation in Bosnia and Herzegovina, along with eighteen other officials for criminal and drug trafficking, in addition to several other changes.[2]

Such criminal networks have a distinctly territorial flavor. According to Binder (2002), in the twenty-first century organized crime in the Balkans accomplished what empires like the Romans, Byzantines, Ottomans, Hapsburgs, and, briefly, Hitler's Third Reich had achieved in the past, which is to compel the myriad, rival ethnic groups of the region to work together for a common purpose. The scale of state involvement and complicity in criminal networks in the Western Balkans became clearer in the autumn of 2002; an international sweep of sex trafficking operations in BiH had to be aborted when it was revealed that a dozen Bosnian police officers were patrons and protectors of brothels (ibid.). In addition, the Balkan Route is the transit for narcotics traffickers moving Afghan heroin and opium from Central Asia to Western Europe; it crosses over Albania, Bulgaria, Kosovo, Serbia, Croatia, and Bosnia and Herzegovina (Maftei 2012). In short, the territorial dimension of Balkan regionalism is recognized and utilized by both the international organizations and global structures of governance deployed in the region, as well as by criminal networks, most of which are deeply intertwined with the states in the region (Binder 2002; Andreas 2005; Ivan-Cucu interview 2012).

Parallel to the territorial dimension of Balkan regionalism is the functionalism prevalent in the region. In contrast to the picture presented in the literature on regional studies, in the Western Balkans functional ties as regional markers are deeply rooted in the geographic proximity of the states, where the functional ties between countries have been largely developed around shared problems. European structures have played a key role in fostering such issue-based and governance-focused regional ties such as those needed to provide security in the region.

Meanwhile, despite the weakness of local civil societies in these states, a variety of professional associations have been forming in the region. The Balkan Society of Geometers, Balkan Women's Coalition, Balkan Alliance of Hotel Associations, Association of Balkan Athletics Federations, and Network of Education Policy are some examples. Transnational nongovernmental organizations also have been important conduits of functionally based ties in the region, because most of the large NGOs, such as Mercy Corps, CARE International, and World Vision, maintain offices in the member countries, thereby facilitating cross-country policy diffusion in various issue areas (Ohanyan 2008). Some of these initiatives have been strategically supported by the European Union, while others have more organic roots of origin. Perhaps the most vivid and consequential example of functionally organized regional cooperation is the Regional Cooperation Council, which is discussed later in this chapter. The RCC has been utilizing its technical skills to overcome the political obstacles to regional cooperation.

Are State or Nonstate Actors Shaping Regionalism?

The second division within regional studies is whether state or nonstate actors are shaping and moving regionalism. Balkan regionalism, as an example of a PDA, captures the multilayered and highly complex nature of regionalism in terms of its actors and drivers. Some regional arrangements are promoted by external players—mostly states or state-centric actors such as international governmental organizations. The European Union has been a key driver in this respect, cultivating agreements and the political will for engagement between the often reluctant governments of the states in the region. Regional cooperation was enforced through both bilateral and multilateral instruments. The Royaumont scheme, an initiative in multilateral cooperation promoted by the EU that included Bulgaria, Romania, Slovenia, and the Western Balkans, was meant to match U.S. activities in southeastern Europe (Schtonova 1998; Bechev 2011). It resulted in meetings among parliaments, municipalities, civil society, the media, and trade unions, but it fell short of convening a summit of foreign ministers (Bechev 2011). In addition, in 2001 the EU launched the Community Assistance for Reconstruction, Development and Stabilization (CARDS) program for the Western Balkans. Under this program with a strong regional component, the Western Balkans received 4.9 billion in 2001–6. It was later replaced by the Instrument for Pre-Accession Assistance (IPA). Subsequently, the Stabilization and Association Process offered the Western Balkans Stabilization and Association Agreements (SAAs). Although SAAs were bilateral in nature, they also included a strong endorsement for regional cooperation.

These and other EU efforts at regional cooperation were joined by NATO's Partnership for Peace Program, which was launched in January 1994 to focus on postcommunist countries. In addition, the United States was promoting cooperation in the Balkans through its Southeast European Cooperative Initiative (SECI), which began in July 1996. This initiative operated in parallel with the South Balkans Development Initiative (SBDI), comprising Albania, Macedonia, and Bulgaria. SBDI was an effort to link the energy corridor between the Black Sea and the Adriatic (ibid.; Andreev 2009).

Trends of bottom-up regionalism crossing interethnic divides, largely driven by nonstate actors such as businesses and civil society groups, are evident as well. According to the regional Technical Assistance for Civil Society Organizations (TACSO) database, just in the area of "Education and Research" there are more than 250 NGOs in the region. In the "Business, Professional and Specialist

Interests" area alone, over eighty NGOs are listed in the region.[3] The fact that the number of civil society groups is steadily rising tells the story of strong nonstate sector involvement in region-building processes.

The state versus nonstate actor involvement in promoting regionalism also reflects "soft" and "hard" regionalisms. Soft regionalism is led by nonstate actors and through grassroots efforts. Hard regionalism emerges from state-to-state agreements and governmental initiatives. The distinction between the two obscures the deep institutional engagement between state and nonstate actors in the process of region building in the Balkans. A large number of soft regional initiatives have been carried out within the frameworks of hard regionalism, as negotiated by governments and international organizations. The network approach to regional studies discussed in the next section reveals the institutional pathways through which soft and hard regional initiatives interconnect and interface.

Such interrelationships are particularly important in PDAs. In the Western Balkans region, international governmental initiatives in regionalism have facilitated nonstate actor involvement in regional cooperation through specific mechanisms. A good example is the establishment of TACSO, which has created in the Western Balkans an important forum and a space in which cross-conflict regional contacts can develop. It has enhanced the efficiency of information flow between civil society actors, while also creating and spreading norms of issue-based and problem-driven engagement across conflict lines (Westergaard interview 2012). Most important, TACSO seems to have transformed itself into a process of regionalism, as opposed to remaining at an organizational level: the TACSO website allows new NGOs and networks to register, which helps to build the regional community of civil society actors in the Western Balkans.

In short, the Balkan case of regionalism demonstrates that in PDAs the relationship between state and nonstate actors in building regionalism is rather symbiotic. Although promoting regional engagement may be politically challenging for state actors, resorting to civil society actors provides government officials with an important tool for building apolitical engagement with a counterpart. The opposite is also true. At times, NGOs need state actors to build legitimacy for their projects, as well as the funding that is often a concern for the civil society sector in the region (Carlarne and Carlarne 2006). Thus the dichotomy between state and nonstate actors in regional politics may be analytically sustainable in regions that are not politically divided or recovering from deep divisions in an aftermath of a war, but in PDAs with fractured political systems and disintegrated social fabric the networks of state and nonstate actors are the drivers of regionalism that matter the most. The Balkan case is illustrative of region building in other PDAs, where strategic network cultivation and the sporadic, separate, and perhaps more organic state and nonstate initiatives are advancing parallel to one another. To understand regional integration in a PDA one must explore the network-based organization of regional arrangements in it.

Is Conflict or Cooperation the Dominant Regional Marker?

The third division prevalent within regional studies is whether conflict or cooperation is the dominant regional marker, as discussed in Chapter 1. In the Western Balkans, more often than not politics has been a source of conflict and insecurity, while the mechanisms for cooperation have been found among the functional ties between the states. The great efforts in region building by European structures are focused on transforming regional politics from a force of conflict into a force of cooperation. Building structures of regional governance is important to this effort, but it has been realized unevenly and sporadically by the European Union (Andreev 2009).

Since the violent breakup of Yugoslavia, and in the post-Dayton era, the Western Balkans has more often been viewed as a regional complex, defined by negative interdependencies of disorder, than as a regional order, characterized by institutions of regional security. The post-Dayton infrastructure of governance in the region is specifically geared toward transforming the region from a security complex to a security order. The political-military tools provided by NATO and the Organization for Security and Co-operation in Europe (OSCE) are particularly noteworthy in this regard. OSCE's work in security cooperation in Bosnia and Herzegovina has centered on assisting in state-level capacity building to ensure democratic control of the armed forces in the states; monitoring and coordination of arms-control activities as well as the safe disposal of stockpiles of surplus and unstable ammunition; and organizing arms-control activities in cooperation with local and regional partners.[4]

In addition to the plethora of other security actors in the Western Balkans, NATO has been central in transferring political conflicts to an institutional forum. It has also played a key role in defense and security reform in the countries. The promise of NATO membership, similar to the prospect of EU accession, has been an effective carrot for fostering political consensus among political elites in the region, although the consensus for NATO membership within Bosnia and Herzegovina has been slow to develop (Anonymous Senior Official from OSCE, interview 2012). Republika Srpska has been revisiting the issue, primarily questioning whether the high cost of joining NATO is a worthwhile investment. If BiH does develop a consensus for NATO membership, then its political leaders in both entities have to agree to register the immovable defense property as state property.[5] In December 2004, implementation of the General Framework Agreement for Peace in Bosnia and Herzegovina was handed over from NATO to European Union Force (EUFOR), but NATO remains central in assisting the state to carry out its reforms and commitments related to the Partnership for Peace Program and closer integration with NATO, as well as in supporting the International Tribunal for the former Yugoslavia on a case-by-case basis.

In short, in the Western Balkans OSCE and NATO have evolved into key nodes within the security networks in the region, created to transform the region into a security order but with a range of bilateral issues remaining unsettled. At the same time, the Balkan case illustrates that such categorizations of a region as either a regional security complex or a regional security order can be limiting. This PDA, in particular, is currently a moving target. In some dimensions, it has remained a regional security complex, as evidenced by the stubborn persistence of conflict lines between and within the countries, as well as the emerging regional security problems such as transnational criminality. Still, the steady spread of regional and international security institutions in the Balkans is indisputable, even if the process has been tumultuous. The lack of domestic political will among the elites to come together and the absence of deep coordination among international actors are just some of the problems (Stefanova 2009; Ohanyan 2008, 2009; Paris 2000). OSCE's work in the region is carried out in partnership with the EU Delegation, UNDP, NATO, and EUFOR, in addition to The Regional Arms Control Verification and Implementation Assistance Center (RACVIAC), the South Eastern and Eastern Europe Clearinghouse for the Control of Small Arms and Light Weapons (SEESAC), and The Regional Approach to Stockpile Reduction (RASR), among others,[6] and a clear regional approach to security reform is still lacking. Bilateral engagement continues to dominate OSCE operations in both the Western Balkans and South Caucasus.

The theoretical distinctions and divisions within regional studies discussed so far in the context of Western Balkans matter, and they are helpful to the extent that they can direct policy interventions and reform packages. At the same time, the distinctions are limiting because they challenge our ability to appreciate the dynamic nature of regionalism and regionalization in the Western Balkans. The processes of regionalism have been a moving target in this PDA. In this respect, in the context of the Western Balkans, "region" is better understood as a process than as an entity. The question as to whether the Western Balkans is a region needs to be replaced with one that asks which parts of the Balkan societies and policy areas are becoming integrated, by manifesting the confidence, political will, and capacities to develop regional approaches in various policy fields (Ohanyan 2007), and which ones have been looking inward to the state for solutions to increasingly regional problems.

Regional Network Politics in the Western Balkans

The broad patterns of regionalism in the Western Balkans reveal that it is *deliberate,* and that it is a *process.* What matters is that, in contrast to the patterns of regional integration in other parts of the world, in PDAs regionalism is a deliberate process as opposed to an organic structure. Although organically developed ties, particularly in the business sector, are emerging in PDAs, including the Western Balkans, maintaining a consistent process of political regionalism is needed to facilitate the economic and political interfaces between the conflict societies (Biščević interview 2012).

To manage the process of regionalism in PDAs, one has to understand the composition of the networks supporting regional cooperation. Networks have been a tool in the deliberate cultivation of regional ties across conflict lines in PDAs, and in the Balkans in particular. Study of the network composition of regionalism in the Western Balkans also reveals just how unevenly the processes of regional integration are advancing in the spheres of politics, business, and civil society, as well as across policy areas. This section is a modest attempt to uncover some of the general patterns in network-driven region building in the Western Balkans, mapping the process as opposed to the structure of regionalism in this particular PDA. It is by no means an exhaustive account of all the existing regional networks in the Western Balkans. This section now opens with a look at the network attributes most consequential for patterns of peace and conflict management on the ground. These attributes were developed earlier, in the theoretical chapters of this book.

Patterns of Regional Mobilization

The first of the network attributes, *patterns of regional mobilization* of networks, reveals a rather mixed picture in the Balkans. In particular, the fieldwork of this study shows that both top-down and bottom-up networks have been developed, but it also appears that such regional networks are insufficiently connected with one another. In the economic sphere, respondents generally agreed that the prewar ties of the former Yugoslavia played a key role in pushing for economic regionalism across the member countries of the Western Balkans. These countries are too small to project any economic weight on their own, thereby creating urgent imperatives for cross-border engagement. In Yugoslavia, most companies had sister organizations and branches in the other republics of the country. Since the war, some of these companies have reemerged under different names. The people working in these companies then revived their prewar ties, which have become crucial lubricant in facilitating economic regionalism in the Western Balkans (Mišlović and Grujić interview 2012). Indeed, the former Yugoslavia was more integrated in its trade patterns than the rest of the countries in southeastern Europe: in 1987 (prior to the breakup of the country) most republics were exporting more than half of their products to other Yugoslav republics (European Bank for Reconstruction and Development 2004). Even though the trade structure changed after the war, with trade levels falling to less than one-third of prewar levels in most cases, over time the countries of the former Yugoslavia maintained and in some cases increased their shares of trade with other former republics (ibid.). Economists often cite geographical proximity and cultural affinity as key determinants of trade and investment flows in the region (Resmini 2000; Basu, Chakraborty, and Reagle 2003). Such regional networks in the Balkans are rather organic, with distinct bottom-up processes of development. Most of these networks have been developed with little, if any, political support from the top, with the exception of the Central European Free Trade Agreement, which provided the political framework for such connections to function by lifting the tariff barriers between states (Kapetanovich interview 2012).

And what is the role of politics in networks? They are far from being empty institutional vessels devoid of politics. The advancement of regional networks translates into a loss of power for political elites, who derive their political support from exclusionary rhetoric and the blame game across the border. A respondent from the government of BiH pointed out that the political elites in

BiH within all three ethnic groups have learned to use the ethnically charged blame game as an electoral tactic, often as a way of disguising their own lack of competence in governance processes between election cycles (anonymous interview with author 2012). By contrast, the bottom-up networks, mostly in the business sector, are driven by the potential benefits of greater regional cooperation. Large companies, in particular, are eager to overcome the small size of the markets by accessing neighboring states. As noted earlier, the Croatian company Agrokor is an example of how the regional approach translates directly into higher profits (Kapetanovich interview 2012). The regional strategy of Agrokor entailed expanding its operations in the region by acquiring a number of large companies in southeastern Europe as well as by establishing branches across the region. The company currently employs nearly forty thousand people, and its business operations range from water bottling to ice cream and frozen food production.

In short, despite the persistence of ethnically driven political divisions in the region (particularly inside BiH), the bottom-up processes of economic regionalism inside the Western Balkans and in southeastern Europe, as well as in the EU, continue to develop. At times, the oppositional flows of political and economic networks constitute the core of regionalism as a process of political and socioeconomic engagement and state building among the member countries. Overall, the balance between top-down and bottom-up network development is rather mixed, with both patterns dominant in the region formation processes in the Western Balkans.

Institutional Density

In terms of *institutional density*, the business sector networks are understandably highly institutionalized. The trends in the level of network institutionalization in spheres beyond the business sector are rather different. Although a comprehensive regional governance infrastructure across the Balkans is still beyond reach, significant steps to that end are being undertaken. Currently, the prospects of EU accession are the dominant incentive for building regional structures of governance from the top down. At the same time, very real regional problems are requiring joint collective action at the regional level, and this realization is slowly dawning on the political elites (Minić interview 2012).

Highly institutionalized regional networked governance has been emerging in the justice and home affairs area and the security area (both issue areas of the RCC), driven in part by the imminent problem of criminal activities in the region, which have emerged as one of the crippling war legacies in the Western Balkans. It poses a threat to the governance of not only the countries in the region but also the EU. Respondent Ivan-Cucu (interview 2012) noted that organized crime and corruption are part of the economic and political life of states in the region. This criminalization of the state in the Western Balkans, also noted by Andreas (2005), reflects the continued weakness of states in the region: the stronger the criminal networks, the weaker the institutions of state (Anonymous Senior Official from OSCE, interview 2012). Indeed, many government officials have had to step down because of their alleged connections in criminal activities, raising even more questions about the governance capacities of the individual states.

Against this backdrop, the specialized institutions of the EU, along with NATO, RACVIAC, and OSCE, have joined forces in an ad hoc network to create a sustainable regional infrastructure on security-related issues, ranging from defense to intelligence cooperation. Cooperation in this network has tended toward greater, not less, institutionalization. Often, all the international organizations making up the security network in the Western Balkans cooperate and coordinate their efforts for greater impact. An anonymous respondent (ibid.), who serves with OSCE in BiH, pointed out that the OSCE resources in BiH in the security area are small, and that the organization cooperates with the other international organizations to achieve greater leverage and maximize its impact on the ground.

The regional networks in security cooperation have a strong organizational infrastructure, but they are also supported by political agreements that facilitate such cooperation. Ivan-Cucu (2012) pointed out that the organizations of criminal networks in the Western Balkans are very powerful, and fighting them requires the rapid sharing of information in real time and an ability to obtain acceptable evidence from Ankara, Dubrovnik, and Paris. The respondent also pointed out that the regional security network among international organizations has evolved into a strong tool for fighting organized crime. Although this respondent said that having an organization that could pressure individual governments to cut links with organized criminal networks would be a great accomplishment and a good measure of institutionalization that is not feasible at the moment.

Figure 5.1 depicts the existing regional infrastructure in the justice and home affairs policy areas in BiH, as perceived by the RCC. It captures the chal-

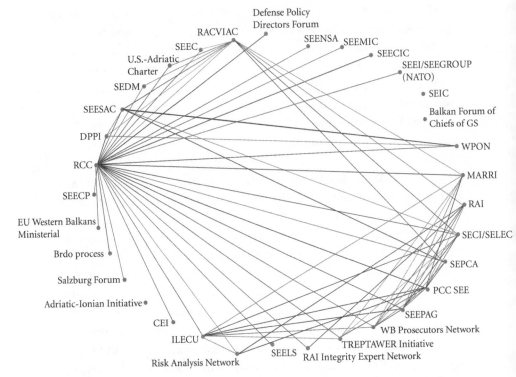

FIG. 5.1. Policy Network in the Security and Justice and Home Affairs Areas in the Balkans, Based on RCC Perception of Initiatives, 2012. (Source: Prezelj, Iztok. 2013. "Challenges of Multilateral Regional Security and Defence Cooperation in South East Europe." *European Perspectives* 5 (2): 83–112.)

lenges and opportunities presented by network mode of governance, which I have examined elsewhere (see Ohanyan 2008, 2009, 2012). The network form of governance creates problems of duplicate efforts and coordination problems among so many actors, as reflected in the figure. Ivan-Cucu of the RCC likened building networks in various issue areas in the Western Balkans to digging tunnels and finding it difficult to tell whether the people in those tunnels are even moving in the same direction (interview 2012). Consolidation and coordination are needed, but at the same time the network mode of regionalism also allows the practitioners and policy-makers involved in a given issue area to address a specific problem in each country. Often, the regional organizations have state-based memberships, which creates a layer of transgovernmental networks (Slaughter 2004). In the security area, Justice and Home Affairs Unit within RCC, transgovernmental networks jump-started a particular form of governance at the regional level: they connected substate levels of public agencies with international and regional organizations, fragmenting and limiting state sovereignty in some respects and enhancing it in others. Some analysts even argue that such subregional cooperation allows "rescue" of the state in the context of globalization (Andreev 2009; Milward 1992) by strengthening its governance capacities. Thus the regional networks play a crucial role in fostering substate regionalism, which is issue-based, highly institutionalized, albeit top-down and often lacking in heteropolarity, as discussed later in this chapter.

Heteropolarity

Heteropolarity is a regional network feature that describes whether a network that has multisectoral membership is also connecting local actors with national and global levels of governance (Der Derian 2011). Such networks in the Western Balkans are observed more in some issue areas than others. Higher levels of heteropolarity, along with higher levels of institutional density, are associated with networked governance. Parker (2007) makes a distinction between networks and networked governance, arguing that in contrast to fragmented network operations, networked governance processes result in steering, setting directions, and influencing behavior. Heteropolar networks produce stronger grounds for networked governance because they provide both the public and private sectors of the society with various access points. Combined with engagement from the local to the global levels of governance, heteropolar networks legitimize network-based governance processes and enhance their policy implementation capacities (Ohanyan 2009).

Indeed, in addition to the presence of public and private sectors in regional networks, the extent to which local levels of governance are connected to global ones is important. One particular organization, the Network of Associations of Local Authorities of South-East Europe (NALAS), is a good example. NALAS's heteropolar credentials are manifest in its ability to connect both local and global actors to its governance structure. Empowered local structures of governance are a key ingredient in fostering cross-border trade as well as regional integration models in general. NALAS acts as a crucial forum and a voice for local authorities; it connects them to the global levels of politics. Similar regional networks are numerous. The issue of heteropolarity matters to the extent that such regional networks add up to regional governance processes.

Another example of a heteropolar network is in the higher education sector. In July 2008, the South East Europe Regional Network for Qualifications

Frameworks was established to provide a platform for exchanging ideas and experiences and promoting good practice among member countries in developing and implementing their national qualifications frameworks in accordance with the European Higher Education Area.[7] The network connects both governmental authorities and institutions of higher education, thereby serving as an institutional mechanism to connect public and private actors in the higher education sector with international governmental organizations—namely, the EU. The network is financed by its membership dues, which reflects the fact that the concrete rationale for regional cooperation in an otherwise highly sensitive area of higher education has been realized by its members.

Like patterns of mobilization and institutional density, levels of heteropolarity tend to vary from one issue area to the next. Regional cooperation in political and military areas is more contingent on the capacity and political will of national administrations, whereas in the sphere of economic and social development successful regional networks, particularly the ones deployed through top-down patterns of mobilization, are heavily reliant on the private sector for successful implementation. It is the critical mass of heteropolar networks that will leave its mark on the fabric of regional governance in the Western Balkans. The case study of the Regional Cooperation Council presented later in this chapter elaborates further the organizational fabric of a heteropolar network and its added value for governance processes and conflict management in the region. At this point, it is sufficient to say that the region is peppered with issue-based networks, and some of them exhibit higher levels of heteropolarity than others.

Degree of Power Concentration

The *degree of power concentration* within networks is a measure used to determine whether a particular network is driven by one or two large players (that is, institutional hegemons), or whether the network derives its resources from a variety of actors (Ohanyan 2008, 2009). In any discussions of this particular regional attribute, the role of international organizations, and the EU in particular, is highly significant. Up to this point, the EU has been critical in spanning regional networks in various issue areas. The EU largely plays the role of the institutional hegemon in the form of providing political, financial, or institutional support to a network. In parallel, though, as the EU financial support begins to decline, networks begin to diversify their funding lines, and some move toward collecting membership dues to consolidate their regional structure. The fact that membership dues are the primary source of income of the South East Europe Regional Network for Qualifications Frameworks reflects the general trend toward greater institutionalization of such networks and their transformation from a centered network with power clearly concentrated in one or two organizations to a stretched network with a more diffuse power base.

A good example of a stretched network is the central and southeastern European higher education institutions related to the life sciences (agriculture, food, biotechnology, natural resources, rural development, and the environment), known as CASEE.[8] This network stands out with its highly institutionalized membership and governance structure, which has contributed to its widespread political and financial resources. With open membership and membership fees, the network is consolidating its global engagement in research and development and education in the life sciences. The network lists three main objectives: (1) supporting the development and implementation of the EU strategy for the Danube region; (2) strengthening research and education and university development in the region; and (3) developing joint research, educational, and other projects among its member universities. Important for understanding the degree of power concentration in the network is its internal organization. It is run by the CASEE General Assembly, composed of the rectors and deans of its member institutions, board members, and executive officers. In addition, CASEE itself is part of a larger European network of more than sixty universities from the EU and neighboring countries. The Association for the European Life Science Universities (ICA) has institutionalized membership-based links with NGOs and private enterprises. As a standing committee within the ICA, CASEE, then, is not only an example of a stretched issue-based network but also one that is highly heteropolar. Such a dynamic in institutionalizing regional cooperation in the Western Balkans is a type of regionalism that is developed brick by brick, one network connection at a time (Ahmed and Bhatnagar 2008; Minić interview 2012; Biščević interview 2012).

Summary

Table 5.1 summarizes the general patterns of networked regionalism in the Western Balkans. The cumulative effect of the network-based regional integration dynamics in the Western Balkans is the overall disaggregation of the Balkan states through transgovernmental and transnational networks, which are constantly evolving into higher levels of institutionalized structures of gov-

TABLE 5.1. General Patterns of Networked Regionalism, Western Balkans

Network attribute	General Patterns
Patterns of regional mobilization: top-down or bottom-up	• Overall balance between top-down and bottom-up network development rather mixed • Both patterns dominant in the region formation processes in the Balkans
Extent of institutional density	• Highly institutionalized in business sector • Issue-specific • Moving toward institutionalization of regional governance structures • Transgovernmental networks, short of regional governance structures.
Heteropolarity	• Growing presence of heteropolar and sustainable regional networks • Heteropolarity credentials largely showcased with EU support as well as through integration in the Balkan societies
Degree of power concentration and power centers	• Linking of regional networks with wider European networks and internal institutionalization of the networks, reflecting their stretched as opposed to centered nature • Prevalence of apolitical issue-based networks • Evidence of stretched networks, which are less politicized and more expert driven

ernance, or disappearing with the decline of the external sources feeding them. Although in some respects state disaggregation is viewed as a weakening of the institutions of state, in many others it is a measure of pulled, as opposed to weakened, sovereignty. For example, research and development in the field of biotechnology is otherwise a very costly exercise, but by pooling resources with other universities in the region, individual states gain unique access to both the regional and European structures supporting the biotechnology sector.

This chapter now turns to exploring the general patterns of network-driven region-building processes in the Western Balkans in greater detail by taking an in-depth look at the Regional Cooperation Council, one of the central networks of regional cooperation in the Western Balkans.

To Network or Not to Network? Regional Cooperation Council

The RCC is the successor of the Stability Pact for Southeastern Europe, which was launched in 1999 as a peace-building tool by the international community. It focused on supporting initiatives for fostering democratic peace,

human rights, and economic development in the region. Regional cooperation was the cornerstone of Stability Pact activities. It was viewed partly as a
tool to integrate the countries in the region into European and Euro-Atlantic
structures. It was succeeded by the RCC during the RCC's inaugural meeting in
Sofia, on February 27, 2008. The RCC was launched as a tool to provide operational capacities for the South-East European Cooperation Process (SEECP).
SEECP is not a treaty: at the end of the 1990s, ratification of a treaty on regional
cooperation by the members in the region would have been difficult (Ivan-
Cucu interview 2012). SEECP was a more flexible tool for pulling countries together for enhanced regional cooperation despite the range of bilateral political
disputes still pending and persistently fragmenting the region at the time.

The RCC has forty-six members, which include countries, international organizations, and financial institutions. Its secretariat is in Sarajevo, BiH. The
RCC is headed by a secretary general, Goran Svilanovic, who took over from
Hido Bisevic in 2012. RCC members that contribute to the RCC budget are
members of the RCC board, which currently consists of the representatives
of twenty-seven countries.[9] In addition to the contributions it receives from
RCC board members, other members, and the European Commission, the organization receives project-based grants from various foundations and international organizations (ibid.). The West Balkan countries, which benefit from
the RCC, are board members. This status reflects their financial contributions
to the operation of the RCC and their socioeconomic and political interests in
regional cooperation. The RCC has evolved into a regional platform for guid-
ing and monitoring processes of regional cooperation in southeastern Europe
(Regional Cooperation Council 2012. Although it is supported by international
actors, the RCC derives its operational strength from its regional ownership
and from the region itself (Regional Cooperation Council 2012; Minić interview 2012).

Indeed, the key difference between the Stability Pact and the RCC is the
regional ownership of the latter; the entire staff of the RCC is from the region.
The RCC itself is a source of new regional initiatives in various issue areas,
which strengthens the local ownership of the organization. Moreover, in its
early years of formation, the RCC was often casually referred to as that "aboriginal organization," and so its critics thought it would not succeed (Minić
interview 2012). Today, the RCC stands out as a locally driven organization, but
its "aboriginal" posture constitutes its main strength. Being in the field and able
to identify projects from the bottom up, the RCC has managed to generate con-

crete ideas and initiatives to apply to very real and tangible problems requiring regional solutions (ibid.). By yielding concrete results, the RCC has increased its visibility in the region and generated much-needed trust as an "aboriginal" regional organization.

The work of the RCC is organized around the following priority areas: economic and social development; infrastructure and energy; justice and home affairs; security cooperation; and building human capital and parliamentary cooperation. Each priority area is structured as a unit and is headed by a senior expert in a given issue area.[10] A key feature of the RCC as both an *organization* and a *method of region building* is its unique balancing act between its technical expertise and the political implications of such technical engagement in the Balkans. Respondent Ivan-Cucu, head of its justice and home affairs unit and a senior expert, noted:

> We are not a political organization. Most of our activities are at the level of experts. . . . Our work is a combination of both expert activities and politics. Our Secretary General is a very political position though. We are intergovernmental but we do not have a direct political influence (from the states) because we are working under the umbrella of another intergovernmental process, South East European Cooperation Process (SEECP). RCC practically is the operational arm of SEECP. SEECP is the political organization/tool of the region. It is a process. RCC is the operational structure of SEECP. SEECP consists of couple of meetings, summits. SEECP has no secretariat. We are the secretariat of SEECP. We are implementing SEECP's political decisions. (Ivan-Cucu interview 2012)

It emerged in this interview that the RCC is able to shield itself from deep political divisions in the region by serving as an operational arm of SEECP. However, in reality the distinction between technical expertise and politics is rather blurred. To marshal support for a particular issue area between experts across the region the RCC is all but technical in its engagement. Politics is at the heart of building coalitions between experts and stakeholders in the region. Once an issue area is identified by the RCC as crucial, it builds a network of stakeholders from the region, at times moving around the national authorities, who are often reluctant to lend their political or administrative support to a regional initiative (Minić interview 2012; Biščević interview 2012). Such a coalition-building strategy has served the RCC well over the years, and can be described as a specific region-building strategy in PDAs. Jelica Minić, deputy secretary general at the RCC at the time, described it as "the guerilla approach" to region building, highlighting that RCC tactic in building coalitions with stakeholders on the ground and setting up the specific issue-based networks *prior* to approaching the national administrations for their otherwise lacking political support. This approach will be described in greater detail in the next section.

RCC Network Profile: Institutional Hegemon and Guerilla Fighter

The RCC's network profile has two dimensions: the RCC internal structure (1) as an organizational network on its own, and (2) as a method of region building through network cultivations with other agencies and stakeholders of regional integration. As a mechanism and a method of region building, the RCC echoes the earlier discussions about regions and regionalism in PDAs as processes as opposed to established structures. Throughout this section, when analyzing the RCC's network profile, I will distinguish the RCC as a networked organization from its role as a network development instrument in the Western Balkans.

As a networked organization, and in terms of the main network attributes presented in this study, the RCC is developed from the top down with the political support of the EU and as an operational arm of SEECP. It enjoys unique access to structures of global governance as well as to national administrations in the region: each national government in the region has an administrative position, usually within the Ministry of Foreign Affairs, that serves as a liaison with the RCC. As a networked organization, the RCC is relatively heteropolar. It enjoys access to both the public and private sectors, and international financial institutions (such as the World Bank, the European Bank for Reconstruction and Development, and the European Investment Bank) as participating members. Representatives of civil society are routinely invited and provided access to the variety of regional forums organized by the RCC.

In terms of the degree of power concentration inside this networked organization, the RCC is a stretched as opposed to a centered network—that is, benefiting from financial contributions from the European Commission as well as project-driven funding, the organization is beyond the sole control of a single donor or a player. The policy initiatives are fed into the organization both from annual meetings at a high political level and RCC board meetings, which represent various countries with relatively diverse sectoral representation. At the same time, members of the administrative staff of the RCC, who are closely embedded in the region, are also sources of project initiatives and policy proposals:

RCC is one of the most, if not the most, important regional organization because of the number of issue areas it covers. We [develop] strategic approaches, we have a vision, and we proved that we are very helpful for EU integration process. We also proved that regional issues are easier understood and focused on from interior, meaning we proved that we do not compete but complete other regional players. We have been able to protect the country and its regional interests. (Ivan-Cucu interview 2012)

As a networked organization, the RCC is an institutional hegemon because it is able to drive initiatives on its own, and it has specific mechanisms to shield itself from the political interests of donor states as well as those in the Western Balkans. As for exerting autonomy relative to its Western stakeholders, mostly donor governments and international organizations, the RCC has specific tools for maintaining an institutional distance. Its ability to develop internal administrative capacities, which the RCC has done rather effectively, and its skill in withstanding political pressures from outside stakeholders, are important measures of its autonomy as an organization and indicators of its institutional hegemony relative to its immediate organizational environment. The role of the RCC as an institutional hegemon relative to outside players takes the form of highly institutionalized consultation mechanisms. The RCC has various instruments of coordination and consultation that allow it to generate feedback from various external and internal stakeholders. There are at least two coordination meetings with all the actors (regional, national, EU, and UN) that also serve as forums of consultation (ibid.). In addition, the RCC organizes ministerial meetings. The RCC staff then collects all the information and drafts strategic documents based on the consultation received. Its unique "aboriginal" access to the locality counterbalances any political positions articulated from the top down, and allows it to generate balanced, highly pragmatic solutions to regional problems. It is this institutional autonomy from its stakeholders—its position as an institutional hegemon in its network—that is one of its main strengths.

When exerting an institutional distance and autonomy from the national governments, the RCC always points to its "status-neutral" position in the persistent political disputes in the region (Biščević interview 2012), as well as to the SEECP agreement for regional cooperation among the national governments. Indeed, "preserving flexibility and 'distance' from many mutually opposing views in the region . . . to ensure effective functionality of cooperation" is considered key to the development of the RCC as a formidable regional structure

(Regional Cooperation Council 2012, 25). One step in this direction has been integrating the relevant experts from the national governments, thereby slowly minimizing over the years the political pressure and influence from the ministers within national authorities. According to Biščević (interview 2012):

> At the beginning the shadow of politics [was prevalent]. By way of example, we would invite representatives of countries from the region to participate in the environmental meeting to discuss this or that project. At the beginning these representatives would seek the approval from Ministers of Foreign Affairs. We have been through that process and we are done with that period. At the beginning the regional cooperation was politicized and politically sensitive domestically. I, as a chief of department of environment in Zagreb, would not dare to go to a regional meeting without the approval of the Minister of Foreign Affairs.

While as a networked organization the RCC is an institutional hegemon, as a mechanism or a method of region building, the RCC is a true guerilla fighter, according to Minić (interview 2012). To reiterate, "guerilla tactics" refers to its unique ability to forge regional issue-based networks within a persistently inhabitable political environment for such regional contacts. Although the EU's carrots for eventual accession played a big role in garnering political support for regionalism by national governments, that support is mostly confined to the level of rhetoric (Biščević interview 2012). It is its specific networking tools that allow the RCC to push for the rhetoric that it can translate into concrete administrative support by national governments. The next section examines the RCC as a method and a process of region building, emphasizing the types of regional networks it spans.

Region Building and Networked Peace: The RCC Way

When the RCC is viewed as an instrument of network development, a consistent strategy of region building emerges. Although the RCC is itself a regional organization developed from the top down, its approach to networking the region is rather diverse. The organization routinely works with national authorities within the SEECP framework, thereby relying on top-down patterns of network mobilization. National authorities are among its most direct stakeholders in region building. Although the role of national authorities as a bridge to issue-based stakeholders has declined over the years (ibid.), its political importance is still a factor. The already discussed mismatch between the political rhetoric for regionalism and the actual political will for concrete, region-based cooperation within the national authorities remains an area of concern for the organization (Regional Cooperation Council 2012). Over the years, by learning to sideline and sidestep national authorities, the RCC was able to create issue-based networks between stakeholders across the region before approaching the national government for its political blessing:

> But there is intrinsic, basic interest in cooperation by states and other stakeholders, so whenever we had problems with state officials, we would circumvent the state officials and approach the final beneficiaries. And only after that we would approach state officials, and they would have no choice. Very often we would organize regional meetings, where national officials were participants. They were not in a position to impose their conditionality, to blackmail anybody. We became skilled in this process of involving national administrators and still let them feel comfortable. We always try not to confront national administrations. At times the national structures are so strong that it is almost impossible to make a breakthrough, especially in areas where there is big money circulating, like infrastructure and energy, where the European Commission did not empower and encourage our organization appropriately to make a breakthrough. (Minić interview 2012)

One of the implicit assumptions in the regional studies literature is that if there is an intergovernmental agreement on a given regional initiative, implementation follows easily. It appears from Minić's response that even if parties have agreed on broad political cooperation, the political will at the national or even at the level of an intergovernmental organization may be lacking. Top-down network mobilization is not any easier than bottom-up mobilization, although each has its own set of difficulties, challenges, and opportunities. In cases in which even top-down network mobilization is a challenge, particularly with "big money circulating," the RCC builds networks with the bigger players. For example, in an energy-related project in which the Energy Community Treaty Secretariat lacked the will to cooperate, the RCC sidestepped that organization. According to Minić, the Energy Community Secretariat even blocked the RCC's efforts to diversify its stakeholders. The RCC then moved to forge an alliance with the Central European Initiative, and this partnership paved the way for a sustainable energy development in the region. The shared country membership between the Central European Initiative and the RCC played a key role in advancing the initiative. A regional conference on energy sustainability was organized, and the European Energy Community took part: "They had no choice because we had many other stakeholders present on the issue," said Minić in an interview (ibid.).

The situation just described was a kind of "guerilla struggle" using the top-down approach. The RCC also applies that strategy using a bottom-up approach. A good example is the reform initiative in higher education, which in PDA countries is particularly sensitive in political terms. With political support from national authorities in the region not forthcoming, the RCC, building on the initiatives for regional cooperation from the universities themselves, organized a regional conference on the issue, and, together with the universities, developed a questionnaire that was sent to national administrations. According to Minić (ibid.):

> They [the national administrations] answered us, as an inter-governmental organization, but they would not answer the Universities at the national level. The questionnaire became the basis for a project, financed by TEMPUS, and subsequently supported by national Ministries. RCC was used as a leverage by Universities from the region, to involve administrations in the sensitive area of higher education reform. We were able to approach some issues that otherwise we could not, had we approached national administrations directly.

In short, in this "guerilla approach" to region building the RCC skillfully utilized both top-down and bottom-up approaches to regionalism. The RCC strategy of network development is heavily dependent on the political opportunities available on the ground. In both approaches, the RCC plays a facilitating role, and once a network is established, the RCC seems to pull out.

Institutional Density of RCC Networks

As a method of region building, the institutional density of the networks created and facilitated by the RCC can be analyzed in both quantitative and qualitative terms. In quantitative terms, the number of regional institutions facilitated by the RCC and the opportunities for regional engagement shaped by the organization are indeed numerous. However, the quality and the institutional sustainability of such regional forums are critical at this stage of regional cooperation in the Western Balkans. Higher institutional density is associated with the transformation of existing regional networks into more sustainable structures of regional governance that can function with or without the EU umbrella and its incentive system (Parker 2007). Higher levels of institutional density ultimately entail reshaping the current pattern of regional cooperation (Biščević interview 2012) so that the existing ad hoc and problem-driven support for regional cooperation can permeate the political structures and political circles. This process will entail recalibrating and recalculating national interests through a more complex and sophisticated prism of regional cooperation. Redefining and recasting the national interests in regional terms will be an ultimate measure of institutionally dense regional networks, but one that calls for solutions to political problems, according to (ibid.).

Achieving higher institutional density of networks also entails consolidating the existing "vibrations of regional cooperation" into more mature and institutionalized arrangements that can function in the long term (ibid.). Transforming sporadic structures of regional cooperation, ranging from sparse top-down and single-sector networks (such as in South Caucasus) to institutionalization and trans-governmentalism (such as in the Balkans) into fully consolidated regional structures (such as in Northern Ireland) seems to be evolving as a template for using regional cooperation for conflict management purposes. To date, the RCC's role in this process has been significant. It has been focusing on building regional efforts network by network (Minić interview 2012), and brick by brick (Biščević interview 2012). The RCC strategy has been to demonstrate the organizational utility of the RCC to donors, beneficiary governments, and functional stakeholders (Minić interview 2012), and respondents from the RCC have indicated that it succeeded in showing its use in making more effective the Multibeneficiary Instrument for Pre-Accession Assistance of the EU. Biščević spoke of a "pebbles effect": "You have to work brick by brick—. . . forestry, education, museums—so you can have a pebbles effect across the region to have more and more grassroots inclusion, [which ultimately] creates a new atmosphere" (Biščević interview 2012).

Minić (interview 2012) echoed this sentiment. In answering a question about how the RCC manages to forge cooperation in a region in which geopolitical differences and political tensions are still unresolved, Minić alluded to the growing institutional density in developing regional cooperation:

> Yes, we are used to live and operate in these circumstances [that is, unresolved political issues]. For us, it is normal. . . . For us, it is how we breathe. You have to overcome [political tensions] on a daily basis. Sometimes you cannot attack the problem directly. Sometimes you have to formulate achievements and proofs that problems can be solved. It is not by the book. You have to go around. You have to make a living body/corpus of cooperation and then you can put on the crown. You cannot put on the crown and then develop the body. (Ibid.)

The institutional density of the regional initiatives created and facilitated by the RCC can be described as moderate. Overall, the RCC has created a substantial "corpus" of regional initiatives, but Minić (ibid.), Biščević (interview 2012), and Ivan-Cucu (interview 2012) believe that there is a need to consolidate the existing institutional infrastructure of regional cooperation. Minić (interview 2012) maintains that the instruments, mechanisms, projects, and programs of regional cooperation have been established, but that they are fragile: "They have to be nurtured. Lots of care and commitment is needed to consolidate all of those, the established structures" (ibid.).

The RCC has been very active as an instrument of region building. It initiated or co-organized more than sixty events just in 2011 (ibid.). These project-based events are implemented through RCC networks with a variety of other international organizations and private institutions.[11] The impressive list of RCC projects in 2011 reflects the quantitative institutional density of the networks the RCC is spanning. However, as a method of region building, the mechanisms to ensure sustainability in such regional efforts are less assuring. Indeed, the RCC recognizes that its areas of intervention remain broad, which complicates the prospects of making these initiatives more sustainable in the long run (Regional Cooperation Council 2012). To this end, the secretariat is seeking to transform its activities into coherent "flagship initiatives that involve other partners as needed, rather than being driven by these partners and their interests" (ibid., 12).

One major issue when thinking about the prospects of consolidating existing regional cooperation networks is the political will of the governments; it tends to oscillate with the changing domestic political landscapes and unresolved bilateral issues (Regional Cooperation Council 2012). Greater institutional density entails embedding regional contacts in the national governments by strengthening transgovernmental networks and making them less vulnerable to the political elites within national authorities. In a way, strengthening the institutional density of the RCC networks involves supporting transgovernmental networks between international actors and national authorities, while trying to depoliticize such functional linkages.

Another challenge in strengthening the institutional density of regional networks, both transgovernmental and subnational, is that the contact persons with the RCC within the national authorities are often lower-ranking officials in the ministries of foreign affairs, such as chiefs of departments, who do not have the required influence with other parts of the government (Biščević interview 2012). This factor is a serious institutional impediment to greater regional cooperation and one that reflects the insufficient political support in governments for regional cooperation projects. As Biščević (ibid.) described the problem:

> When I was talking about the lack of administrative follow-up, when the national coordinator comes to the RCC meeting in the area of Justice and Home Affairs, he is acquainted with the program of trafficking but he is not influential within the Ministry of Justice and Home Affairs to influence their own attitudes towards the program. This is what is lacking. Twice I sent a letter to Prime Ministers asking to upgrade the role of RCC coordinator to the level of Prime Minister's office. They have not been very receptive. In some cases, some countries upgraded the role of national coordinators to the level of State Secretary, very positive for RCC, but in most cases it is just an official from the Ministry of Foreign Affairs.

Greater institutional density of transgovernmental networks as facilitated by the RCC will require the depoliticization of regional projects within the domestic settings of member countries. Biščević (ibid.) pointed out that the resolution of bilateral political issues is needed to depoliticize the regional initiatives, whereas Minić (interview 2012) indicated that such political issues will always remain, and that learning to build regional projects within such politically charged settings is crucial. The broader theoretical implication is whether institutional cooperation and institutional ties can be powerful enough to help address the political tensions in a given PDA.

Heteropolarity of RCC Networks

As for the levels of heteropolarity within the networks built or facilitated by the RCC, the picture is brighter. The RCC has been highly effective in forging partnerships and regional networks among various stakeholders and sectors—that is, governments, the business sector and market structures, and NGOs and civil society organizations. Even a cursory glance at the RCC's key achievements highlighted in its 2011–12 annual report quickly reveals the highly heteropolar nature of the RCC mechanism in region building.[12] Examples of RCC initiatives are the following: (1) taking over management of the South East Europe Investment Committee from OECD; (2) helping to create a platform for joint action of stock exchanges in southeastern Europe to strengthen links among regional capital markets; (3) launching the Women's Entrepreneurship Project as a mechanism of job creation in southeastern Europe with the SEE Centre for Entrepreneurial Learning and Gender Task Force; (4) working with the Regional Anti-Corruption Initiative to establish the Integrity Experts Network, which evolved into a regional structure of national agencies specializing in public officials' assets declaration; (5) initiating a regional cooperation mechanism among the chiefs of military intelligence; (6) supporting development of the Building Capacity for Structural Reforms in Higher Education of Western Balkan Countries program ; and (7) helping to establish the European Association of Public Service Media in South East Europe as a nonprofit professional body of public broadcasters (Regional Cooperation Council 2012b). This incomplete list reflects the slow but steady development of issue-based networks that are highly heteropolar in nature (Regional Cooperation Council 2012a). Moreover, heteropolarity is deeply appreciated within the RCC as a political tool for building support for regional cooperation when dealing with the European Commission as well as the national authorities. Heteropolarity is at the heart of the guerilla fighting mechanism for region building, as practiced by the RCC. The efforts to develop a social agenda for the Western Balkans and enhance social inclusion in the region are particularly instructive for showing the skillful use of heteropolarity by the RCC in its region-building initiatives. To this end, Minić (interview 2012) notes the following:

> In regards to labor regulations and social agenda for the Western Balkans, it did not exist in the previous pre-accession assistance program for the region. We introduced a social agenda dealing with employment, poverty reduction and Roma issues. Now we are putting a stress on employment policies and labor market institutions, with support of the Friedrich Ebert Stiftung Foundation (FES) as it was close to its mission. They gave us funding to organize events in order to develop an operational regional platform. But to have these events backed by analytical work, we made a memorandum of understanding with the London School of Economics that provided support of the network of experts from the region dealing with social issues and poverty reduction in the Western Balkans.

According to Minić, "networking is the keyword." But heteropolarity was no less important in building an issue-based network with significant leverage and legitimacy—enough in fact to ultimately win the support of the European Commission, which did not support the initiative at first: "The European Commission suddenly understood that we set and developed the whole structure already and now it is appropriately addressed by the new Multi-beneficiary Instrument for Pre-accession Assistance (IPA II)" (ibid.). To the question of why the EC failed to support the initiative in the first place, Minić said that the EC did not know how to support it. "What we learned was that if we pushed hard with clear goals, and we put the structure of stakeholders together and it looked reliable, the Commission would always say yes, even after long struggle.

At the end, it lasted two years before we developed a common ground with the EC in this case. The same was true when introducing the Joint Strategy for Research and Development for Innovation for the Western Balkans, and in the end, a blessing came [from the European Commission]" (ibid.).

Heteropolarity in building networks in the region has been useful not only in dealing with the European institutions but also in making inroads inside the member countries. Partnering with the NGO sector has opened new doors for the RCC (ibid.) and allowed it to access the local and grassroots levels of engagement. This have provided the RCC with unique political access to the grassroots, thereby creating concrete tools to build legitimacy within the public for regional projects. "The local level is all about democracy, governance and development. Thanks to some specific activities, we are also approaching the local level and the NGO sector: the whole 'building' is here, the government, the businesses and the civil society" (ibid.).

The extent to which the emergent networks are centered or stretched varies from one issue area to the next. In broad strokes, depending on the urgency of the issue, the RCC was able to overcome political divisions with more ease in some issue areas than in others, thereby building stretched networks with diverse power centers in those issue areas with the least political resistance from national or European stakeholders. For example, because of the strength of criminal networks in the Western Balkans and the proximity of the region to the EU, cooperation in the justice and home affairs and security areas has probably been easier to forge than in other areas (Ivan-Cucu interview 2012). This ease is reflected in the rich diversity and high number of players in this area. By contrast, in the infrastructure and energy area the networks include one or two major powers and are centered. The earlier discussion of the Energy Community Secretariat and the challenge of gaining its participation in some related regional projects is indicative of a trend: in high-stakes regional initiatives, building bottom-up and stretched networks is politically more complicated.

Because the RCC operates as a mechanism to facilitate accession of the Balkan countries into the European Union, and thus membership is a major carrot to facilitate political will of regional cooperation, one could argue that the European Commission provides much-needed legitimacy (that is, political resources) within the regional networks facilitated by the RCC. However, within its various units the RCC has also forged partnerships with other major political players in global governance, thereby adding new layers and sources of political legitimacy within its regional networks. For example, within the justice and home affairs unit, the RCC has partnered with implementing agencies such as the Regional Anticorruption Initiative (RAI), Deutsche Gesellschaft für Internationale Zusammenarbeit (GIZ) GmbH, the German and Austrian Federal Police, Federal Ministry of the Interior of the Republic of Austria, and the United Nations Office on Drugs and Crime (UNODC). This diversity of implementing actors is in contrast to the Security Cooperation Unit, where there are fewer implementing agencies in the region (RACVIAC, SEESAC, the Disaster Preparedness and Prevention Initiative [DPPI]), reflecting greater RCC reliance on a few organizations in this issue area in 2011. In the Building Human Capital and Parliamentary Cooperation Unit, the main implementing partners and supporting organizations were numerous and growing exponentially.

In financial terms, the degree of power concentration also varies from one unit or issue area to the next. For example, in 2011–13 the Economic and Social Development Unit leveraged 3,120,000, of which the EC provided only about a quarter (800,000); the Swedish International Development Agency provided most of the rest (2,200,000). In the Infrastructure and Energy Unit, the fundraising continues, and, according to the 2011–12 RCC Annual Report, it has raised 2,589,900 to date (Regional Cooperation Council 2012a).

Within the Justice and Home Affairs Unit, the United States (10,750,000) and the European Union (12,376,981) are the main donors. It appears that in financial terms the RCC has been supporting more centered networks within Justice and Home Affairs than in other issue areas. Within the Security Cooperation Unit, Norway is the main donor, with 5,050,000 out of the total 7,350,000, and SEESAC is one of the main implementing partners. Like the Justice and Home Affairs Unit, the Security Cooperation Unit is also relatively centered, with organizational and financial resources provided by two main organizations within the emergent networks. Within the Building Human Capital and Parliamentary Cooperation Unit, in 2011 the European Commission was the only financial contributor, with a total of 5,600,000. Within the Media Unit, the European Commission is also the only financial contributor, with a total of 2,938,000, with subsequent support of the Friedrich Ebert Foundation for the Media Law School.

In very broad strokes, it appears that in terms of organizational resources the RCC has built relatively stretched networks, with a variety of actors assisting in the implementation of projects. In financial terms, the European Commission is the dominant financial contributor to the Justice and Home Affairs Unit and Economic and Social Development Unit: in financial terms the networks within the Economic and Social Development, and Infrastructure and Energy units are more diverse, which indicates that they are stretched as opposed to centered networks. Indeed, the EC continues to be a major champion or an institutional hegemon driving regional integration projects in the Western Balkans. However, because the RCC is reconsidering mechanisms and the prospects of consolidating regional cooperation, the patterns of regional networking may change. Both Minić and Biščević have indicated the growing legitimacy of the RCC in the region, with the result that more partners are approaching the RCC for assistance to foster regional networks with counterparts. Although the EU provides the political umbrella under which regional cooperative networks are created by the RCC, there are also local interests in such cooperation, irrespective of EU support. Minić notes that when building regional cooperative structures, the RCC faced very few obstacles when approaching stakeholders to try to "activate" regional interests.

Conclusion

The Western Balkans is a PDA with some general patterns of regionalism that are also prevalent in other PDAs. First, as in other PDAs, regionalism in the Western Balkans is a deliberate process as opposed to an organically developed one. The Balkan case study reveals the centrality of international actors—the European Union in particular—in providing the general political umbrella under which to nurture regional contacts. Second, the case study of the RCC reveals the existing pragmatic grounds for regional cooperation in this PDA; the RCC was able to activate the already existing deep interests in regional cooperation across conflict lines. Third, this case study of the Western Balkans also shows the two speeds of regional integration in this PDA. In the political track, the gains are less visible and slower to develop, whereas progress has been greater in the business sector. The development of issue-based, transgovernmental networks is also emerging as a consistent pattern within regional integration in the Western Balkans.

In conclusion, the Balkan region as a PDA is characterized by the significant role of market forces of integration and regional problems as drivers of regional cooperation. However, a meticulous, deliberate process is needed to cultivate regional contacts and networks across conflict lines in this PDA, and in this respect, study of the RCC both as an organization as well as a method of region building has much to offer to other PDAs, and to South Caucasus in particular. Chapter 7 delineates the specific opportunities and constraints provided by the type of regionalism developed in the Western Balkans. That analysis will create the groundwork for a deeper theoretical understanding of peace building as region building in such PDAs as the Western Balkans and South Caucasus.

6   The South Caucasus: Weak States or a Broken Region?

The Ukrainian government's decision on November 21, 2013, to abandon negotiations with the EU on its Eastern Partnership Agreements in favor of Russia-led Eurasian Union/Customs Union was quite explosive. It galvanized a public protest over a foreign policy decision, which in itself is very significant for the postcommunist world. However, the scale of the public protest and its bloody aftermath obscured the similar yet silent detour few months earlier, but this time by the Armenian government, which, in September of 2013, also had abandoned the EU negotiations in favor of the Customs Union—Russia's significantly more restrictive regional bloc. Indeed, like Ukraine, the South Caucasus also was in the eye of the storm that was produced by clashing regionalisms of Russia and the West, and partly was driven by the Cold War hangover (Terterov interview 2012).

This state of flux in regional politics in the South Caucasus is ominous and symptomatic on several fronts. First, according to the power-based geopolitical analysis more fashionable in the region, Russia's geopolitical superiority and control over Armenia's security agenda ultimately prevailed over Armenia's ability to independently chart its course toward Europe, as it originally had intended. From this perspective, might is right. Against this backdrop, the tacit support of the West for Azerbaijan and Turkey in isolating Armenia by bypassing the regional pipelines and railroads around Armenia, backfired: Russia easily divided the region, strengthening the status quo in regional politics, which currently suits Russian interests quite well (ibid.). Georgia seems to be lost to Russia, but Russia, (re)gained Armenia and at the time of this writing, is flirting with Azerbaijan, and continues to sell arms to the oil-rich state, despite the fact that the latter is in conflict with Armenia—Russia's ostensible ally in the region. The use of the conflicts in the South Caucasus by Russia is acknowledged by analysts across the region (Isazade interview 2012; Giragosian interview 2012; Gegeshidze interview 2012).

To clarify, the frequently touted strategic alliance among Georgia, Azerbaijan, and Turkey is one regional axis (Zakareishvili interview 2013), which has been driven mostly by the energy needs of the European Union, in an effort to reduce its reliance on Russian energy supplies. According to the World Trade Organization,[1] major oil and gas pipelines, such as the Baku-Tbilisi-Ceyhan and South Caucasus pipelines, and railways and roads have elevated Georgia's position as a transit country in the region, excluding Armenia from such initiatives. Limiting its regional engagement in the South Caucasus to its status as a transport, energy, and trade transit state benefits Georgia in the short term,[2] but it hurts all three countries' long-term political and economic interests, as I argue in this chapter. According to Bagratyan (interview 2013), Georgia, in this current form of "regionalism," is just a territory invaded by Turkish and Azerbaijani capital, rather than an area of sustained and job-creating economic growth.

An understandably fatalistic and deterministic regional prognosis emerges from this narrative. While the rest of the world has adapted regional development templates and formed regional groupings to secure better access to the global economy, the South Caucasus has remained stuck in unresolved conflicts, strengthening the hand of external powers in the region. Indeed, the lack of a shared value system and the density of conflict fault lines are frequently cited reasons for why the South Caucasus is failing to come together as a region (Gegeshidze interview 2012; Ter-Gabrielyan interview 2013; Torosyan interview 2013). Some even considered the South Caucasus to be an artificially created postcolonial legacy that has outlived its usefulness (De Waal 2012). Others have pointed out that the existing cultural similarities fail to serve as the glue needed to hold the region together (Broers interview 2013). Marat Terterov of the European Geopolitical Forum maintained (interview 2012) that the relations between Russia and the West continue to suffer from a lack of trust, and any improvement on that front would spill over into the South Caucasus, making regional integration there more realistic and feasible. It is against this backdrop that the region often is described as "broken," "locked," and "fragmented." Regionalism is often viewed as anathema to the South Caucasus (Armenia, Azerbaijan, and Georgia).[3]

The second and alternative narrative to the flux in regional politics in the South Caucasus is a story of a region of weak states. The weakness of regional structures and near absence of regional thinking in the South Caucasus prevented the individual countries, and Armenia in particular, from negotiating better terms with external powers, and maintaining foreign policy autonomy relative to such powers.

> There are some interests that great powers have in the region, and this is not just Russia. Other large powers have been able to maintain influence by connecting bilaterally. If there was regional connection, this region has amazing resources being at a crossroads, so the regional collective group could be very strong in dealing with Iran, Russia, EU, as to what the region wants. . . . And it is not just institutions, but also the cultural shift that needs to happen. People are looking for permission from central authority to connect regionally, as opposed to saying, "I want to do this." People matter, they can be agents of change. (Allen interview 2013)

More, each of the three countries has been searching for external patrons for enhanced security. This, paradoxically, makes the region less secure. Hrant Bagratyan, the former prime minister of Armenia and a current member of the parliament, maintains that "desire in trading with one's neighbor's neighbor at the expense of one's neighbor" is a unique regional disease in the South Caucasus (Bagratyan interview 2013). It reflects the zero-sum thinking within the political elite in all three countries (as opposed to primarily external geopolitical calculations), and the unfortunate dominance of purely military security in public discourse (Allen interview 2013). Significant human security issues, ranging from poverty to forest fire prevention, which often require regional cooperation, fail to reach the national agendas in the three countries and fail to be defined as policy problems requiring attention (ibid.; Oliphant interview 2013). Some of the respondents noted that the governments ignore such human security issues at their own peril (Oliphant interview 2013; Giragosian interview 2012).

The South Caucasus is not a fatalistically broken region, but a very real collection of weak states. This shift in the "diagnosis" I argue is more accurate and is also crucial because it opens up numerous new opportunities for conflict management. This is a region with weak civil societies and young states (Torosyan interview 2013), poorly consolidated democratic institutions (ibid.; Giragosian interview 2012), and visible authoritarian currents, and most important, rather basic and unsophisticated administrative structures of governance (Yedigaryan interview 2013). These factors are often unnoticed as significant hurdles against regionalism in the South Caucasus, where the unresolved conflicts are the most visible factors "credited" in hindering regional integration. While the policy and public debate has been binary, forcing a choice between the West/EU's Eastern Partnership on the one hand, and Russia/Eurasian Union, almost no one speaks and advocates for regional integration in the South Caucasus itself, which is mostly seen as part of a larger geopolitical game.

According to Armenia's former ambassador to the United States, Mr. Shougarian, regional as opposed to individualist thinking was part of the policy discussions in the immediate aftermath of the Soviet disintegration. According to Shougarian, the idea was championed by several advocates, including Eduard Shevarnadze, the Georgian president at the time, the Baltic presidents, and even Zbigniew Brzezinski, U.S. national security adviser to President Jimmy Carter (Shougarian interview 2014). It appears that the idea was ahead of its time, lacking the needed institutional support and the right political chemistry to be moved forward. Yet regional integration next to great powers with intrusive habits is not without a precedent. The comparative regional analysis developed throughout this research allows us to draw parallels between contemporary regional politics in the South Caucasus and those of Central America throughout much of the twentieth century and Southeast Asia throughout much of the Cold War. From this perspective, the state of regional politics in the South Caucasus is better told as a story of weak states than a failed region.

This chapter discusses the overall outlines of regional politics in the South Caucasus. It then moves to applying the key theoretical themes from the regional studies literature, as reviewed in Chapter 1, to the South Caucasus. In doing so, it examines the case of the South Caucasus relative to that of the Western Balkans. The key objective here is to generate comparative regional theory on politically divided areas (PDAs), building on the cases of the Western Balkans and the South Caucasus. The chapter then discusses the region in terms of the network approach, with a focus on the existing peace-building infrastructure as currently deployed in the region. The chapter concludes with two case studies: the Regional Environmental Centre for the Caucasus (REC) and the South Caucasus Business and Development Network.

Regional Vibrations in the South Caucasus

Energy transport in the South Caucasus is currently considered the most regionalized policy area, although so far Armenia has been excluded from it. And yet contrary to public statements by Azerbaijani, Georgian, and Turkish trade officials, the formation of an energy transport alliance among the three countries has yielded limited results in terms of their socioeconomic development. In 2013, Shahin Mustafayev, Azerbaijan's minister of economic development, commented during a joint business forum in Gabala, Azerbaijan, on SOCAR (State Oil Company of Azerbaijan Republic) investments in Georgia by saying that SOCAR had created "conducive conditions for the opening of 7,700 new jobs."[4] However, these jobs have not yet been created, and this projected number is quite modest for the population of nearly 5 million, excluding Abkhazia and South Ossetia. Although the trade turnover between Azerbaijan and Georgia increased in 2012 by 12 percent and some 150 Georgian companies operate in Azerbaijan, three hundred Azerbaijani entrepreneurs are working in Georgia, according to Mustafayev.[5]

A cursory view of trade relations (exports in particular) among Armenia, Azerbaijan, and Georgia reveals that the levels of integration between Georgia and Azerbaijan are quite low. According to statistics provided by World Trade Organization, as of 2012 Azerbaijan's primary export destinations were the European Union (59.6 percent), United States (8.6 percent), Russian Federation (4.5 percent), Indonesia (3.4 percent), and Ukraine (3.4 percent). Interestingly, neither Georgia nor Turkey is among the top five export destinations for Azerbaijan. This is explained in part by the fact that oil is Azerbaijan's primary export, destined to go to larger markets beyond the South Caucasus. For Georgia, the top five export destinations are Azerbaijan (19.5 percent), European Union (19.4 percent), Turkey (10.4 percent), Armenia (10.2 percent), and Kazakhstan (7.2 percent). Armenia's top five export destinations are the European Union (46 percent), Russian Federation (16.7 percent), United States (7.1 percent), and Canada (5.3 percent).[6] Overall, it appears that in terms of exports, the Azerbaijan-Georgia-Turkey energy/security triangle has failed to translate into other areas of investment and trade in significant levels—that is, a tightly integrated regional economic bloc failed to develop between these countries. Instead, Georgia's exports are more integrated regionally, while the Azerbaijani and Armenian export trade profiles are geared toward the EU, the United States, and Russia. By contrast, the regional economic ties in exports among Bosnia and Herzegovina, Serbia, and Croatia reflect greater integration, with each country among the top five export destinations of the others, with the exception of the Serbia-Croatia link—Croatia is not a top-five export destination for Serbia.[7] In short, it appears that communities and countries have learned to adapt to closed borders and restrictions, and the pull of more distant capitals seems to have contributed to it, as the case of Armenia demonstrates (Ter-Gabrielyan interview 2013).

Grounds for Skepticism

The skepticism about the prospects for greater regional integration in the South Caucasus is economic and political in nature. In economic terms, Giragosian (interview 2012) notes that Armenia's biggest export to Turkey is scrap metal, and no product is waiting to be exported and no sector would immediately benefit from greater openness in the region (Iskandaryan interview 2012). In terms of political and security needs, Yakobashvili (Yakobashvili 2013) speaks for many observers in the region when arguing that Georgia, Armenia, Turkey, and Azerbaijan have different threat perceptions and security needs. According to Yakobashvili, Georgia continues to see Russia as its main security threat because Russia recognized the independence of Abkhazia and South Ossetia after the Georgia-Russia war in 2008, and Russian troops were stationed just forty miles from Tbilisi. For Armenia, the threat is the Turkey and Azerbaijan axis, cemented by a special agreement between the two countries on military collaboration and security assistance in case of an external military confrontation. For Turkey, there is the legacy of Armenian genocide carried out in the Ottoman Empire at the beginning of the twentieth century and the refusal of the Turkish government to recognize the atrocity as such. This lack of recognition is perceived by the Armenian government to be an existential threat to Armenia's security, as stated by Armenia's president in 2013.[8] Finally, as for Azerbaijan, the cease-fire with Armenia that ended the war between the two countries over the Nagorno Karabakh (NK) territory in 1994 remains fragile, and the lack of a political solution continues to feed significant insecurity in Armenia. The NK conflict pushed Armenia toward Russia in search of security guarantees. According to Yakobashvili (ibid.), Azerbaijan also sees the unresolved state of NK as its main security threat, in addition to Iran, which is home to large populations of ethnic Azeris. Indeed, the three countries embrace security guarantors from outside the region, which has activated patron-client relationships at a regional level (Broers interview 2013; Ter-Gabrielyan interview 2013) and made the region particularly vulnerable to external overlay and great power penetration (Buzan and Wæver 2003).

Beyond the "Frozen" Conflicts: Reasons for Poor Regional Integration

Several analytical challenges surround the argument that the political and economic prospects for greater regional integration in the South Caucasus are weak. First, the skeptics of greater regional integration discount the complex interplay between domestic and foreign policies within these countries when they claim that the existing interstate conflicts make greater regional integration impossible and unrealistic. Indeed, Giragosian maintained in an interview in 2012 that there is a threat misperception in these countries: elites and others have failed to acknowledge that the weak governance institutions internally have fueled oligarchic and highly monopolized economies. In Azerbaijan and Armenia, in particular, this is a bigger threat than any of the external ones that the governments and their publics may consider (Giragosian interview 2012; Bagratyan interview 2013).

Second, the argument linking unresolved regional conflicts and lack of regionalism in the South Caucasus discounts the internal complexity and diversity of the actors that make up these very states. Ter-Gabrielyan (interview 2013) puts it vividly when he states that there is a sovereignty gap in the region, with no country able to provide for its own security:

> Countries are sovereign, actually and potentially, potentially more than actually because they do not feel that sovereignty, their rulers do not allow their populations to feel that sovereignty. . . . There is a huge sovereignty capacity in the region, indeed. Funnily enough, and that's the pluralism of this region, which is a multi-colored carpet, there are several sovereign entities, inside and outside of societies. For example, oligarchs in Armenia are sovereign; Armenia as a state is to a certain extent sovereign; NK [Nagorno Karabakh] as an unrecognized territory is to a certain extent sovereign; Kurds that live at the other side of the border in Turkey are to a certain extent sovereign. When there is lot of anarchy, all these types and shades of sovereignty exist and the individual is the most sovereign, the migrant is the most sovereign, she is the state for herself, because they have nobody to rely on.

In short, the reasons for poor regional integration are currently misunderstood in their complexity and are overshadowed by the visibility of unresolved conflicts. This, in turn, leads to a significantly slimmer menu of choices when it comes to possible interventions and conflict management strategies in the South Caucasus.

Third, a related criticism coming from the human security perspective is that the existing economic disparities and high levels of poverty, combined with the high number of refugees in the region (Oliphant interview 2013), create enormous internal conflict fault lines (Giragosian interview 2012), which the governments ignore at their own peril.

Fourth, skepticism about the prospects and value of greater regionalism in the South Caucasus also underestimates the potential of the global economy to continue creating incentives for regionalism: in many parts of the world the regional blocs are being used as steppingstones to integration with the global economy. The poor levels of economic integration in the region are more a reflection of their underdeveloped business culture (Makaryan interview 2013) than of their divergent economic interests. Isazade highlighted in an interview (2012) that Armenian and Azerbaijani businesspeople are working well together in Russia and Georgia, indicating a serious interest in the business community for greater engagement. Moreover, building economic and political alliances with external powers or strengthening regional cooperation is not necessarily a dichotomous choice, as evidenced by the experiences with regionalism in the developing world.

Fifth, constructivist criticism of such analysis in terms of ideas having political power is best captured in the words of Ter-Gabrielyan (interview 2013): "I am against realpolitik not because it does not have explanatory power. When explaining things through geopolitical approaches, people take the capacity to act themselves, away from themselves." It follows from this position that the South Caucasus is poorly integrated not just because of its varied geopolitical interests and external threat perceptions, as maintained by local analysts in the region, but also because of its lack of administrative capacity to engage regionally, from the local to national levels of government. Anyone who maintains that the South Caucasus is not integrated because there is no objective basis for it to do so obscures the real issues and weaknesses related to administrative capacities in all three states. Realizing the value of regional governance entails developing a strong regional dimension to one's statehood, which requires states to be sophisticated administratively and institutionally. Political solutions to ongoing conflicts may be necessary, but they are not a sufficient condition for developing regional mechanisms and regional governance structures for seemingly domestic political and economic problems.

Reasons for Regions

Proponents and skeptics of regionalism in the South Caucasus have been equally passionate about the issue in the past. Analysts have pointed out that the Caucasus civilization is distinct because of its common anthropological and ethnographic characteristics, geographical locations, common cultural patterns, and similar historical experiences in terms of interrupted independence efforts and short experiences with statehood. According to many analysts, these are some of the features that distinguish the South Caucasus from the Baltics or from Central Asia (De Waal 2012; Broers interview 2013; Ter-Gabrielyan interview 2013). Georgia's minister of reconciliation and civil equality, Paata Zakareishvili, has noted:

> When you look at the region, it seems as if God ordered that these countries join into a common region to be strong on their own. They have Caucasus Range in the North, two Seas, powerful resources to create a common and contained security area. There are historical neighbors, such as Turkey and Iran, with whom there are histories and experience of communication. This objective situation seems to dictate these countries to join their resources for common security, more efficient security, which would allow each member to reduce its security expenses. In reality the opposite is happening. (Zakareishvili interview 2013)

Laurence Broers of the Conciliation Resources (interview 2013) indicated that it may be hard to persuade Abkhazia or South Ossetia of the value of greater regional integration, but in the end "it is the difference between being a player in your own region as opposed to being an appendage to some other economic or political system." The respondent further pointed out that greater regional integration enhances the sovereignty of individual states because it is ultimately about the benefits of sovereignty at a practical level: traveling shorter distances between Azerbaijan and Turkey, between Armenia and Azerbaijan (not necessarily going through Georgia), and between Georgia and Russia. He further noted that it is ultimately about having economic agency as opposed to existing as an economic periphery to some distant capitals such as Moscow, Washington, or Ankara. As of the summer of 2013, all three countries in the region seem to be moving toward Europe, and regionalism manifested at that level allows envisioning congruence between political and economic development, and security orientations of the member countries (ibid.).

Indeed, the regional dynamics in the South Caucasus is complex, but statecentric geopolitical explanations are inefficient at capturing that complexity (Allen interview 2013). All three member countries of the South Caucasus are newcomers to political independence (Torosyan interview 2013), and decoupling from Soviet and post-Soviet structures is still under way. In the words of Terterov (interview 2012), it is impossible to expect that nearly century-long integration within the Soviet space will simply disappear in the span of merely twenty years. This dynamic is effectively captured by Giragosian:

> The problem is that we have a schizophrenic situation where in terms of identity and religion, in terms of inward and external identity, the region is less of a region, more

artificial. But that is offset by the seventy years of the Soviet experience of rather artificially forced regional not just integration but co-dependence, especially in the economic structures of Soviet economy. Delinking from those 7 decades is institutionally hard whether it is railways, pipelines, or economic structures. If we look at the competitive and comparative advantages of the three countries, they still have to overcome the 7 decades of experience. (Giragosian interview 2012)

Finally, the European integrative model of the Eastern Partnership and the Russian-led Eurasian Union are competing visions of remaking the South Caucasus (Kempe 2013). As a result, the prospects of greater regional integration in the South Caucasus, and the political fabric and organizational support for such regional integration in Caucasus, remain in flux. The European model places significant emphasis on the regional cooperation of the South Caucasus within the Eastern Partnership framework. Terterov (interview 2012) notes that the EU is heavily lobbied by businesses who are interested in larger markets of several tens of millions. This crystallizes the EU's interest in regional integration in the South Caucasus. Terterov (ibid.) continues that Russia is happy with the status quo in terms of regional disjointed "integration" in the South Caucasus, where Russian capital has already invaded, albeit bringing very little development with it.

Beyond this, there is little recognition of regional cooperation in the South Caucasus among the respondents in this study. This research, at a very minimum, is a call to reconceptualize and to rethink the regional discourse in the South Caucasus. Instead of engaging in unending debates over whether the South Caucasus is a region and whether it was invented by Russians or the West, a more constructive question to ask of governmental authorities and the donor community alike is, Should the region become a region in the full sense of the word? Ultimately, what matters is whether the states have developed strong, sophisticated regional dimensions to their state-building processes. Region building is a necessary albeit not sufficient condition for engaging in global structures and global policies effectively. The shared characteristics and unrealized economic potential in the South Caucasus are abundant (De Waal 2012; Allen interview 2013). However, a more nuanced understanding is needed of the layers of politics and politicization of governance that are blocking any significant progress to that end. To date, one-dimensional geopolitical analysis has failed to capture the complexity of the regional politics in the South Caucasus.

The Political Chemistry of Regionalism in the South Caucasus: A Comparative Look

Factors internal and external to states in PDAs tend to shape regional politics. Some of them are shared by the Western Balkans and the South Caucasus, while others are unique to each region. The first factor—the existing political culture within states in both regions—is consequential in shaping both foreign policy directions as well as public attitudes toward their immediate regional neighborhoods. Like the Western Balkans, the South Caucasus reemerged from the ruins of an integrative model that was cultivated and engineered from the top down (De Waal 2012) through the forces of sword and word (ideology). As in the Western Balkans, regionalism is politically discredited in the South Caucasus: the public is suspicious of any talk of regional integration after witnessing the relatively recent decline of one of several attempts at regional integration in the South Caucasus—the collapse of the Soviet Union (ibid.). Prior attempts at regional integration were short-lived, including that long-ago attempt to form, in the spring of 1918, a Transcaucasian state, which lasted only a month. The Soviet Transcaucasian Federation then formed in 1923 lasted only until 1936 (ibid.). In short, the region's prior experience with bottom-up regional integration is very limited and the political divisions significant. The fragmented hub-and-spoke pattern of regionalism in the South Caucasus contributed to consolidation of conflict structures within the region (De Waal 2010).

The weakness of regional ties among the three countries is deeply associated with the current conflict systems in the region, which have been described as "frozen" by some analysts. The 2008 war between Georgia and Russia painfully illustrated just how quickly these "frozen" conflicts can come undone. De Waal cautions that the current "no-war no-peace" situation around the NK conflict and the steady military buildup in Azerbaijan, with its military budget alone exceeding Armenia's national budget, creates conditions conducive to the eruption of a war, accidental or predetermined (ibid.). In some respects, the "Georgian conflicts" are less explosive for the region, despite the recent Georgia-Russia war; the de facto loss of territories of Georgia has left the country with a single choice: to democratize and to develop economically in order to attract and entice the breakaway region back into Georgia (Gegeshidze interview 2012; Zakareishvili interview 2013). In addition, within this no-war no-peace situation in the region, the peace-building infrastructure is rather underdeveloped, as I discuss later in this chapter. By contrast, there is a consistent pattern of "conflict building" (Ter-Gabrielyan interview 2013) that tends to ultimately result in war and violence. Moreover, the existing few peace-building structures are often politicized by national authorities in the region, according to Ter-Gabrielyan (interview 2013).

The second factor shaping regional politics is the weakness of civil societies. That weakness leaves these processes virtually unchecked, and the national authorities remain the dominant, if not the only, players in shaping the foreign policies of their countries. Indeed, the second internal factor explaining regional dynamics in the South Caucasus is the weakness of institutions of governance (Torosyan interview 2013; Bagratyan interview 2013). Similar to the situation in the Western Balkans, state institutions are weak, and a serious sovereignty capacity gap exists in the South Caucasus (Ter-Gabrielyan interview 2013). The weakness of state institutions is correlated with the strength of nationalist rhetoric as a political tool in domestic politics, mostly used to cover up administrative incompetency (Özkan 2008; Caspersen 2012; Huseynov interview 2012; Broers interviewinterview 2013; Bagratyan interview 2013). As in the Western Balkans, analysts across conflict lines in NK maintain that although the conflict emerged mostly through forces of ethnic identity and nationalism, the political elites have been instrumental in its perpetuation (Giragosian interview 2012; Iskandaryan interview 2012; Abbasov 2013; Bagratyan interview 2013).

A third factor with regional repercussions and also related to the political culture is value systems. Former speaker of the Armenian parliament Tigran Torosyan mentioned in a 2013 interview (Torosyan interview 2013) that the Caucasus countries do not share a value system similar to that in the EU that would sustain greater regional engagement. He further clarified that in terms of their democratic credentials each of the three countries is quite different, and that this nuance is often lost on Western observers. Indeed, the regional politics in the South Caucasus remains deeply affected by the politics of the sword and military security promises and threats, while the space otherwise used for regional ideology is filled with nationalist rhetoric and nation-building initiatives. And yet ASEAN, a relatively successful model of regionalism, includes countries with different types of political systems, political cultures, and levels of economic development (McMahon and Western 2009). The lack of a regional ideology or a shared value system is less of a factor in the Western Balkans than in the South Caucasus because the uncontested European presence in the region has offered a powerful ideology of democratization and integration, which is an alternative to the often divisive national rhetoric in the member countries in the Western Balkans. To clarify, as an ideology, regionalism is not as discredited in the Western Balkans as it is in the South Caucasus. In the Western Balkans, the European Union is a grounded institutional force, supporting and bolstering the ideology of regional engagement with carrots and sticks. While weak institutions of statehood are a shared problem in both regions and a serious obstacle for regional engagement, the South Caucasus lacks a deep supranational institutional presence with serious governance functions to offset the institutional weakness of the states. Biščević (interview 2012) was skeptical that the Western Balkans could remain regionally engaged if the European factor were taken out of the equation. The question for the South Caucasus is whether regional engagement can be cultivated without the carrots and sticks of European membership on the table.

Indeed, one of the main external factors with regional implications in both the Western Balkans and the South Caucasus is the European Union. It is significant for regional politics because of its ability to cultivate transgovernmental networks between countries in regions where it is active, thereby institutionalizing ties of interdependence between them. The South Caucasus lacks any transgovernmental network infrastructure, and the international connections at the regional level are rather fragmented, mostly omitting either Armenia or Azerbaijan from the equation. The Regional Environmental Center for the Caucasus (REC), one of the exceptions, is covered later in this chapter.

The European Union's Eastern Partnership promotes regional cooperation in the South Caucasus, but the Russian model is quite ambiguous on that front, to say the least. Although the EU falls short in offering countries in the South Caucasus security arrangements (Kempe 2013), it does offer a normative framework, and, as such, it is a technical construct (Zakareishvili interview 2013). By contrast, the Russia-led Eurasian Union and Customs Union are widely perceived as politically driven models, which has obscured their economic rationale (Libman 2007). Regardless, the European approach to region building in both the Western Balkans and the South Caucasus has been criticized for building regions with one hand and undoing them with the other, with the promise of broader integration in the EU space. In this respect, whether the pull of integration within the region will be to Georgia or Germany remains a question, and the prospects for parallel and multifaceted regional integration both within the South Caucasus as well as within wider frameworks remain underexplored.

In conclusion, the overall internal reluctance in the South Caucasus to define itself as a region stands in contrast to the strong identification of the South Caucasus as a region by external actors. Lack of complementarity in economic structures between the states, power imbalances and multiple conflict lines, and the perpetual search by each member state for external patrons are some of the most frequently cited reasons for the sustained lack of "regionness" in the South Caucasus. In contrast to the Western Balkans, where regional integration has more institutional support from the EU and is locally more anchored, few segments of society in the South Caucasus are currently viewing regionalism favorably. Interestingly, conflicts are the most visible but far from the only or even the major reason for poor levels of regional engagement in the South Caucasus. Lack of democratic institutions, heavily centralized states, weak administrative capacities, and weak civil societies are some of the factors undermining any prospects for regional integration. Although the need for cross-border cooperation between local levels of government across two entities may be great, in undemocratic/Westphalian states the centers usually discourage local initiatives of autonomous engagement across the border. Combined with lack of financial support as well as the capacity to engage across the border, the local levels of governments are disempowered from promoting greater engagement with their neighbors. However, the local levels of governance are important players in fostering microregionalism and in harnessing the developmental potential of regionalism at the community level. With an emphasis on grand economics, this level of regionalism and development is often skipped over in the regionalism discourse in the South Caucasus.

Theory of Regionalism for the South Caucasus

This section examines the South Caucasus as another empirical case study for testing the conceptual limits of the regional theories reviewed in Chapter 1.

Geographical Proximity or Functional Ties?

Territory versus functional ties as regional markers was the first theoretical division in the regional studies literature identified in Chapter 1. Although the case of the Western Balkans illustrates that geography and functional ties are mutually reinforcing in region-building processes there, in the South Caucasus the space and geographical location are currently being exploited for festering conflict as opposed to realizing shared economic goals. Zero-sum thinking is prevalent in the region (Gegeshidze interview 2012), primarily within the discourse of policy-makers and local analysts, which, by extension, blocks any avenues for alternative ideas to percolate into the public domain. Functional ties at the regional level are sporadic, ad hoc, and fragmented, lacking any consistent strategic support on the part of national authorities in all three countries.

In terms of geography, the South Caucasus is tightly bound by the Black Sea on the west and the Caspian Sea on the east, and it is laced with the Caucasus Mountains on the north. "Traveling from sea to sea, while crisscrossing three countries" has been cited as an obvious tourist advantage for the region (Allen interview 2013). Today, geography plays a role in cementing the South Caucasus together as a regional security complex—a system of division and fragmentation. Should war break out in the Georgian territory, it will immediately affect Armenia's socioeconomic development and survival. The breakout of war in NK would jeopardize the security of the oil and gas pipelines that carry Azerbaijani hydrocarbons to Europe, threatening economic devastation in both countries as well as in NK. Moreover, its geographic proximity to the North Caucasus makes the poorly integrated South Caucasus particularly vulnerable to any elements of Islamic fundamentalism that may enter from that region. The regionally and transnationally organized drug cartels operating from Afghanistan through Central Asia and the South Caucasus (Giragosian interview 2012) add yet another layer to the regional governance gap, driven by geography and yet insufficiently acknowledged by the member states in the region (ibid.).

The informal markets of Sadakhlo, Ergneti, and Bagratashen, which were in border areas and allowed traders across conflict lines to meet, have been closed down by state authorities, citing the need to clamp down on informal trade and criminality. These markets, which are often cited as excellent cases of grassroots-driven pragmatic cooperation, were formed in part because of their proximity to borders. Indeed, geographical proximity is insufficiently utilized to build efficient economic systems. Instead, it is used to isolate and interfere. For example, Azerbaijan and Turkey have played an active role in ensuring that oil pipelines and transportation routes bypass Armenia in an effort to isolate that state. In doing so, however, they have increased the transaction costs for the companies building and transporting oil and gas from Azerbaijan to Europe.

Instead, Shougarian has been advocating the creation and use of Qualified Industrial Zones (QIZ) in border areas between Armenia and Turkey, and Armenia and Azerbaijan. QIZs are similar to free trade zones, which have been used as a way to build trust and deeper ties among local officials on both sides of the conflict.[9] Shougarian (interview 2014) calls on the U.S. government to revitalize the project of QIZs, originally introduced by the Clinton administration for the Middle East (Israel, Palestine, Egypt, and Jordan) in 1996. Shougarian highlights that this trade format has been designed to promote peace in the Middle East by encouraging regional economic integration and cooperation primarily between countries in political conflict, and advocates for its application in the South Caucasus and its immediate neighborhood. Turkey has long been eager to get a free trade agreement with the United States—notoriously difficult to get. Placing a QIZ in a politically divided area may offer a possibility to place such a proposal on the fast track in the U.S. Congress.

Are State or Nonstate Actors Shaping Regionalism?

The second theoretical distinction discussed in Chapter 1 is between regional arrangements driven by states and nonstates. This distinction is quite stark in the South Caucasus. The existing regional frameworks are very few, and, particularly in the political sphere, are led by the state, with almost nonexistent mechanisms for spillover into other sectors of society or levels of governance. One such arrangement is the EuroNest Parliamentary Assembly, which is the parliamentary component of the Eastern Partnership. It includes members from the European Parliament and the parliaments of Armenia, Azerbaijan, Georgia, Moldova, and Ukraine. This is a rare forum in which all three the South Caucasus countries come together, but it excludes the nonrecognized territories (Nagorno-Karabakh, Abkhazia, and South Ossetia). Most of the other political and economic regional forums in which all three countries take part extend beyond the boundaries of the South Caucasus, reaching the larger region of the Black Sea and Mediterranean. Examples of these forums are the Organization of the Black Sea Economic Cooperation (BSEC) and Georgia Ukraine Azerbaijan Moldova Organization for Democracy and Economic Development (GUAM), which excludes Armenia, and the Commonwealth of Independent States (CIS), which excludes Georgia. In parallel, there are a variety of nonstate actor–led initiatives at the regional level, funded and driven by the European Union, Great Britain, and several Western European bilateral funding structures, that have brought together nonstate actors from the region. Both state-led and nonstate actor–led networks have virtually no mechanisms for interfacing with one another, which, as I will discuss later in this chapter, is counterproductive when attempting to structure a responsive and strategic conflict management infrastructure in PDAs.

Yedigaryan (interview 2013), drawing from her decades-long experience with donor structures in the South Caucasus, highlights that the donors tend to seek out the same civil society groups in nearly all projects. These are usually groups that are ready to work with their counterparts from other states. More, donors have been more drawn toward bringing togethercivil society actors between Armenia and Georgia, and Georgia and Azerbaijan, with very few cases of trilateral projects. Instead, she advocates for engaging in trilateral models, particularly because they are more challenging, but in an effort to bring in new actors and accessing new layers in civil societies across different states.

Is Conflict or Cooperation the Dominant Regional Marker?

The third division in regional analysis covered in Chapter 1 is whether a region is defined by conflict or cooperation. As we have seen, the South Caucasus is more of a regional complex than a regional security order. Because of the zero-sum thinking prevalent within policy-making circles, the acute security interdependencies between the states, minorities, and unrecognized territories is not acknowledged, nor is it translated into a modicum of cooperation around regional security issues. The existing instruments of security management are externally created and externally supported. Whether it is the Organization for Security and Co-operation in Europe (OSCE) Minsk Group (mediation regime created for management of the Nagorno-Karabakh conflict) or the Geneva Process (mediation and conflict management efforts involving Georgia, its breakaway regions of Abkhazia and South Ossetia, and Russia, created after the 2008 war between Georgia and Russia), it is the external players who are playing a central role in maintaining the fragile and tenuous security in the region.

External efforts at security provision are important, but the local and home-grown efforts of security management should not be discounted, particularly between Armenians and Azerbaijanis (Broers interviewinterview 2013). The mandate of the OSCE Minsk Group is fairly limited. They have to notify both sides several days in advance when visiting the cease-fire line. Therefore, on its own, the OSCE Minsk Group could not have achieved much without Armenia's and Azerbaijan's cooperation. The gap left by the external security actors as well as the home-grown measures continues to be significant if the high number of cease-fire violations across the Line of Contact between Armenia and Azerbaijan are considered.

Regional Autonomy

It is in terms of the level of regional autonomy that the South Caucasus has been particularly striking in challenging the existing theories of regional studies. Almost all of the respondents in this study pointed out the significance of the external influences of the regional and global powers. The gravitational pull to external power centers is evident in the region. Respondents also highlighted a clear pattern of quasi-self-help among the states: in an effort to provide its own security, each state is seeking an outside power and building bilateral coalitions. Examples are Armenia-Russia, Azerbaijan-Turkey, and Georgia–United States/European Union, although Zakareishvili (interview 2013), the minister of reconciliation and civil equality of the Republic of Georgia, noted that Georgia's relationships with the West are poorly institutionalized, if at all, and that Georgia is the least protected state within the region. Ironically, the patron-client relationships that are so characteristic of internal state-society relations in all three countries are being replicated at the foreign policy level in all three countries. One could thus argue that the region has very little autonomy, and that there is a thick blanket of overlay by outside powers seeking to exert influence over the region.

While popular in the region, power-based arguments that emphasize the role of external players (Russia, the United States, and the EU) in depriving the region of autonomy fail to capture the complexity of the situation on the ground. It appears that the South Caucasus as a region has acquired "negative autonomy"—that is, none of the external powers interested in the region have been able to advance a coherent agenda there. Analysts and international policy-makers and diplomats on the ground concede that the local states and societies need to find a way to agree on solutions to their conflicts, and that the outside powers should play only a facilitating role (anonymous interview with a senior Western diplomat 2013).

The negative autonomy in the region—the ability to maintain and consolidate the existing conflict structures, thereby delaying regional and national development—is increasingly explained by domestic factors. The observers and analysts of the region interviewed for this study, as well as the academic literature, concur that the lack of legitimacy of national authorities, the lack of rule of law, and the politicized economies have evolved into security threats in the region. Internal governance problems and the politically unrecognized human dimension of security have created a condition of threat misconception (Giragosian interview 2012). The oligarchic economy in Armenia (ibid., Ter-Gabrielyan interview 2013) and strong control of dissent in Azerbaijan are emerging as key sources of instability.

In the "negative autonomy" argument, the availability of competing regional models—the Russian-led Customs Union and Eurasian Union versus the EU's Eastern Partnership—created room for the political elites in all three countries to maneuver in dealing with their external powers. For example, Giragosian (interview 2012) maintains that the more the Armenian government engages with the EU, the more it is able to gain from the Russian government. The ability of regional elites to carve out room to maneuver has also been supported by the "regional empowerment" argument within regional studies. This argument supports the position that regions in developing countries are slowly emerging on their own and that the great power overlay is diminishing in some instances. Still, as the Balkan experience shows, regardless of the kind of regional model toward which a country may gravitate, the need for cooperating with one's neighbor remains a political and socioeconomic constant. Hido Biščević, secretary general of the Regional Cooperation Council at the time of his interview, noted that one needs to move away from the mentality that joining the EU will change one's geography and eliminate the need to engage with one's immediate neighbor (Biščević interview 2012).

The Issue of Overlay

In terms of overlay, the South Caucasus challenges the regional studies literature in one significant way. Scholars of regional studies often associate regional maturity with the ability of the members of the region to overcome zero-sum thinking and collective action problems. Regional maturity is understood to be the foreign policy exercised by states when they come together and push against external actors seeking to maintain influence in the region. The South Caucasus experience, however, reveals the false dichotomy between regional maturity and overlay. Instead, national authorities and political elites are able to dictate their terms of engagement without the region as a whole coming together and without the region as a whole developing any solid regional engagement structures, economic or political. The Nagorno-Karabagh conflict between Armenia and Azerbaijan is instructive. The OSCE Minsk Group has tried many times to foster cooperation between Azerbaijan and Armenia on nonpolitical technical issues, and it has put forth measures to build the confidence of the two states. Small-number and small-scale second-track initiatives between Armenia and Azerbaijan notwithstanding (Ter-Gabrielyan interview 2013; Huseynov interview 2012), overall, the respondents from international NGOs and international governmental organizations have pointed out that Azerbaijan refuses to engage with Armenia until there is a resolution to the conflict (anonymous interview with a senior diplomat from an international organization 2012; Christensen interview 2012; Bagratyan interview 2013). Questions posed to a senior official from the EU delegation in Armenia (anonymous interview with a senior EU diplomat in Armenia 2012) and to a senior official from the OSCE office in Armenia (anonymous interview with a senior Western diplomat in Armenia 2012) about why the international community is not exerting greater pressure on Azerbaijan to open up avenues of engagement beyond the official negotiation channels always produced similar answers: Azerbaijan is a sovereign state, and ultimately it will decide how to proceed with negotiation processes. The fact that Azerbaijan is an important source of energy for Europe undoubtedly constrains the position of the international community relative to Azerbaijan. The internal implications of the reliance of the Azeri government on oil are yet another factor. Azerbaijan has evolved into a "rentier" state that is not dependent on the public for revenues. As a result, the government is fully capable of shielding its policy-making from domestic influences. In this case, the great powers have been unable to push the Azerbaijan–OSCE Minsk Group negotiation process in any direction.

Network Attributes of the Regional Peace-building Infrastructure in the South Caucasus

Bottom-up or Top-down?

Compared with the Western Balkans, the South Caucasus is an institutional desert in terms of regional structures of governance dealing with concrete problems. At the same time, it shares some of the same patterns and trends in regional network development observed in the Western Balkans. Indeed, as discussed earlier in this chapter, the South Caucasus can be characterized as a case of "hard" regionalism, in which the few initiatives are driven by intergovernmental agreements and are state led. Its regional frameworks, while very small in number, are also very thin institutionally. Most of the trilateral interactions between the three countries in the South Caucasus occurs within broader regional and multilateral settings, ranging from BSEC to EuroNest. If bilateral political and economic initiatives are considered, then the regionalism is the "hub-and-spoke" type.

The unresolved nature of the conflicts perpetuates the existing governance gaps in the unrecognized territories, which are often left out of even the hub-and-spoke models of regionalism observed in the South Caucasus. It is "as if those territories should not move ahead in terms of democratization and free elections, governance," said one respondent. "Such territories are like white spots on the map" (Torosyan interview 2013), completely cut off from international reform efforts in the region (ibid.). The engagement with these territories by international and regional organizations has also been heavily politicized, and any significant economic and political engagement with them has halted (Weaver 2010). Finding ways of building engagement with such territories is far from granting them political status (Torosyan interview 2013). Indeed, in the Western Balkans the decoupling of engagement from political legitimacy and its depoliticization have been carried out through the diverse techniques and strategies employed by regional organizations, most notably the RCC.

Bottom-up and more organic efforts of regionalism are sparse, in part because of the unresolved conflicts, with Azerbaijan making conflict resolution a precondition for any engagement with Armenia. At the same time, although there is no conflict between Armenia and Georgia, their relationship is quite primitive, lacking any institutional sophistication or any political priority by the governments. Overall, the pull of external actors is a major impediment to regionalism, which is similar to the dynamics in the Western Balkans immediately after signing the Dayton Accords. As a region, the Western Balkans has achieved greater regional maturity in multilayered governance: it engages with the European Union, and the Balkan states are driven by the EU membership, but this factor is resonating less and less as a replacement for regional engagement with immediate neighbors.

The scarcity of regional state-driven initiatives in the South Caucasus also stems from the weak states in that area. Against the backdrop of an increasingly globalized economic and political environment, the states in advanced and mature regions have developed a distinct regional profile, as expressed in their abilities to foster national governance through national structures and to use regional structures to address problems that are internal in nature. As described in the previous chapter on the Western Balkans, an ability to forge transgovernmental networks between governments has been the RCC's key accomplishment. Against this background, the South Caucasus experience is stark. Either because of their weak administrative structures and highly centralized states, or because of their lack of political will, the states in the region have very few mechanisms for using regional engagements in addressing their national problems. Interviews with governmental officials in both Armenia and Georgia indicated that neither government has any special priority in its foreign policy related to its neighbor. Having "friendly" relations was how such relations were usually characterized.

The gap is often filled by regional organizations, such as OSCE and the EU, which also are pathways of top-down region building in the South Caucasus. OSCE's work in environmental security is a good case in point. Acting on a request from Azerbaijan, OSCE conducted a wildfire management project because the issue was a concern for everyone in the region. Regional training on this front, usually organized in Turkey, connects representatives and midlevel civil servants and professionals from all countries in the region (anonymous interview with a senior Western diplomat 2012). Unfortunately, such top-down initiatives are seldom seen, but they offer many lessons learned in terms of building transgovernmental networks and strengthening professional networks across conflict lines. As this study argues, such measures are crucial for diffusing the conflict, but also for strengthening the administrative capacities of nation-states at the regional level.

In peace-building initiatives, the existing regional networks are also top-down, but largely initiated by the donor communities as opposed to the governments of the member states. Recently, the European Union has been emerging as the lead donor in funding peace-building projects in the South Caucasus, whereas earlier the British government was the dominant financial supporter of these initiatives (anonymous interview with a senior Western diplomat 2013; Broers interviewinterview 2013). As the EU emerges as a leading donor in the South Caucasus (Ter-Gabrielyan interview 2013), the issue of accountability remains central (ibid.). About ten years ago, the EU began to channel its funding through governments, directing it away from NGOs (ibid.), which generated a big outcry from the latter (ibid.). Although governments are more accountable on paper, in reality the practice of channeling funds through governments has created significant corruption and money laundering. The growing EU presence within peace-building initiatives also creates the problem of donor-driven agendas (ibid.), which, for the reasons given shortly, are often counterproductive for peace-building initiatives (ibid.). "Often people [in NK] want civic advocacy and computer training, and we come in offering dialogue with Azerbaijanis," said Broers (interview 2013).

The rise of the European Union as the main financial supporter of peace building in the South Caucasus did not alter the overall structure of donor-NGO networks. The interface between donors and the NGO sector is significant for peace building at this point. An anonymous NGO practitioner interviewed for this study said that NGOs are increasingly important in helping shape the agenda because NGOs have the most direct contact with local actors and partners (anonymous interview 2013). Today, the NGO sector has evolved into a mechanism for giving voice to local communities, which in general are left out of the third-party intervention regimes established in the region. Donors working in international capitals are reliant on embassy staff for information, but these officials tend to have heavy workloads and only little information on the situation:

> International NGOs must not . . . come with already established templates [that they try] to impose locally. My own sense as a practitioner and a former policymaker is that that approach does not work and alienates local partners. Efforts and work have to be built around proper collaborative and fully consultative processes that take into account . . . how the locals see their situation and their needs." (Anonymous interview 2013)

Echoing this statement, Broers (interview 2013) maintained in an interview that the NGO sector is emerging as the key institutional memory in the region because donor staff members tend to rotate and change positions quite frequently. Educating each donor about peace building takes time and effort, and in the long run it can degrade peace-building initiatives. In short, within the existing top-down regional patterns of network mobilization the NGO sector plays a pivotal role in representing local voices and serving as an institutional memory. Donors, however, to meet the growing emphasis on monitoring and impact evaluation, must rely on technical and quantifiable information such as the number of training participants and gender breakdown, which has rarely been effective in capturing the complex effects of peace-building initiatives on the ground (ibid.). Overall, Broers (ibid.) noted, the ongoing conflicts have placed the peace-building civic initiatives on track II (diplomacy), and they have been a target of criticism (ibid.) because they have been perceived as not delivering. And yet "Track I has not delivered because of basic methodological misconceptions of how it works" (ibid.).

In terms of the patterns of mobilization of peace-building networks, there is also a clear distinction in terms of track I and II dynamics in the NK conflict, on the one hand, and the Georgian-Abkhaz and Georgian-Ossetian conflicts, on the other. Indeed, in the NK conflict, tracks I and II developed in different realms, with occasional attempts to link them up (ibid.). Overall, the OSCE Minsk Group is criticized for being elitist with no interface with track II efforts, and calls to bolster and beef it up are heard often from the practitioner and policy community (anonymous interview 2013; Broers interview 2013).

Institutional Density: Binding Ties?

In terms of institutional density, the levels of regional trade, including between Georgia and Armenia, are quite limited. Unrealized regional potential was cited by many respondents (Giragosian interview 2012; anonymous interview with a senior EU diplomat 2012; anonymous interview with a senior Western diplomat 2013). Limited economic cooperation has been observed, such as when Georgia simplified small and medium enterprise (SME) registration, and some Armenian businesses relocated there (Ter-Gabrielyan interview 2013). Similarly, Armenian tourists are routinely spending their vacations at the Georgian seaside. Cooperation between Georgia and Azerbaijan in the regional networks in the economic and political sectors is quite thin, despite the fact that the two countries are linked by their strategic interests (Zakareishvili interview 2013), with Georgia serving as an energy route for exporting Azerbaijani oil and gas (ibid.). According to Ter-Gabrielyan (interview 2013), there are few joint enterprises between Georgia and Azerbaijan, and the economic dividends from the pipeline routes through Georgia remain limited.

Within peace-building initiatives, the institutional density of the existing regional networks remains limited. Over the years, the number of actors in the peace-building field has not increased, and the number of beneficiaries from their initiatives remains small (Broers interview 2013). Increasing the institutional density of a given regional network is at times politically and practically difficult. Broers (ibid.) has noted:

> Peace-building initiatives do tend to be insular. They only reach a limited number of beneficiaries or constituencies. There are a number of reasons for that. On the one hand, peace-building NGOs do not understand PR, how to broaden the impact and public awareness around key issues. This is internal to how NGOs work. Even with public awareness initiatives such as our films, we do not often reach as many people as we would like. It is labor-intensive to organize screening of films across Azerbaijan, Armenia and NK. . . . When we create resources like this, there is not necessarily

follow-up from local partners, to take this and run with it, unless it has project ties, with salaries, and that becomes a labor-intensive project into itself. (Ibid.)

Broers (ibid.) also listed turf wars, different ethos, and different comfort levels with the public profiles of NGOs as factors complicating the prospects of multiplying outcomes and reaching a higher number of people in conflict communities. Although some of the factors working against increasing the numbers of nodes and networks in peace building have top-down dynamics (NGO competition, donor reliance on the same NGOs to maintain high levels of capacity in program management, and so forth), there are also bottom-up obstacles. "Creating portals for people to enter the peacebuilding effort" remains a challenge, Broers (ibid.) observed. The peace initiatives advanced by international community are often perceived as illegitimate. In addition, the peace agenda faces the same challenges of coordination and public mobilization as any other political party in all three countries. The ability to access tacit networks with peace-building agendas and generate political participation remains a major challenge in these countries (ibid.). In short, although the unresolved status of conflicts is a frequently cited reason for greater cross-conflict engagement in other issue areas (Torosyan interview 2013), there are also numerous administrative and other issues related to the political cultures in these countries that have been equally powerful obstacles to cross-conflict engagement. Therefore, the issue of low institutional density of regional networks in peace building can perhaps be alleviated by greater donor risk taking in bringing new NGOs into the field, thereby generating programs that are more embedded in the social and political fabric of these conflict societies.

Heteropolarity: Diversifying Stakeholders

As for heteropolarity within the peace-building initiatives, the picture in the South Caucasus and the Western Balkans is bleak. The existing NGO-donor networks are quite rudimentary and often highly politicized, which makes it almost impossible to enhance their heteropolarity by bringing in the private sector. The International Alert's Caucasus Business and Development Network, one of the few exceptions, is reviewed later in this chapter.

The broader political context in the three countries is a major consideration here. In an interview in 2013, Tigran Torosyan, former Speaker of Armenia's Parliament, observed (ibid.) that although the West treats the three countries in the same way, there are marked differences in the extent of democratization in the countries, particularly Armenia and Azerbaijan: "I am fully aware of the flaws and problems in the Armenian political system in regards to its democratic credentials. However, it is not comparable to the ones prevalent in Azerbaijan" (ibid.). This statement is supported by other respondents who pointed out that Azerbaijani participants in track II initiatives tend to be under heavy political pressure back home. Often constructive postures and constructive engagements are sanctioned heavily by the Azerbaijani government. An anonymous respondent from an NGO sector noted many mostly arbitrary cases in which international officials who had visited NK through Armenia and then tried to visit Azerbaijan were denied visas at the airport (anonymous interview 2013). Broers (interview 2013) said Azerbaijani authorities have never forbidden him to initiate a particular project, but he did explain that "there is an active advocacy for specific formats they want to see in Track II initiatives" (ibid.). Broers also noted that the increased number of high-level official visits to NK from around the world is perceived by the Azerbaijani government as tantamount to granting legitimacy to NK. Such a perception prompts retaliatory acts on the diplomatic and track II fronts by Azerbaijan. The most important implication is the increased politicization of track II efforts, which precludes any prospects of institutional evolution and sophistication in conflict management infrastructures on the ground. The very low levels of heteropolarity, reflected in the lack of sectoral diversity in conflict management networks, as well as the absence of links between the local, national, and regional levels of government, are highly characteristic of peace-building networks in the South Caucasus.

The lack of heteropolarity in the peace-building and other types of regional networks in the South Caucasus is mostly a function of the politicization of the economic sector (Makaryan interview 2013). The business sector not only has not been involved in peace-building initiatives, but also has been actively shut down by the governments, particularly that of Azerbaijan, for being a "risk factor" in conflict management processes. According to Makaryan (ibid.), the situation has worsened in Azerbaijan. As for Turkey, contrary to the image that it tries to project, the political influence over economic relations with Armenia is still quite predominant. The highly controlled and orchestrated relationships with the business sector to date have limited any potential for their role in peace-building processes. As the case study of the Caucasus Business and Development Network illustrates, a deep commitment from business actors is needed to build and nurture the relationships between networks and their counterparts across the conflict lines.

When building heteropolar networks in the South Caucasus, greater economic engagement at the regional level is imperative. Some local respondents in Armenia often cited the lack of complementarities between the economies of Armenia and Georgia (Bekirski interview 2012; Iskandaryan interview 2012), arguing that there is no basis for a regional economic interface. By contrast, all Western respondents and some of the local ones clarified that regional engagement is a prerequisite for economic development. Issues such as the ability to ensure the "rhythmic supply of resources and products" (Makaryan interview 2013) and "more efficient linkages" (Giragosian interview 2012) are cited as crucial for region building in the South Caucasus. Makaryan, the executive director of the Union of Manufacturers and Businessmen Employers of Armenia, noted that the pressure for greater regional engagement will only increase with time, and that issues of complementarity are not sustained by the market forces that push locally, regionally, and globally (Makaryan interview 2013).

Power Concentration: Follow the Money

The last network attribute for assessing the peace-building infrastructure in the South Caucasus is the degree of power concentration—that is, whether the existing peace-building networks are centered (supported by one or two organizations that play the role of institutional hegemon and dominate the provision of financial and institutional resources within the network), or stretched (whether the resource supply is more broad based). For peace-building purposes, the presence of an institutional hegemon allows greater coordination and complementarities in resources and efforts. The lack of an institutional hegemon leaves the network more vulnerable to political pressures and fluctuations on the ground.

As discussed earlier, within the peace-building infrastructure in the South Caucasus, and particularly within NK, the European Union is gradually replacing the British government as the main source of financial support in track II efforts. Almost all of these initiatives are heavily dependent on funding because most of them are donor led, even though grassroots initiatives tend to be more sustainable in the long run (Ohanyan 2012).

Although there has always been a clear institutional hegemon providing financial resources in the peace-building networks in the South Caucasus (whether it is the EU or British government), it is the NGO community, local and international, that plays the key role in the sustainability of initiatives. According one respondent who chose to remain anonymous:

One lesson I would draw, from having been in the government side, previously working in the Foreign Ministry and now working in the practitioner/NGO sector, is that it is the importance of sustained programs and sustained efforts in terms of having the most impact in the region. I think you can have fireworks of impressive one-off single episode kind of initiatives, but actually it seems to be what people are mainly looking for is sustained efforts and credible efforts. (Anonymous interview 2013)

The respondent further emphasized that the issue of trust is central in sustaining such initiatives in the long term. That trust is created by establishing a reliable pattern of behavior. Therefore, in both stretched and centered networks, the sustainable financial support is needed to nourish these networks, but it is the deep commitment at the grassroots level that makes a difference in peace processes: "[T]he staying power of local partners . . . has been remarkable. One day this is going to produce a breakthrough because it is working in a common sense and pragmatic way. This is the way, I think, to try and affect people's lives" (ibid.).

In contrast to Armenia-Azerbaijan relations (or lack thereof), the Turkey-Armenia track II interface has been particularly promising. This is a rare initiative in which business associations from Turkey and Armenia have been steering the process. Over the past decade, the Turkish-Armenian Business Development Council (TABDC) has been pushing for the border opening between Turkey and Armenia, but with only mild success. TABDC has initiated several projects and networks and has acted as a key institutional hegemon in such initiatives. Among them are the Kars-Akhalkalaki initiative, Arax project, Satr project, Rotary and Caucasian Friendship Days, and Virtual Agricultural Wholesale Market. Even with the recent setback in Turkey-Armenia engagement,[10] there is enough energy and momentum for many other initiatives to develop across the border.

In the context of the conflicts in the South Caucasus, the presence of an institutional hegemon—the British government or the EU—is essential to sustain the existing efforts. However, in contrast to Turkey-Armenia initiatives, there is little evidence to show that these initiatives can replicate and proliferate without funding. The weakness of civil societies in the region is one explanation for such an outcome. Still, if greater regional engagement is achieved in the South Caucasus, new portals and windows of opportunity will be created for some of these existing peace-building initiatives to scale up and down to the grassroots level. Transition from centered to stretched networks in peace-building infrastructures will signal a maturity in peace-building initiatives as well as in the region as a whole.

The prevalence of centered networks in the South Caucasus peace-building infrastructure renders the initiatives vulnerable to a global financial crisis. Many respondents from the NGO sector noted that "there are hard times for peace building" in terms of diverted energy and attention from the South Caucasus to the Arab Spring and Syrian uprising, as well as the global financial crisis, which threatens to undermine financial commitments to the region's peace-building efforts. In this respect, the presence of heteropolar and stretched networks would have made the peace-building infrastructure less vulnerable to political and economic fluctuations in the global polity and economy.

Regional Network Profiles in the South Caucasus

The two regional networks profiled in this section highlight both the opportunities for and the vulnerabilities of peace building exhibited by state-centric models of "hard regionalism," such as the REC, and society-focused models of "soft regionalism," driven by civil society and the business sector, such as the Caucasus Business and Development Network (CBDN).

REC

The REC was established to address the very concrete and real problems surrounding the environment. It offers a unique opportunity for researchers to understand how cooperation develops in this politically divided region and how political divisions between the governments and societies are negotiated within the daily work around environmental protection. The REC focuses on concrete environmental problems and the regional governance gaps around them. The regional dimension of the areas it covers—water, land, forest/biodiversity, green economy, disaster, climate change, and waste—is quite pronounced. For example, the countries in the South Caucasus lie within the Kura-Araks River Basin. The shared problem is water quality, quantity, flood, habitat protection, and bioresources. The REC concentrates on problems such as "inadequate monitoring, low data reliability and accessibility, poor infrastructures, low awareness and inadequate capacities to contribute to defective water-related eco-systems." The REC also tackles specific issues with a definite regional dimension, such as the different approaches to and standards and methods for management of water resources between the countries, and the absence of a reference laboratory in the Kura River Basin and of a harmonized classification scheme in the South Caucasus.

The REC was initiated by the European Union. It is the only example of a regional forum in which the three countries in the region participate at the governmental level (Sahakyan interview 2013). Indeed, the environment has been noted by the respondents in this study as probably the only area in which it has been possible to cultivate true regional cooperation in the South Caucasus (anonymous interview with a senior diplomat from an international organization 2012; anonymous interview with a senior Western diplomat 2012). The REC is registered as a not-for-profit organization, with the goal of addressing environmental problems in the South Caucasus as well as developing civil society in the member countries of the region.[11] The REC was established within the framework of the "Environment for Europe Process" as a follow-up to the Sofia Ministerial Conference in 1995. The charter of the organization—its main founding document—was signed in September 1999 by the governments of Azerbaijan, Armenia, and Georgia, and the European Union. The organization is headquartered in Tbilisi, Georgia, with offices in Baku and Yerevan.

In terms of its main network attributes, the REC is a top-down regional network, centered in terms of its internal power structure, with medium to highly institutionalized links within the societies. It is highly heteropolar in its ties to various sectors (market, civil society, and government), and it has solid connections from the local to regional levels of governance (Sahakyan interview 2013).

Its top-down pattern of operation is on view in its decision-making processes. The REC is governed by a board of directors composed of members of the governments from the three countries, as well as representatives of the civil society sector. The regional executive director position rotates periodically among the executive directors of REC offices in all three countries. Although the decision-making and policy development processes are top-down, problem formulation and agenda setting are quite open to input from ordinary citizens. Also, as a top-down, state-centric network, the REC has been able to develop a track record of engaging with local levels of government, important beneficiaries of REC projects and reports. Sahakyan (ibid.) noted that local levels of government have been quite responsive and effective in implementing and supporting the sustainability of REC projects in Armenia.

As for its institutional density, the REC's contacts in the societies are quite extensive. Within its green economy priority area, the REC has been working with the SME sector in the region (ibid.). Lessons learned from one country are usually transferred to neighboring countries. For example, the REC is developing adaptive mechanisms for climate change, which is already affecting agricultural production in the region, by offering substitute crops for those affected. In developing such adaptive mechanisms, the REC works closely with farmers and rural communities, thereby registering a high level of societal involvement in its program as well as in its follow-up and sustainability efforts. "We always tell the communities that through our programs we are doing your job and after we finish, you need to support the programs and initiatives that we have created in your community" (ibid.).

However, despite the high level of societal engagement and institutional density, in terms of solid networks built with local levels of government, the REC falls short of qualifying as a transgovernmental network. Members of the governments of all three countries meet within the institutional domain of the REC, as opposed to operating within the transgovernmental networks they create themselves. As a result, the REC recognizes that there is a lack of policy coordination in the environmental policy area. The locus of authority is outside of governments and outside of any institutional space supported by contacts between governments directly. Instead, the REC serves as an intermediary, which, for PDAs, may be the only available model to structure and nurture regional cooperation and governance around specific problem areas.

Levels of heteropolarity within the REC network are high, as demonstrated by its highly institutionalized contacts with the central and local levels of governments in the three countries, as well as with the civil society. However, connections with the business sector have only recently begun to evolve, and they exhibit a program-based, as opposed to institutionalized, character. In particular, the REC has developed and is currently implementing the Promotion of Cleaner Production and Energy Efficiency Technology through Development of Business Planning Practices for Cleaner Production and Energy Efficiency Project. The main objective of this project is to advance sustainable development and minimize environmental impact from the industrial sector.[12] Stimulating SMEs is a tool thought to be essential to this end.

The heteropolarity of this network has been strengthened by one of its pilot projects: the Local Environmental Action Plan (LEAP). LEAP has been implemented in three cities in the South Caucasus: Ararat, Ganja, and Kutaisi. The notable aspect of this work is that it has been developed in close cooperation with local authorities and the involved communities alike. In this program, local governments receive small grants to build partnerships between business and NGOs. The grants translate into projects to improve drinking water supplies and irrigation systems, thereby improving waste management, encouraging the planting of greenery, and raising environmental awareness. The REC's strategic emphasis on heteropolarity is best captured by its efforts to serve as a bridge between the public and the governments,[13] which it does through capacity building and the provision of information, advice, and expertise to encourage dialogue and enhance public participation in environmental decision-making.[14]

Finally, in the distribution of power resources within the network, the REC is a centered network. The bulk of its financial resources are provided by the European Commission, and additional bilateral funding is supplied by the governments of Germany, the Netherlands, Norway, the United States, and Liechtenstein, as well as the OSCE. The REC also receives financial support from the national governments of the three countries, most of which is used to cover administrative costs of the offices in each capital. The political legitimacy of this regional effort is ensured through a range of international agreements signed by the EU and the member countries in the region. The political support and credibility are generated through a range of conventions that support REC's activities in the South Caucasus.[15]

An example of "hard regionalism" led through top-down efforts, the REC is a unique arrangement that has created an institutional space for the national authorities from all three countries to work together in an effort to address environmental problems and enhance their environmental security. It is also a unique instrument for building a professional community through creating transgovernmental ties. Therefore, as a mode of governance, the REC is very innovative in the context of the South Caucasus, where the institutional isolation of the national authorities of the three countries is the norm.

The peace-building opportunities that this arrangement creates in the region may seem marginal at first glance. However, by creating and consolidating a network of professionals built around a concrete set of problems, the REC has evolved into a useful mechanism for depoliticizing relationships among the three countries, particularly between Armenia and Azerbaijan. Respondents from the REC have noted on several occasions that it is not a political organization (Harutyunyan 2013; Sahakyan interview 2013). The Regional Cooperation Council's neutral status is significantly more evolved, politically explicit, and institutionalized through day-to-day programmatic actions. As a mechanism of regional governance, which could almost be described as transgovernmental, the REC is a useful model for building similar professional communities in other issue areas. As the RCC experience demonstrates, this model helps to decouple political relations between conflict parties from their relationships in other areas of shared concern, ranging from the environment to drug trafficking. The REC can also become a useful tool through which to demonstrate the peace dividend to local communities that otherwise are beyond reach. Creating a new track of engagement between conflict parties, in this case Armenia and Azerbaijan, through a regional forum of engagement does not add up to granting a status to disputed territories (Torosyan interview 2013). But it does produce strengthened governance capacities in all three countries. Strengthening state capacities in environmental policy and administration, from central to local levels of governance, through regional cooperation as fostered by the REC, is a major accomplishment and highly consequential for peace-building purposes. It creates the possibility of peace building through region building, an argument covered more extensively in Chapter 7.

The obvious limitation for peace-building purposes within the REC regional network is the fact that the REC, at least to date, has engaged only the state entities in the region: Armenia, Azerbaijan, and Georgia. Although peace building and conflict management are not a REC objective, the fact that the REC has stayed out of the disputed territories supports the argument that it has a state-centric bias in building regional ties. By contrast, International Alert's Caucasus Business and Development Network, which is building more inclusive regional arrangements, albeit with no state support, is a case of "soft regionalism."

Caucasus Business and Development Network (CBDN)

International Alert's Caucasus Business and Development Network was selected for greater analysis in this study because it differs organizationally from the REC when it comes to fostering regional cooperation. The REC as a model of regional cooperation has features of transgovernmental network governance, whereas the CBDN is largely a nonstate-centric regional process of cooperation. As I argue in this section, both models possess unique opportunities for peace-building processes while also posing certain challenges to it.

The regional methodology was a strategic choice by International Alert (IA), which established the CBDN. The CBDN is a top-down network with low to medium levels of institutionalization, and it is highly heteropolar, and with stretched power centers within the network (Ter-Gabrielyan interview 2013).

The current successes by the CBDN are largely derived from the IA's earlier extensive experience with applying the regional methodology of peace building to the South Caucasus (Klein and Pentikainen 2012, 228). The IA experimented with regional approaches by establishing the Caucasus Forum 1998 with EU funding (Ter-Gabrielyan 2012). This was a confidence-building measure between Georgians and the Abkhaz in the city of Nalchik, near Mount Elbrus in Kabardino-Balkaria (Krikorova 2012). The regional methodology of peace building employed by the IA was based on the rationale that conflict parties often hesitate to come together in bilateral formats (Ter-Gabrielyan interview 2013; Krikorova 2012). A format that applied to the entirety of the South Caucasus allowed significant flexibility and reassured the conflict parties that a peacebuilding initiative would not add to their opponent's legitimacy in some way.

Both the CBDN and Caucasus Forum were envisioned and created as loose, semistructured networks, giving them great flexibility in building relationships and attracting participants. The Caucasus Forum did, however, establish a coordinating body, the Coordinating Council, that was staffed by one NGO representative from each of the Caucasus regions. The coordinating activities were carried out by the executive secretary on a rotating basis (Krikorova 2012).

The Caucasus Forum carried out a range of peace-building projects at the regional level, which included organizing a meeting of the former combatants, the All-Caucasus Creative Youth Games, and the "Forgotten Regions" project, aimed at supporting and developing civil society in Nagorno Karabakh, South Ossetia, and North Caucasus (Ter-Gabrielyan 2012). Although the Caucasus Forum continues to exist through virtual contacts maintained between partners and individuals (and is still formally registered in the Netherlands), the forum has ceased to exist in a more formal capacity (Ter-Gabrielyan interview 2013; Krikorova 2012). The cessation of funding and the growing complexity of the political situation in the region are some of the factors often cited behind the decline of the Caucasus Forum (Ter-Gabrielyan interview 2013; Krikorova 2012).

In terms of its network attributes, the CBDN is supported financially by the IA and its donor network, but there is no local financial support to sustain its operation. However, its top-down patterns of mobilization in financial and organizational terms in the early stages of its formation were accompanied by strong local involvement in developing program priorities and shaping agendas for operation. Indeed, whether a given network is top-down or bottom-up can be quite relative. Taking the societies in the region as referents, one could argue that the CBDN evolved through top-down measures, driven by the IA and its international donor networks. However, as the CBDN network supported by the IA developed and matured over time, the CBDN and its local partners began to take on leadership roles in fund-raising efforts as well. Participants in and close observers of the CBDN argue that, without the IA, the CBDN probably would not have survived (Klein and Pentikainen 2012). Over time, the top-down patterns of network mobilization in the CBDN gave way to greater institutional maturity and differentiations in the roles of network members. Perhaps it is more useful to think of the IA's initial role in the network as one of intermediating between locally developed and nurtured ideas and initiatives, on the one hand, and donor preferences and priorities, on the other. In this respect, the IA, at least within this network, played a role similar to that of the RCC in the Western Balkans in cultivating regional functional ties between the societies in this conflict region. The main distinction between the two is scale: the RCC's scope of operation in terms of issue areas as well as institutional depth was significantly more expansive than that of the IA, but that was largely because of the political support that the RCC received in the Western Balkans as part of the EU's involvement in the region.

In terms of institutional density, the IA's CBDN network is quite instructive. The network has thought long and hard about the proper levels of institutionalization needed for the CBDN presence in the region, drawing partly from the experience of the Caucasus Forum. Prior to creating the CBDN, the IA had a relatively dense institutional presence in the region, which, observers of the CBDN note, allowed a more comprehensive analysis of the situation on the ground as well as more effective development of relationships and partner selection in the network (ibid.). While the Business and Conflict team within the IA was working in Azerbaijan on oil-related issues, the North and the South Caucasus team was engaged with the civil society organizations in the region. The network was thus in tune with the needs and interests of the ultimate stakeholders in regional approaches within the network.

Indeed, the high level of institutional density of the IA within the region proved to be an asset for subsequent structuring of the CBDN, which, interestingly, opted for relatively low levels of institutional presence in the region. To what extent to formalize and institutionalize the CBDN was debated openly, and the IA's experience with the Caucasus Forum served as a point of reference:

> We had seen the Caucasus Forum struggle through designing statues—a process which took endless days of negotiating over semantics and grammar. We realized

that we could not get involved in such a process, as neither we nor the participants had the time, interest or patience for such activities. Therefore, we steered the group towards a loose and informal network. (Ibid.)

While the IA opted for a loosely organized information network as a supporting structure for the CBDN, it still grounded its presence in the region in institutional terms. In particular, the IA and CBDN established "Business Centers" in each of the seven entities (Armenia, Azerbaijan, Georgia, and Turkey, as well as Abkhazia, Nagorno-Karabakh, and South Ossetia). By contrast, the Caucasus Forum, despite its internal institutionalization, was never properly rooted in the region (ibid.). The level of institutionalization in terms of field presence provided the CBDN with a regional perspective and created real channels for local input to enter into the peace-building process as driven by the IA and CBDN. In addition, albeit on a low level, the field presence helped to integrate the peace-building process into the mainstream by bringing business initiatives and business communities into the network. This was an effective strategy for developing larger peace communities and increasing the number of people from new segments of the conflict societies (ibid.). In short, although the CBDN maintained a low institutional profile internally, it opted for an institutionalized field presence in the entities, thereby expanding its reach within the societies and building "peace pressure points" within the region.

The CBDN's heteropolarity is one of its key features by default. The CBDN was designed to build networks between business communities across the political divide. In capitalizing on the political and economic opportunities provided by heteropolarity, the CBDN made a strategic choice to focus on the SME sector as opposed to large businesses, which tend to be more politicized in conflict regions and more capable of overcoming the geographic distances to reach distant markets. Most important, SMEs were appreciated within the IA and CBDN because they were embedded in their communities and thus could become more effective as "peace pressure points" within the conflict society.

Caucasus Tea and Caucasus Cheese are some of the most visible CBDN initiatives, with several others in the making. However, the CBDN ran into the problem of whether to market the Caucasus Cheese and Caucasus Tea as political or economic brands. Ultimately, the decision was made to consider the context in each case. Regardless, this dilemma raises the question of whether to place a given peace-building initiative within broad governance-focused processes or ones with a direct emphasis on peace building. The first one relates to the broader notion of developing the involved communities, whereas the latter is specifically and directly focused on peace processes on the ground. In a way, heteropolar networks create opportunities to move on both tracks in conflict regions, which is a necessary condition for sustainable and successful peace-building initiatives. The major outcome of the CBDN's high level of heteropolarity on the ground was the development of numerous mechanisms and avenues of depoliticizing. The best evidence of the significance of such depoliticized networks was the fact that the CBDN survived the Georgia-Russia war in 2008.

Although it is highly heteropolar in sectoral terms, the CBDN has lacked the mechanisms to reach out to different levels of government, from local to national, and this has been a major strength of the REC network. The CBDN has had strong access to the European Union and the bilateral donor community, which have been involved in the network primarily in terms of providing the finances needed for network maintenance and operation. And yet the local and national structures of governance are missing from the network, which could be one area in which the CBDN could magnify its presence.

The last network attribute is the extent to which the power resources within the network are diffused or concentrated—that is, whether the network is stretched or centered. This particular network dimension of the IA's CBDN network has been highly variable. In terms of financial resources, in the early stages of the network formation and consolidation the IA played a key role in fund raising for the CBDN from European capitals. The IA was also central in providing the necessary political resources—that is, placing the International Alert label on projects, which, as the observers argued, is central to gaining legitimacy for the initiative (ibid.). In view of its institutional support for the initiative, particularly in terms of intermediating between the CBDN and the international donor community, one could argue that the IA was the key political center within the network and the institutional hegemon that played a key role in consolidating the CBDN.

Over time, the CBDN matured and was able to stand on its own, with occasional IA support. In fact, it gained enough legitimacy and credibility to raise funds independently, with marginal support from the IA. This shift of the power locus to the CBDN was viewed as a measure of success and an indicator of sustainability by the IA, which in some ways was in contrast to donors' emphasis on the establishment of sustainable businesses as an ultimate success indicator (ibid.).

The shift of power to the CBDN, in both financial and institutional/organizational terms, reflected the changing dynamics within the network. The IA's facilitating role slowly evolved into a more genuine partnership with the CBDN. The network-based structure of the IA-CBDN relationship in terms of its evolving and fluid nature has been a key factor in strategically shifting the power center within the network from the IA to the CBDN. The question of who is leading, and when, has been debated and discussed directly within the network, and the appropriate decisions, particularly on delegating greater power and competencies to the CBDN, have been made along the way:

> There was also the pragmatic consideration of devolving competencies that were held more tightly before by Alert. At some point, "devolving" the responsibility to lead became the only way to cope with the workload and maintain the dynamic of the process. Had this not happened, Alert would probably have begun to hinder the process. Some of the decisions that have derived from this "devolution" have not been the ones that Alert would have made—but nor should they be. (Ibid.)

Although the IA has been effective in devolving responsibilities and shifting greater power to the CBDN, its role in facilitation, coordination, and intellectual support of network members and its ability to visit all entities in the region have been instrumental (ibid.). The responsible devolution of power and competencies to the CBDN has proven a great move toward the long-term sustainability of the CBDN initiative in the region.

Conclusion: The Search for "Sophisticated Statehood" in the South Caucasus

A closer comparative analysis of the Western Balkans and the South Caucasus produces an important lesson on the dynamics of regionalism in PDAs: the visibility of conflicts in such regions often masks underlying and deeper obstacles to regional integration that may or may not be related to active or "frozen" political conflicts. One obstacle is the weakness of institutions of governance, or their rudimentary and underdeveloped nature. Put differently, the lack of regional thinking among public sector officials in Armenia and Georgia is largely associated with the lack of "sophisticated statehood" in those countries. The domestic governance weaknesses, mostly expressed in highly centralized governance models and weak civil society engagement with governance structures, are major factors blocking the political activation of regional stakeholders and regional interests, which are currently unrecognized in political and institutional terms. The opportunities that more sophisticated and smarter statehood can offer for conflict management processes are quite real. Regional layers of governance to address domestic problems offer opportunities to limit the institutional and political space of "frozen" political conflicts in such regions. Countries in the Western Balkans are blanketed with a heavy layer of European institutions that are actively involved in building the administrative capacities of the state, whereas in the South Caucasus such a layer is almost nonexistent at the moment. For example, international organizations as well as Armenian diaspora groups play a range of governance roles in the country, but their aggregate impacts on the governance capacities of Armenian statehood are quite random and highly uneven.

An issue related to the lack of sophisticated statehood is the state of the discourse on regional politics in the South Caucasus. As in many developing countries, in the countries in the South Caucasus, regionalism is mostly understood by the local respondents in this study to be an EU experience, with deeply integrated economic space and pulled sovereignty to a supranational institution. The layered institutional pathways and possibilities in regional engagement have not entered the discourse of regional politics. Understanding and appreciating such diversity are an important step toward realizing the opportunities for enhanced problem solving in domestic politics presented by regional arrangements of cooperation.

7   Peace-Building as Region-Building:
Theory and Practice

Studies in comparative regionalism are dominated by discussions on the extent to which emerging regions in the developing world possess any autonomy. Neorealists tend to argue for an era of hegemonic regionalism, with a particular regional or global power advancing its interests through regional structures. Regionalism without integration is often an outcome of this pattern of region building (Kelly 2007). A related argument focuses on the internal weakness of states in the developing world, making overlay by great powers possible and inevitable. The lack of public legitimacy of the governments in these countries does create internal security problems (ibid.). Such domestic pressures then often push governments to gravitate more toward regional arrangements of joint and coordinated government action aimed at suppressing domestic dissent than toward pooling state sovereignty for enhanced domestic governance—the approach adopted by the advanced industrialized countries. This approach often translates into a lack of incentives for constructive conflict management in such regions. At the other end of the spectrum of this debate, the proponents of "new regionalism" point out that nonstate actors can play an independent role in region building, and that they often produce multilayered processes of regional integration. Developing new analytical tools to explain such processes is considered urgent in this line of research.

This debate is consequential for the theory and practice of conflict resolution. Theories based on hegemonic and power-driven understandings of regional politics tend to translate into policies that allow little rationale, if any, for regional approaches to conflict management. Regional organizations as pivots and focal points of regional cooperation have only marginal value for conflict management from this perspective. By contrast, theories that recognize the rise of regional politics on an autonomous level offer more hope to regional actors and regional intervention strategies for conflict management purposes.

This study argues that for conflict resolution the question is less about whether regions exist as independent constructs and more about the processes of regional building—that is, whether broad-based diverse regional links are being cultivated by peace builders and policy-makers alike. As I argue in this chapter, the question for the field is not whether a given politically divided area (PDA) is a region. It is more about the process: whether to undertake region building or not. If the decision is made to go forward with region building, then what types of regionalism matter the most for catalyzing effective conflict management processes?

This chapter begins by describing the regionally networked peace paradigm as it moves from theory to practice. The next section features the key theoretical implications of this study, specifically focusing on the field of conflict analysis and resolution. The chapter then examines the general policy implications for region building as a peace-building strategy, and offers specific policy recommendations for South Caucasus, where region-building processes are embryonic and the structures of regional governance are nearly nonexistent.

The Regionally Networked Peace Paradigm: From Theory to Practice

The regionally networked peace paradigm is essentially an interdisciplinary approach to regional studies with an emphasis on conflict management. It was developed to evaluate regional politics in terms of the opportunities and limits a particular regional arrangement presents for conflict management processes in a PDA. Its starting point is the acknowledgment that not all regions are created equal in their impacts on conflict management processes. Some are institutionally multilayered and flexible in offering spaces and instruments for different tracks of conflict management. Others are institutionally primitive and state-dominated, with few openings and opportunities for conflict management.

Regions, as highly networked peace systems, are essentially regional arrangements with specific attributes. They are decoupled enough from the global structures of conflict management to exert autonomous institutional power vis-à-vis the great power rivalry. In conflict management, this decoupling entails reconfigured connections and links among international donors, national political elites, and local actors such as "peace entrepreneurs" and "peace constituencies" within societies affected by conflicts (Mouly 2008). Regionally networked peace systems are nourished by inclusive and multilayered governance structures populated by various players such as regional organizations, municipal governments, civil society organizations, business associations, and national governments. The roles that these actors play are equally diverse, ranging from defining problems to exerting accountability over governments, conducting analysis and research, undertaking advocacy, building coalitions, forming dialogue groups, and implementing policy implementation. Such regionally networked peace systems offer political opportunities for diverse instruments, transcending the more traditional conflict management tool kit. Examples are negotiation, mediation, arbitration, and problem solving.

In contrast to traditional conflict management instruments, regionally networked peace systems create a solid track of cross-conflict engagement that is highly technocratic and depoliticized. The deliberate strategic cultivation of broad, deep partnerships between professional communities across conflict lines can offer enhanced governance capacities of the national governments. Such regionally networked peace systems are associated with the regional dimension of state governance, which is currently neglected by both the national political elites and policy-makers, as well as the multilateral and bilateral donor agencies supporting them.

Regionally networked peace systems are dramatically different from conventional conflict management systems and state-centric peace processes. Selby introduces a rather critical description of peace processes:

> Peace processes are inter-elite political accommodations whose aim is often not so much "peace" as the reconfiguration of domestic hegemony and/or international legitimacy; peace processes are reformist, conservative and far from revolutionary phenomena, and often therefore do not provide a basis for the social transformations necessary for sustainable peace. (Selby 2008, 13)

The regionally networked peace paradigm, as a theoretical tool, recognizes that deeply illiberal and semidemocratic political systems tend to populate PDAs in the developing world. Contemporary conflict management systems and peace processes are superbly oblivious to that fact, often falling victim to power struggles and realist power politics. Selby further notes that as historically novel phenomena, peace processes readily provide "breeding grounds for the entire gamut of regressive political developments" (ibid., 25). By contrast, regionally networked peace systems reflect postsovereign models of governance that transcend the centrality of states and recognize the limits of their sovereignty (Richmond 2007). They are plural structures of governance at the regional level that create new political spaces and instruments of empowerment for a larger number of communities across conflict lines, thereby offering new opportunities and untapped potential for sustainable peace-building processes to take place.

The policy dimension of the regionally networked peace system is essentially a call for region building (at times in addition to state building) as a developmental strategy implemented by the donor community in PDAs around the world. In policy terms, the regionally networked peace paradigm is about building regional social capital—an institutionally thick quilt of connections and tiers across conflict lines. It is a policy framework for organizing conflict management at the regional level, largely through building interorganizational coalitions and partnerships across conflict lines that are diverse, institutionalized, multisectoral, and from different levels of governance. The policy dimension of the regionally networked peace paradigm is the set of *principles* for regional network development that are most conducive to and supportive of conflict management processes in PDAs. In particular, regionally networked peace systems offer the following opportunities in terms of conflict management:

- Creating institutional spaces for engagement across conflict lines
- Depoliticizing issue areas of regional import: by building political technocratic ties one can reduce the political space of the conflict(s) dividing the region
- Creating intermediary regional institutions such as the RCC that can depoliticize regional governance, building up the technocratic power of regional organizations
- Applying multiple new pressure points to political elites for constructive conflict management
- Scaling up often isolated track II efforts
- Developing communities and recruiting stakeholders for peace
- Ending the institutional dominance of narrow political elites in narrowly defined "conflict management" processes
- Increasing cross-conflict line societal interdependencies and multiplying the pressure points in conflict societies for constructive engagement
- Adopting region building as a state-building strategy that is a more responsive approach to the rapidly changing dynamics in PDAs in the form of increasingly active and mobilized publics who are often questioning the legitimacy of their authorities.

Theoretical Implications

At a general level, this study echoes liberal institutionalism in arguing that institutions are essential if states are to sustain cooperation, particularly in PDAs (Keohane and Martin 1995). The empirical sections of this study examined the Western Balkans and South Caucasus as two regions endowed with different institutional environments at the regional level, and yet confronted with similar structural conditions—that is, persistently "frozen" structures of conflict (ibid.).

At its core, the regionally networked peace paradigm is functionalist (Selby 2008): it is based on the rich literature advocating the pacifying effects of regional economic cooperation (Fishelson 1989; Fisher et al. 1993; Fisher et al. 1994). It also shares a key principle with functionalist theories: the role of professional communities and issue-based networks in cultivating consensus and cooperation across conflict lines. However, the model developed here departs from functionalist analysis in one key dimension. Functionalist theories argue for spillover from one low-stakes area of cooperation to another, whereas this study maintains that the political environments in PDAs are complex, and that technical spillovers rarely develop and cannot be relied on as a conflict management strategy. Instead, the regionally networked peace paradigm developed in this study shows that it is not the spillover effects that can pacify a region; rather, it is the strategically and explicitly cultivated regional networks that can empower new voices beyond the government and create new political spaces for engagement across conflict lines. They add up to multiple new novel pressure points for peace. The peace process that grows out of this approach is far from harmonious and even technical, as envisioned by the "spillover" argument. Instead, the peace processes that emerge from regionally networked peace can be politically contentious, often unpredictable, but necessary for the long-term sustainability of conflict management and the coexistence of conflict societies and groups in PDAs.

Several other concrete theoretical outcomes stemming from this study also merit further research: (1) the introduction of politically divided areas as a distinct analytical category; (2) a framework of comparative analysis of PDAs, largely informed by the regional studies of international political economy and security; and (3) network analysis of the regional organizations pivoting a particular PDA (this relates to the regional dimension of state governance and transgovernmental networks).

Delineation of PDAs as a Distinct Analytical Category

The first theoretical outcome of this study that merits further research is the delineation of PDAs as a distinct analytical category. Such research has been possible from the cross-fertilization of international political economy and security studies with the field of conflict analysis and resolution. To echo Selby (2008), issues of political economy are "pivotal to the form and functioning of peace processes." The recognition of PDAs as a distinct analytical category allows one not only to uncover how existing conflicts politicize economic interactions and the prospects of broad-based development in the region, but also to understand the ways in which economic forces can constrain or empower peace-building processes in the region (ibid., 21). In short, the broad rationale for an analytically distinct category of PDA depends on the rather politicized dynamics between politics and economy in each state. The role that states usually play in promoting economic development is different in PDAs, where peace processes and conflict dynamics become important dimensions of such decisions. PDAs are distinct because the existing frozen or active conflicts affect the broader legal, political, economic, and institutional environment in which global and local market forces can operate. Active conflict fault lines create certain kinds of incentives for regional engagement for particular types of groups, such as drug cartels or monopolistic oligarchs. Active conflicts provide the oligarchs with perfect cover to push for protected economic spaces in an otherwise free trade regime toward which the global community has been slowly moving. Overall, the recognition of PDAs as a distinct analytical category calls for greater scholarly attention to the ways in which conflict-induced political dynamics can influence the activities of market forces, often creating rather perverse spaces of economic activities, which can be best described as negative regionalism.

PDAs are also distinct from other regions because of the politicization of economic spaces. Respondents in the Western Balkans and South Caucasus often pointed out that political solutions to addressing a particular conflict are needed before economic and social cooperative structures can be built. The fieldwork in this study indicated that this assertion is correct up to a point. Greater understanding is needed of the conditions in which cooperation between business sectors across conflict lines tends to occur. For example, an interface among large businesses across conflict lines would be harder to forge because of their political visibility. However, that does not preclude the possibility of smaller-scale and rather low key cooperation between small and medium enterprises, and several examples of such engagements are covered in the empirical chapters of this book, such as the South Caucasus Business and Development Network, profiled in Chapter 6.

Recognizing their analytical distinction allows one to appreciate in PDAs the extent to which conflicts are central or marginal to the formation and operation of a region. In PDAs, the structures of conflict and peace can coexist in an uneasy but relatively stable relationship. However, this coexistence is often ignored in the literature on conflict resolution, which sees the relationship between conflict and peace as linear and evolutionary—that is, peace is possible only when conflict ends (Richmond 2007).

Some PDAs have succeeded in containing conflicts by creating regional organizations and thereby building institutional spaces for addressing some of these conflicts (see Chapter 4). At the other end of the spectrum, when states in PDAs fail to forge even basic and institutionally thin regional structures of governance, they become subject to hegemonic regionalism, which often cements the hold of the existing governments over them. Ad hoc regional coalitions are in between (Lepgold 2003). Put more simply, creative, effective management of regional structures of governance requires vibrant civil societies and strong administrative structures. In states with hybrid regimes (illiberal democracies and electoral authoritarian states), such regional engagement creates a political environment that is hard to control and manage for their narrow political goals. Therefore, genuine regional cooperation at times conflicts with the political and even economic incentives of the ruling governments in PDAs.

Finally, the study of PDAs as a distinct analytical category raises issues about the scales of regionalism. Within both academic and policy discourse, regionalism is equated with regional free trade blocs, often obscuring the value of microlevel regionalism between communities in border areas or functional ties between professional communities at the regional level, which can be of greater value in development terms for states with high levels of poverty than a free trade bloc that may favor particular segments and sectors of the economy.

A Framework of Comparative Analysis of PDAs

The second theoretical outcome of this study warranting further research is the framework of comparative analysis of PDAs—specifically: (1) levels of regional autonomy versus great power overlay; (2) territorial proximity versus functional ties as a regional marker; (3) conflict or cooperation as a regional marker; and (4) the extent of nonstate actor involvement in regionalism. The resulting framework of regionalism developed for PDAs allows an interdisciplinary conversation between the students and scholars of regional studies, on the one hand, and of conflict analysis and resolution, on the other. The framework allows one to delineate the various levels of maturity of regional structures in a PDA. The broad overview of regional arrangements covered in Chapter 4 illustrates that stronger regional structures do not always evolve only when the great power overlay recedes. In some cases, such as Southeast Asia or Central America, the rudimentary structures of regional cooperation can be formed even when the overlay from great powers is significant. In Southeast Asia, the preexisting regional structures prepared the region for taking advantage of the end of the Cold War, thereby claiming more regional autonomy and demonstrating greater regional maturity. Similarly, Central America, which was defined by great power influences for much of the twentieth century and before, succeeded in building rudimentary regional structures and experimenting with various regional models of integration. Once the political opening was available at the end of the Cold War, Central America moved ahead with sophisticated structures of regional cooperation, while continually working toward greater integration in broader regional arrangements with North America, the EU, and Asia.

This framework of comparative regional analysis is also valuable for the theory and practice of conflict analysis and resolution. Comparing PDAs in the dimensions just listed provides a granular understanding of possible opportunities and roadblocks in building regional structures of conflict management. For example, regions with lower levels of autonomy and greater overlay may call for low-stakes and low-visibility regional projects, while those with greater maturity of regional governance structures gravitate toward more comprehensive regional conflict management systems.

Network Analysis of Regional Organizations Pivoting a PDA

Network analysis of the regional organizations pivoting a particular PDA is the third theoretical outcome of this study deserving more research. Such analysis focuses attention on the organizational locus of authority in a PDA and its role in fostering a regional conflict management system in the region. As discussed in the early chapters of this book, within the changing and often chaotic and fragmented global governance structures, regional organizations are increasingly in the spotlight for taking over certain tasks from multilateral institutions (Patrick 2014). Although there is overall acknowledgment of the possible political and institutional roles of and value added by regional organizations, little is known about their impacts on governance outcomes. To that end, this study has introduced one framework of analysis, with the specific goal of examining conflict management and the provision of security.

The network dimensions of a regional organization introduced in this study help to determine the extent to which a regional organization is embedded into societies across the region and interwoven into the political and economic fabric of those societies. Most regional organizations in developing countries start from the top down because they are poorly embedded into the political and economic lives of their societies. They are often associated with hegemonic regional projects, such as the Commonwealth of Independent States, in which the organization serves as a mechanism to maintain Russia's influence in its neighborhood (Lepgold 2003). In most cases, such patterns of regionalism fail to produce pluralized structures of governance (Selby 2008), and are driven by regional hegemons. The network approach to studying regional organizations helps to detect the institutional quality of such arrangements, particularly their capacities for conflict management and peace building in the region. It also helps to separate the highly politicized and hegemonic arrangements, such as the Russia-led CIS or newly formed Customs Union, from organizationally more structured, interest-driven, institutionalized models, such as the ones found in Central America.

For the theory of conflict analysis and resolution, this network analysis provides a concrete tool that can be used to study the limits and opportunities presented by regional approaches to conflict management. To date, the literature has been limited to the organizational capacities of regional organizations to deal with conflict management. Very little is understood about what makes a particular regional organization more effective and more constructive as a conflict manager in a region. Such comparative questions are important in determining the various impacts of such organizations on the ground.

The network approach introduced in this study calls for embedding a regional organization in the public by building transgovernmental networks and broader alliances with multiple and institutionally diverse stakeholders. The obvious case of the EU and the role it played in the conflict management processes in Northern Ireland reflect the importance of locally embedded regional ties. For PDAs in the developing world, the network approach reveals that regional organizations with external networks that are mostly state led and lack input from various sectors (such as the business sector and civil society) are less effective in adding value to the quality of governance in a region. Embedding regional organizations in states through transgovernmental and other types of networks can complement the governance capacities of the states in the region. In a world of rapidly changing security environments and increasingly overwhelmed multilateral institutions (Diehl and Cho 2005; Crocker et al. 2011 a, b ; Patrick 2014), the regional dimension of state governance in the developing world is a key consideration. There, the development of regional networks in which the state is one of many institutional players is emerging as a dominant form of problem solving.

The nature of networked governance in various regions, particularly in a comparative context, offers a new frontline of state agency, particularly where highly asymmetric power relations characterize the states in a region. Power imbalances between states are often perceived as a major roadblock to the development of meaningful regional arrangements. However, exercising the regional dimension of statehood through the cultivation of multisectoral, multilayered, and institutionally dense networks with neighboring states can allow smaller states to increase their bargaining power relative to their large neighbors, within as well as outside a regional bloc or a regional organization.

Within PDAs, the power asymmetries between states can be particularly debilitating and destabilizing, and networked governance offers a low-key approach to overcoming possible hegemonic influences for or against local regional ties between smaller states. To a question about whether Georgia can assume a regional leadership position in South Caucasus, a senior Georgian government official said that "Russia would never allow it," and that Georgia would not be willing to confront Russia on the matter (Zakareishvili interview 2013). This position was shared by other analysts in the region, both in Armenia and in Georgia. Regionalism is understood by most to be a grand project, advanced through grand economics and grand power balances between states. The development of the regional dimension of states through various kinds of networks (transgovernmental or transnational within a region) is a policy pathway that is often considered an afterthought. Cursory research on the matter—scanning the news reports as well as interviews with government officials in Armenia (Babayan interview 2012)—reveals that states assign little strategic significance to building ties with their neighbors. As indicated in earlier chapters, the tendency to access a far-flung metropolis often comes at the expense of cultivating regional ties. Even the widely recognized strategic importance of ties between Azerbaijan and Georgia and the lack of active conflicts between them have not been followed by the development of any significant bilateral structures between them strong enough to amount to a joint regional governance structure. In sharp contrast to South Caucasus, the European Union has been actively building such regional ties in the Western Balkans, even when the states themselves fail to realize the administrative value of strong, diverse networks with their immediate neighbors.

In conclusion, comparative analysis of networked governance at the regional level within PDAs raises new questions about state governance. It pushes the analytical boundaries of the sovereignty-focused state-building research paradigm to include the regional dimension of building governance structures in PDAs. The deployment of regional networks between states and their societies introduces new political and administrative spaces of governance, thereby creating new channels of learning and policy development. The creation of such regional networks also can create new instruments and spaces for exercising political accountability over governments, which, ironically, is the very factor inhibiting the rise of regional dimensions of state governance in PDAs in the developing world.

As for the theory of conflict analysis and resolution, this study challenges the sovereignty bias of the field. The existing scholarship in conflict analysis and resolution, with its emphasis on track I diplomacy (the government and political elites), track II diplomacy ("semi-influential representatives outside of the government"), and grassroots negotiations (civil society actors and the broader communities), assumes a clearly defined locus of political power (that is, the state). The resulting intervention strategies and mediation regimes are somewhat limited in their applications. By contrast, the regionally networked peace paradigm calls for regional organizations and governance processes as new and often underexplored political spaces for conflict analysis and resolution. The regional level is important as a source or as a facilitating factor in a conflict, as well as a possible tool and an instrument of conflict management. Simply calling for regional approaches to conflict management, as in the literature, is insufficient. Understanding the diversity of regional models of governance is a necessary first step toward uncovering their impacts on conflict management processes as well.

Policy Implications: The Regionally Networked Peace Paradigm

There is an emerging consensus among academics and policy-makers alike that in the post–Cold War period, the great powers have had little appetite and capacity for engaging one another in small-scale proxy wars, as well as for playing a leading role in conflict management processes (Lepgold 2003). Freedman (1998–99) echoes such sentiments by stating that "the big players have not ruled out fighting each other again, but at the moment it is hard to see why they should. Those among the smaller players, even the smallest, who still have things to fight about must therefore set their own standards." Others maintain that the engineering imposed by outside players on conflict parties in bellicose regions will work less and less (Andréani 2011). Lake and Morgan are more explicit in highlighting the increasing need for arrangements and actions of conflict management devised and implemented at the regional level (Lake and Morgan 1997). Nevertheless, as discussed in earlier chapters of this book, the declining capacity in conflict management at the global level has not been matched with growing activity and movement at the regional level (Diehl and Cho 2005).

Any states moving toward regionalism as a conflict management strategy have numerous institutional options. The minimalist application of regionalism as a conflict management strategy entails a regional context for bilateral peace building, thereby changing the broader context, if not its structure, for key political players across conflict lines. The maximalist application of regionalism as a conflict management strategy is about building institutionally thick, diverse, and multilayered regional structures of governance, which emerge as parallel structures in offering governance and problem solving. In both applications, this regionally networked approach to peace challenges state building as a peace-building paradigm. Indeed, the state-building approach is criticized as a "predatory, neo-liberal, ideological perspective aiming to justify and enhance the governance of unruly others" (Richmond 2007, 287). The state-focused models of conflict management are based on the assumption of a social contract between governments and their societies, which assumes that the government is the most effective locus of economic and political security.

In an increasingly globalized context, this assumption is hard to sustain. The government is no longer the only, or even the key, provider of economic security, and its ability to provide physical security is increasingly challenged by the rise of drug cartels and criminal networks. The empowerment of civil society in peace-building processes is a broadly shared approach for sustainable peace building. And yet in the highly illiberal and semidemocratic political systems of PDAs, the empowerment of civil society is rarely the preferred political outcome because it can threaten the domestic political position of the ruling elites relative to civil society or other professional communities. The gulf between indigenous actors, on the one hand, and the socially engineered and artificially promoted civil society envisioned by international actors, on the other, is a political reality (Sylvester 2006; Richmond 2007).

Both the minimal and maximalist applications of regionally networked peace confer on networks and institutions precisely this kind of civil society empowerment because they open up new political, economic, and social spaces of engagement across conflict lines. The political challenges to building such a regional infrastructure of networked peace are many, but the lack of political incentives by the elites in conflict lines is the dominant one, particularly in semidemocratic domestic contexts. Building regionally networked peace systems entails some loss of control over governance and peace processes by the elites, and often this can undermine their domestic hold on power.

Key Tensions in Applying Regionalism to Conflict Management

An important key tension in applying regionalism to conflict management is the one between a certain level of efficiency and capacity associated with the hierarchy and power of global conflict management tools, on the one hand, and the need to empower those caught in conflict, on the other (Andréani 2011). The network approach to analyzing the regional international organizations often pivoting various PDAs has produced a tangible policy template that can be applied to managing that tension. It calls for strategic cultivation of institutionally dense, multisectoral, and multilayered networks across conflict societies, the ultimate goal of which is to build regional institutions of conflict management that can function on a long-term basis and address conflicts as they become active.

The regionally networked peace system advocated in this study is distinct from the existing policy prescriptions for regional and collective conflict management on several dimensions (Diehl and Cho 2005; Crocker et al. 2011a, b). First, it is based on a broader concept of conflict management, emphasizing the conflict management value of policy interventions in issue areas such as health care or agriculture that seem marginally related to conflict management dynamics. Building deliberate issue-based networks and partnerships between professional communities across conflict lines, while in tune with prescriptions of open trade and open economies as conflict-mitigating factors, is a political rather than an economic exercise. Second, the existing literature on regionally cultivated conflict management emphasizes intervention strategies focused on mostly active conflicts that are often treated in a singular manner. By contrast, the regionally networked peace paradigm is long term in its prescriptions for institution building. It is more about systems and structures than single conflicts. Third, the regionally networked peace paradigm allows delineation of security strategies from conflict management, as well as their parallel treatment on a continuum of possible regional interventions. Within the existing literature in regional studies and conflict management, security and stability are often viewed as coterminous with conflict management. This is problematic because short-term security and stability continue to tax the region economically in the form of lost potential of regional competitiveness and drastically reduced FDI levels. Regional arrangements ensuring security regimes of various intensity and institutionalization do not necessarily reflect strong conflict management capacities in the region. Although security sector reforms, for example, imply strong governmental control and management of security interventions, constructive and long-lasting conflict management strategies are rarely limited by the role played by government in the resolution. The provision of security and stability at the regional level is much more sensitive and dependent on the existing geopolitical rivalries and power calculations and perceptions between states. It is high-stakes and politically visible. By contrast, the regionally networked peace paradigm advocates low-stakes and low-profile instruments, forums, and spaces of cross-conflict engagement geared toward interest-based, as opposed to power-based and principle-driven, approaches to conflict management.

Even though security and conflict management need to be delineated clearly, the regionally networked peace paradigm makes possible their treatment within the same continuum. Depending on the institutional composition of regional networks (levels of institutionalization, patterns of mobilization, degree of power distribution, and levels of heteropolarity), some are more effective in the short-term provision of security and stability but lack long-term sustainability in conflict management. Moreover, although the models of security provision emphasize the political power of national authorities and assume their legitimacy, in PDAs this is rarely the case: lack of legitimacy of authorities and political elites is often a major factor shaping the content and design of intervention strategies at the regional level. The regionally networked peace paradigm, as a conceptual product, is much more nimble in capturing the increasingly eroding nexus between domestic and international/regional policy, which is a broadly recognized theoretical concern within the literature in comparative politics.

Another key tension that takes place within regionally networked peace systems is that between the geographical and institutional centers of conflict states and their geographical and institutional peripheries. The development and sustainability of regionally networked peace systems require solid "infrastructural power," which refers to the strength of the institutions and administrative structures (Mann 2005). As discussed earlier in this book, the poor capacities of civil service and administration, particularly in the local levels of government and in border/peripheral areas, are the biggest obstacle to greater regional integration in PDAs. Although the existing conflicts provide a useful political reason to avoid greater regional engagement, the fieldwork carried out for this study reveals that lack of administrative structures and trained civil service are an even more formidable challenge to undertaking greater regional engagement.

Developing Regional Social Capital

A policy dimension of the regionally networked peace paradigm developed here rests on the principle of building regional social capital in PDAs. The concrete network dimensions developed here (such as patterns of network mobilization, level of institutionalization, heteropolarity, distribution of power resources inside networks) offer concrete tools for determining which regional models are most promising for constructive conflict management in PDAs. Under the network approach introduced in this study, the structure of the network matters for conflict management outcomes. Understanding the network structure helps to delineate the contours of political action for conflict management actors at various levels of analysis. Developing the network analysis of regions and regional organizations is also crucial for differentiating regional arrangements (1) that are more conducive to security provision or to conflict management; (2) that are more politicized and vulnerable to political elites and hegemons or have stronger grassroots involvement; and (3) that are institutionally more complex and integrated into state and local levels of governance or are institutionally shallow or highly politicized.

The network approach to the study of regional organizations and regions therefore generates prescriptions and principles for developing regional social capital. Regions rich in regional social capital have a relatively dense layer of networks and organizations across conflict lines, ranging from those that are issue based and highly technocratic at one end of the spectrum, to the highly political and elite-driven ones at the other end. Regions with social capital are populated with states that have a strong regional dimension to their sovereignty. Such regions are able to exert a certain level of organizational autonomy from hegemonic powers and global structures of governance. Meanwhile, their networks are heteropolar and supported by state as well as nonstate actors in terms of their organizational and financial sustainability.

Developing the regional social capital of PDAs can be divided into three main levels: macro, meso, and micro. The macro level emphasizes the donor community. Developing regional social capital at this level entails relaxing the sovereignty bias of donor institutions. The fieldwork carried out in South Caucasus—regionally the least evolved area in this study—indicates that the dominant approach used by donors in delivering aid is sovereignty based. They work with individual states, and truly regional projects are rather sparse. Jonathan Francis (interview 2012), with the Swedish embassy in Bosnia and Herzegovina, said in an interview that truly regional projects are difficult to carry out because of their administrative challenges and coordination problems. And yet the approach of dispersing multilateral funds among bilateral donors is quite frequently adopted, indicating that designing regional approaches to foreign aid, while politically and administratively challenging, is quite possible. When regional approaches are tried, the participants in regional projects have to go through the representatives of the appropriate donor in their own country (Allen interview 2013). Alternatively, regional organizations, if active in PDAs, tend to implement projects in parallel but unrelated tracks in the countries involved. A good example is the OSCE presence in South Caucasus. Even with the OSCE Minsk Group representing the key mediation regime in the Nagorno Karabakh conflict between Armenia and Azerbaijan, the OSCE branch offices in Armenia and Azerbaijan are cut off from the Minsk Group, which further contributes to the institutional isolation of the OSCE Minsk Group in the region. Developing regional strategies for delivering aid to PDAs is a key component of building regional social capital.

At the meso level, developing regional social capital for a PDA entails building intermediating institutions between the local, national, and regional levels of governance. A good example of this approach is that of the Regional Cooperation Council (RCC) in the Western Balkans. As Chapter 5 on the Western Balkans and the case study of the RCC indicated, even when the national elites in the region broadly agreed politically to undertake regional integration, the actual practice of regionalism was not forthcoming. Indeed, the intermediating nature of the RCC in cultivating regional networks, one issue area and one project at a time, made greater regional integration possible in political and institutional terms in the Balkans.

Building a similar structure for South Caucasus was politically more feasible when Armenia and Georgia were negotiating the signing of the Eastern Partnership agreements and joining the Deep and Comprehensive Free Trade Area. Georgia signed the agreements at the end of November 2013, whereas the Armenian government executed a sudden U-turn: after negotiation with the European Union for nearly four years, the Armenian government suddenly declared its intention to join the Russian-led Customs Union instead of signing the Eastern Partnership agreement with the European Union. Currently, analysts are still calling for greater EU involvement in conflict management in the region, and the terms of EU engagement with Armenia remain uncertain on a pragmatic level, despite the declarations of joint engagement by both sides.

Within the current political climate, such intermediating institutions, while politically still possible, would have to focus on low-stakes issues in order to yield concrete outcomes. In parallel, both the EU and other global donors could concentrate on building regional forums for regional governance, including joint training for economists, engineers, surgeons, and surveyors. In short, developing transgovernmental networks with high institutional density and heteropolarity is one approach to building regional social capital. Moving from state-focused funding to building the regional dimension of governance for the states in PDAs is essential for constructive and sustainable conflict resolution processes to take root.

At the micro level, the principles of building regional social capital require strengthening the local levels of governance. Acknowledging that the weakness of states in PDAs is a serious drawback to regional conflict management efforts is essential. Indeed, often internal governance problems are treated separately from the political processes of conflict management and elite negotiations. Poor local governance within highly centralized states is just as much a formidable challenge to regional integration as the conflicts dividing the region. Weak civil societies and a lack of professional associations that could serve as seeds for regional cross-cutting and pragmatic networks are also related to the micro level of developing regional social capital and devising regionalism as a conflict management strategy.

Conclusion: Broken Regions or Collections of Weak States?

Whether peace and reconciliation can start from economic and societal interdependence or favorable geopolitical conditions is a common, albeit false, choice that the respondents in this study often articulated. Those choosing peace and reconciliation argued that peace is about economics, and those choosing favorable geopolitical conditions argued that it is about politics (Kupchan 2010). This study has tried to show that it is about political economy—the political economy of conflict management, to be precise:

> Only after political elites have succeeded in tamping geopolitical competition do the pacifying effects of economic interdependence make a major contribution to the onset of stable peace. The breakthroughs that lead to stable peace are strategic rather than economic in nature. Diplomacy, not trade or investment, is the currency of peace. (Ibid., 14)

Indeed, economic interdependence on its own will hardly produce a peaceful resolution to a conflict. At the same time, hoping that the strategic stars in the geopolitical universe will align is equally idealistic. Diplomacy matters only if the proper institutional context for it has been created. This study on regionally networked peace argues that, indeed, peace is not just about institutions and interdependencies, as the functionalists maintain, but neither is it just about hegemons, as the neorealists assert. Instead, it is about institutional hegemony. It is about regional organizations that can quietly, or at times quite loudly, develop apolitical and technocratic spaces for cross-conflict engagement in a variety of issues areas. It is not about facilitating spillovers, but about creating political pressures and incentives from the grassroots for conflict management. And it is not about building narrow peace processes or mediation regimes that can get stuck and are vulnerable to geopolitical calculations; it is about building systems of regional governance that can function on a long-term basis and not for a single conflict.

Under the regionally networked peace paradigm, South Caucasus is a collection of weak administrative states rather than a broken region, as is often maintained by analysts (De Waal 2012). The Western Balkans case offers several lessons for South Caucasus: adding region building to state building as a key strategic orientation for the international community active in PDAs is the most central one. Unfortunately, a strategic emphasis on region building in South Caucasus is not present in the foreign policies of the member states as well as efforts of the international organizations and bilateral donors involved in the region. Meanwhile, in contrast to the Western Balkans, South Caucasus as a region has not settled on a single hegemon. The competing European and Russian models of regional integration are often self-serving (Sakwa 2011; Babayan interview 2012), leaving South Caucasus with no genuine champion of regional integration. Moreover, no home-grown foreign policy orientation for regional cooperation is in place in South Caucasus. In the Western Balkans, partly with European encouragement, support, and pressure, the countries in the region are slowly realizing the benefits of regional integration.

As for the influence of external powers, at the moment they are contributing little to the prospects for regional integration in South Caucasus. Russia's Eurasian Union and the EU's Eastern Partnership are politically driven to varying degrees and rather unorganic. The main limitation of the EU's Eastern Partnership is its insufficient attention to regional cooperation in South Caucasus beyond its mere declaratory statements. Its sole emphasis on connecting each individual state to the larger European region did little toward directly enhancing regional integration in South Caucasus. By contrast, the Eurasian Union, Russia's model of regional integration, is explicitly geared toward integrating the states into a broader regional economic bloc in which Russia is the political center.[1]

One could argue that the political enthusiasm for stronger regional cooperation in South Caucasus is at a low point in view of the divergent policies of the three countries. However, Armenia's joining of the Russia-led regional bloc after four years of negotiations with the EU on joining the Eastern Partnership has somewhat rebalanced the political security position of Armenia relative to that of Azerbaijan. This situation is, in a way, conducive to cultivating regional arrangements on a smaller scale among the three countries. Region building, therefore, could become a strategic priority for the states as well as external powers. Genuine regional cooperation is the single long-term remedy for security in South Caucasus.

On a more practical level, the need for a regional intermediating institution in the South Caucasus is palpable. The establishment of an institution that can be "status neutral" in its engagement with the states and nonrecognized territories in South Caucasus is a real possibility. An institution similar to the Regional Cooperation Council could not only enhance the regional dimension of states in South Caucasus and their problem-solving and governance capacities, but also institutionalize new apolitical spaces of engagement between the members. Low-stakes and low-profile regional initiatives on the ground are a solid strategy for decoupling the states in South Caucasus from the top-down and unorganic pressures of post-Soviet politics, largely stemming from Russia's current government. Such regional engagement within South Caucasus would allow renegotiation of the terms of engagement with Russia, and would help to strengthen the political autonomy of individual states relative to external players.

An RCC-style regional intermediating institution that can be status neutral and serve as an engine for developing professional and transgovernmental networks is institutionally unprecedented and unexplored in South Caucasus. Such an initiative would not only add to the administrative capacities of the member states but also help to establish semi-institutionalized mechanisms for more frequent meetings between the political elites in Armenia and Azerbaijan, as well as between Georgia and the unrecognized territories of Abkhazia and South Ossetia. The closest institutional pathway to such an initiative is the Organization of the Black Sea Economic Cooperation (BSEC), and it deserves further exploration to understand the potentials of its enhanced conflict management capacities at the regional level.

South Caucasus is a collection of weak states as opposed to a broken region. And it is an institutional desert compared with the Western Balkans. Region building, as opposed to just state building, is a crucial security strategy that presents many different opportunities for enhanced conflict management impact on the ground. A range of policy tools are available in this area, but the international community active in mediating the conflicts in the region has not been exploring them. It has been my modest hope that this book would generate greater scholarly attention and policy emphasis in this direction. It is high time to make the transition from sporadic, isolated confidence-building models that are state centric to institutionalized regional peace systems that can bring new voices and pressure points into conflict management discourses and practices.

Reference Matter

Notes

Chapter 1

1. World Bank Group, World Governance Indicators, http://info.worldbank.org/governance/wgi/mc_chart.asp.

2. World Trade Organization, www.wto.org/english/tratop_e/region_e/rta_pta_e.htm.

Chapter 2

1. Regional Cooperation Council, accessed January 13, 2014, www.rcc.int/pages/0/35.

Chapter 3

1. From August 2012 to July 2013, I was in Armenia on a Fulbright Fellowship, accompanied by my children.

2. Cited in Ohanyan (2007).

Chapter 4

1. See www.cfr.org/trade/mercosur-south-americas-fractious-trade-bloc/p12762.

2. World Bank, "Central America, Expanding Trade Horizons in Order to Diversify," February 7, 2013, accessed October 17, 2013, www.worldbank.org/en/news/feature/2013/02/07/diversificacion-en-centroamerica.

3. Ibid.

4. See www.parlacen.int/Portals/0/Language/5%20English%202011.pdf, accessed October 21, 2013.

5. See www.sica.int/sica/sica_breve_en.aspx.

Chapter 5

1. Ron Synovitz, "Landmark Belgrade-Pristina Deal Faces Hurdles in Northern Kosovo," *Radio Free Europe Radio Liberty,* April 22, 2013, accessed June 5, 2014, www.rferl.org/content/serbia-kosovo-mitrovica-landmark-deal/24965062.html.

2. Radio Free Europe Radio Liberty, "Bosniak-Croat President Arrested in Corrup-

tion Crackdown," April 26, 2013, accessed June 5, 2014, www.rferl.org/content/police-search-bosnia-federation-head-budimir/24969648.html.

3. Technical Assistance for Civil Society Organizations, accessed June 5, 2014, www.tacso.org/cso-db-res/reg/default.aspx?langTag=en-US#.

4. Organization for Security and Co-operation in Europe, Arms Control, accessed June 5, 2014, www.oscebih.org/Default.aspx?id=11&lang=EN.

5. North Atlantic Treaty Organization, "NATO's Relations with Bosnia and Herzegovina," accessed June 5, 2014, www.nato.int/cps/en/natolive/topics_49127.htm.

6. Ibid.

7. Council of Europe, "South East Europe Regional Network for Qualifications Frameworks," accessed June 5, 2014, www.coe.int/t/dg4/highereducation/ehea2010/QF/SEE%20Network%20QF%20terms%20of%20reference%20ADOPTED.asp#TopOfPage.

8. CASEE (Central and South Eastern Europe), "The ICA Regional Network for Central and South Eastern Europe," accessed June 5, 2014, www.ica-casee.eu/.

9. Regional Cooperation Council, Structure, accessed June 5, 2014, www.rcc.int/pages/7/14/structure.

10. Regional Cooperation Council, Expert Pool, accessed June 5, 2014, www.rcc.int/pages/13/10/expert-pool.

11. Some examples of networks of which the RCC is a part, or that it facilitates, are the Women Entrepreneurship Project Meeting, carried out by the RCC network with SEECEL and GTF; preparatory meeting for the 2nd Sustainable Energy Development Regional Initiative Task Force Meeting, carried out with the RCC and CEI; roundtable on fundraising activities for the International Sava River Basin Commission (ISRBC) Projects, carried out with ISRBC; Evidence Based Policy Making in Education Regional Cluster of Knowledge-Turning Research into Practice, organized by the Ministry of Education and Science of Serbia, Social Inclusion and Poverty Reduction Unit, TF BHC of the RCC; and Kulutur Contakt Austria, ERI SEE, among others (Annex 3, Self-Assessment Report).

12. In its 2011–12 annual report, heteropolarity is highlighted, with an emphasis on the following sectors and stakeholders: the European Commission, specialized units for security cooperation area within the European External Action Service, CEFTA and OECD Investment Compact, donors with an interest in regional projects (UNDP, OSCE, EBRD, SDC, SIDA, FES, GIZ, HBS, USAID, and others), private companies and associations, NGOs and NGO-related organizations (TACSO team, Eco-Social Enterprises Network from SEE, BFPE, ICDT, SEE Change Net, and others), newly established regional networks (SEE Public Private Partnership Network, Regional Network of Investment Promotion Agencies), think tanks, financial institutions, and civil society networks in different areas (Regional Cooperation Council 2012a).

Chapter 6

1. WT/TPR/S/224—Trade Policy Forum. Available at http://search.wto.org/ search?q=cache:-NOPvr2AQB4J:www.wto.org/english/tratop_e/tpr_e/s224-01_e. doc+WT%2FTPR%2FS%2F224&access=p&output=xml_no_dtd&ie=UTF-8&client=english_frontend&site=English_website&proxystylesheet=english_frontend&oe=UTF-8.

2. Ibid.

3. In one conversation, a local analyst started shaking his head negatively as soon as I uttered the word "region," without even waiting to listen to my argument.

4. Aynur Jafarova, "Azerbaijan, Georgia and Turkey Mull Investments, Trade" *Azernews*, July 8, 2013, accessed July 8, 2013, www.azernews.az/business/54501.html.

5. Ibid.

6. World Trade Organization, Statistics Database, http://stat.wto.org/CountryProfile/WSDBCountryPFView.aspx?Language=E&Country=AZ,GE,AM.

7. World Trade Organization, Statistics Database, http://stat.wto.org/CountryProfile/WSDBCountryPFView.aspx?Language=E&Country=BA,HR,RS.

8. *Armenian Weekly*, "Serzh Sargsyan Believes One Day Turkey Will Recognize Armenian Genocide," January 31, 2013, accessed January 9, 2014, www.armenianlife.com/2013/01/31/serzh-sargsyan-believes-one-day-turkey-will-recognize-armenian-genocide/.

9. International Crisis Group Europe Report No. 199, "Turkey and Armenia: Opening Minds, Opening Borders: Europe Report No 199—14 April 2009." Available at http://www.crisisgroup.org/~/media/Files/europe/199_turkey_and_armenia___opening_minds_opening_borders_2.pdf.

10. Plans for Yerevan-Van flights were suspended, and the protocols aimed at normalizing relations between Turkey and Armenia were frozen.

11. See www.rec-caucasus.org/text.php?id=15&lang=en.

12. Ibid.

13. Ibid.

14. Ibid.

15. These conventions include the Convention on Access to Information, Public Participation in Decision-Making, and Access to Justice in Environmental Matters (Arhus Convention); the Convention on Environmental Impact Assessment in Transboundary Context (Espoo Convention); the Convention on the Transboundary Effects of Industrial Accidents; the UN Framework Convention on Climate Change; and the Convention on Long-range Transboundary Air Pollution, among many others.

Chapter 7

1. As noted, Georgia has signed the Eastern Partnership agreements with the EU, and Armenia, after nearly four years of negotiating with the EU, has joined Russia's Customs Union and Eurasian Union. Azerbaijan's involvement with the Eastern Partnership has been limited to the Visa Facilitation Agreement, and the Deep and Comprehensive Free Trade Agreement (DCFTA) has not been signed.

Bibliography

Abbasov, I. 2013. "Patriot Games: Marginalising Political Opponents in Modern Azerbaijan." In *Myths and Conflict in the South Caucasus: Instrumentalisation of Conflict in Political Discourse,* vol. 2, edited by Jana Javakhishvili and Liana Kvarchelia. London: International Alert.

Abbott, Kenneth, and Duncan Snidal. 1998. "Why States Act through Formal International Organizations." *Journal of Conflict Resolution* 42: 3–32.

Acharya, Amitav, and Alastair Iain Johnston. 2008. "Comparing Regional Institutions: An Introduction." In *Crafting Cooperation: Regional International Institutions in Comparative Perspective,* edited by A. Acharya and A. I. Johnston. Boston: Cambridge University Press, 1–28.

Ahmed, Shamima, and David Potter. 2006. *NGOs in International Politics.* Bloomfield, CT: Kumarian Press.

Ahmed, Zahid Shahab, and Stuti Bhatnagar. 2008. "Interstate Conflicts and Regionalism in South Asia: Prospects and Challenges." *Perceptions* (Spring–Summer): 1–19.

Alagappa, Muthiah. 1993. "Regionalism and the Quest for Security: ASEAN and the Cambodian Conflict." *Journal of International Affairs* 46 (2): 439–67.

Alagappa, Muthiah. 1995. "Regionalism and Conflict Management: A Framework of Analysis." *Review of International Studies* 21 (4): 359–87.

Andréani, G. 2011. "Global Conflict Management and the Pursuit of Peace." In *Rewiring Regional Security in a Fragmented World,* edited by C. A. Crocker, F. O. Hampson, and P. Aall. Washington, DC: U.S. Institute of Peace.

Andreas, Peter. 2005. "Criminalizing Consequences of Sanctions: Embargo Busting and Its Legacy." *International Studies Quarterly* 49: 335–60.

Andreev, Svetlozar A. 2009. "Sub-regional Cooperation and the Expanding EU: The Balkans and the Black Sea Area in a Comparative Perspective." *Journal of Balkan and Near Eastern Studies* 11 (1): 83–106.

Askandar, Kamarulzaman, Jacob Bercovitch, and Mikio Oishi. 2002. "The ASEAN Way of Conflict Management: Old Patterns and New Trends." *Asian Journal of Political Science* 10 (2): 21–42.

Ayoob, Mohammed. 1992. "The Security Predicament of the Third World State: Reflections on State Making in a Comparative Perspective." In *The Insecurity Dilemma: National Security of Third World States*, edited by B. Job. Boulder, CO: Lynne Rienner Publishers.

Ayoob, Mohammed. 1999. "From Regional System to Regional Society: Exploring Key Variables in the Construction of Regional Order." *Australian Journal of International Affairs* 53: 247–60.

Bailes, Alison, and Ian Bremmer. 1998. "Sub-regionalism in the Newly Independent States." *International Affairs* 74 (1): 131–47.

Ball, Desmond, and Amitav Acharya, eds. 1999. *The Next Stage: Preventive Diplomacy and Security Cooperation in the Asia-Pacific Region*. Canberra: Strategic and Defense Studies Centre, Research School of Pacific and Asian Studies, Australian National University.

Barash, David P., and Charles P. Weber. 2008. *Peace and Conflict Studies*. SAGE Publications: Thousand Oaks, CA.

Barnett, Michael. 1995. "Partners in Peace? The UN, Regional Organizations, and Peace Keeping." *Review of International Studies* 21 (4): 420–24.

Basu, P., C. Chakraborty, and D. Reagle. 2003. "Liberalisation, FDI and Growth in Developing Countries: A Panel Co-integration Approach." *Economic Inquiry* 41 (3): 510–16.

Becattini, G. 1990. "The Marshallian Industrial Districts as a Socio-economic Notion." In *Industrial Districts and Inter-firm Co-operation in Italy*, edited by F. Pyke. Geneva: International Institute for Labour Studies.

Bechev, Dimitar. 2011. *Constructing South East Europe: The Politics of Balkan Regional Cooperation*. New York: Palgrave Macmillan.

Beeson, Mark. 2003. "ASEAN Plus Three and the Rise of Reactionary Regionalism." *Contemporary Southeast Asia* 25 (2): 251–68.

Belloni, Roberto. 2009. "European Integration and the Western Balkans: Lessons, Prospects and Obstacles." *Journal of Balkan and Near Eastern Studies* 11 (3): 313–31.

Benner, Thorsten, H. Wolfgang Reinicke, and Jan Martin Witte. 2005. "Multisectoral Networks in Global Governance: Towards a Pluralistic System of Accountability." In *Global Governance and Public Accountability*, edited by D. Held and M. Koenig-Archibugi. Malden, MA: Blackwell Publishing.

Berry, Frances Stokes, and William D. Berry. 2007. "Innovation and Diffusion Models in Policy Research." In *Theories of the Policy Process*, edited by P. A. Sabatier. Cambridge, UK: Westview Press.

Binder, David. 2002. *Organized Crime in the Balkans*. Washington, DC: Woodrow Wilson Center for International Center for Scholars.

Birrell, D., and A. Hayes. 2001. *Cross-border Cooperation in Local Government: Development, Management and Reconciliation*. Armagh, Ireland: Centre for Cross Border Studies.

Blanco, Ismael, Vivien Lowndes, and Lawrence Pratchett. 2011. "Policy Networks and Governance Networks: Towards Greater Conceptual Clarity." *Political Studies Review* 9: 297–308.

Bohmelt, Tobias. 2009. "International Mediation and Social Networks: The Importance of Indirect Ties." *International Interactions* 35: 298–319.

Bohmelt, Tobias. 2010. "The Effectiveness of Tracks of Diplomacy Strategies in Third-party Interventions." *Journal of Peace Research* 47 (2): 167–78.

Börzel, Tanja A. 1998. "Organizing Babylon—On Different Conceptions of Policy Networks." *Public Administration* 76: 253–73.

Börzel, Tanja A., and Thomas Risse. 2009. "The Rise of (Inter-) Regionalism: The EU as a Model of Regional Integration." Paper presented to the Annual Convention of the American Political Science Association, Toronto, Canada.

Boschma, Ron A. 2004. "Competitiveness of Regions from an Evolutionary Perspective." *Regional Studies* 38 (9): 1001–14.

Browder, Greg. 2000. "An Analysis of the Negotiations for the 1995 Meking Agreement." *International Negotiation* 5 (2): 237–61.

Bruszt, Laszlo, and Balazs Vedres. 2008. "The Politics of Civic Combinations." *Voluntas: International Journal of Voluntary and Nonprofit Organizations* 19 (2): 140–60.

Bueno de Mesquita, Bruce, James D. Morrow, Randolph M. Siverson, and Alastair Smith. 1999. "An Institutional Explanation of the Democratic Peace." *American Political Science Review* 93 (4): 791–807.

Bueno de Mesquita, Bruce, and Randolph M. Siverson. 1995. "War and the Survival of Political Leaders: A Comparative Study of Regime Types and Political Accountability." *American Political Science Review* 89 (4): 841–55.

Bull, B. 1999. "'New Regionalism' in Central America." *Third World Quarterly* 20 (5): 957–70.

Burton, John W. 1990. *Conflict: Human Needs Theory*. New York: St. Martin's Press.

Buzan, B., and O. Wæver. 2003. *Regions and Powers: The Structure of International Security*. Cambridge: Cambridge University Press.

Buzan, B., and O. Wæver. 2004. *Regions and Powers: The Structure of International Security*. Cambridge: Cambridge University Press.

Byrne, S. 2001. "Consociational and Civil Society Approaches to Peacebuilding in Northern Ireland." *Journal of Peace Research* 38 (3): 327–52.

Cantori, Louis, and Steven Spiegel. 1973. "The International Relations of Regions." In *Regional Politics and World Order*, edited by R. Falk and S. Mendlovitz. San Francisco: W. H. Freeman.

Carlarne, Cinnamon, and John Carlarne. 2006. "In-Credible Government: Legitimacy, Democracy, and Non-Governmental Organizations." *Public Organization Review* 6: 347–71.

Carroll, Toby, and Benjamin Sovacool. 2010. "Pipelines, Crisis and Capital: Understanding the Contested Regionalism of Southeast Asia." *Pacific Review* 23 (5): 625–47.

Caspersen, Nina. 2012. "Regimes and Peace Processes: Democratic (Non)development in Armenia and Azerbaijan and Its Impact on the Nagorno-Karabakh Conflict." *Communist and Post-Communist Studies* 45: 131–39.

Cheng-Chwee, Kuik. 2008. "The Essence of Hedging: Malaysia and Singapore's Response to a Rising China." *Contemporary Southeast Asia* 30 (2): 159–85.

Chiozza, Giacomo, and H. E. Goemans. 2003. "Peace through Insecurity: Tenure and International Conflict." *Journal of Conflict Resolution* 47 (4): 443–67.

Chye, Tan Seng. 2012. "Changing Global Landscape and Enhanced Engagement with Asia—Challenges and Emerging Trends." *Asia-Pacific Review* 19 (1): 108–29.

Collins, Alan. 2008. "A People-Oriented ASEAN: A Door Ajar or Closed for Civil Society Organizations?" *Contemporary Southeast Asia* 30 (2): 313–31.

Courtney, Morgan, Hugh Riddell, John Ewers, Rebecca Linder, and Craig Cohen. 2005. "In the Balance: Measuring Progress in Afghanistan." In *A Report for the International Organization for Migration*. Washington, DC: Center for Strategic and International Studies, Post-Conflict Reconstruction Project.

Crocker, C. A., F. O. Hampson, and P. Aall. 2011a. "Collective Conflict Management: A New Formula for Global Peace and Security Cooperation?" *International Affairs* 87 (1): 39–58.

Crocker, C. A., F. O. Hampson, and P. Aall. 2011b. "The Mosaic of Global Conflict Management." In *Rewiring Regional Security in a Fragmented World*, edited by C. A. Crocker, F. O. Hampson, and P. Aall. Washington, DC: U.S. Institute of Peace Press.

De Waal, T. 2012. "A Broken Region: The Persistent Failure of Integration Projects in the South Caucasus." *Europe-Asia Studies* 64(9): 1709–1723.

De Waal, Thomas. 2010. *The Caucasus: An Introduction*. New York: Oxford University Press.

Der Derian, James. 2011. "Security in an Age of Heteropolarity." In *Regional Dynamics in the South Caucasus Conference*, November 17–19. Yerevan, Armenia. Available at http://securecaucasus.files.wordpress.com/2012/04/james-derderyan.pdf.

Deudney, Daniel. 2011. "How Britain and France Could Reform the UN Security Council." *Survival* 53 (5): 107–28.

Diaz, Elizabeth. 2001. *Towards Comprehensive Peacebuilding*. Paper presented to the International Peace Academy, 2001 New York Seminar, West Point, NY. **International_Peace_Academy_IA_2001_New_York_Sem-1.pdf**

Diehl, P. F., and Y.-I. D. Cho. 2005. "Passing the Buck in Conflict Management: The Role of Regional Organizations in the Post–Cold War Era." *Brown Journal of World Affairs* 22 (2): 191–202.

Diez, T., and K. Hayward. 2008. "Reconfiguring Spaces of Conflict: Northern Ireland and the Impact of European Integration." *Space and Polity* 12 (1): 47–62.

Dosch, Jorn, and Oliver Hensengerth. 2005. "Sub-regional Cooperation in Southeast Asia: The Mekong Basin." *European Journal of East Asian Studies* 4 (2): 264–85.

Duffield, John S. 2006. "International Security Institutions." In *The Oxford Handbook of Political Institutions*, edited by R. A. W. Rhodes, S. A. Binder, and B. A. Rockman. Oxford: Oxford University Press.

Duffield, Mark. 2001. *Global Governance and the New Wars: The Merging of Security and Development*. New York: Zed Books.

Emmerson, Donald K. 2008. "Introduction: Critical Terms: Security, Democracy, and Regionalism in Southeast Asia." In *Hard Choices: Security, Democracy, and Regionalism in Southeast Asia*, edited by Donald K. Emmerson. Stanford: Shorenstein Asia-Pacific Research Center at Stanford University.

European Bank for Reconstruction and Development. 2004. *Spotlight on South-eastern Europe: An Overview of Private Sector Activity and Investment*. London: European Bank for Reconstruction and Development.

Falk, Richard. 1999. "Regionalism and World Order after the Cold War." In *Globalism and the New Regionalism*, edited by B. Hettne, A. Inotai, and O. Sunkel. New York: St. Martin's Press.

Farrell, Mary. 2005. "The Global Politics of Regionalism: An Introduction." In *Global Politics of Regionalism: Theory and Practice*, edited by M. Farrell, B. Hettne, and L. V. Langenhove. London: Pluto Press.

Farrell, Mary, Björn Hettne, and Luk Van Langenhove, eds. 2005. *Global Politics of Regionalism: Theory and Practice*. London: Pluto Press.

Fausett, Elizabeth, and Thomas J. Volgy. 2010. "Intergovernmental Organizations (IGOs) and Interstate Conflict: Parsing out IGO Effects for Alternative Dimensions of Conflict in Postcommunist Space." *International Studies Quarterly* 54: 79–101.

Fawcett, Louise. 1995. "Regionalism in Historical Perspective." In *Regionalism in World Politics*, edited by L. Fawcett and A. Hurrell. Oxford: Oxford University Press.

Fawcett, Louise. 2003. "The Evolving Architecture of Regionalism." In *The United Nations and Regional Security: Europe and Beyond*, edited by M. Pugh and W. Sidhu. Boulder, CO: Lynne Rienner Publishers.

Fawcett, Louise. 2004. "Exploring Regional Domains: A Comparative History of Regionalism." *International Affairs* 80 (3): 429–46.

Findley, Michael, and Peter Rudloff. 2009. "Combatant Fragmentation and the Dynamics of Civil Wars." In *Annual Meeting of the American Political Science Association*. Toronto, Canada. http://papers.ssrn.com/sol3/papers.cfm?abstract_id=1450036.

Finnemore, Martha. 1996. *National Interests in International Society*. Ithaca, NY: Cornell University Press.

Fishelson, G. E. 1989. *Economic Cooperation in the Middle East*. Boulder, CO: Westview Press.

Fisher, S., L. Hausman, A. Karasik, and T. Schelling. 1994. *Securing Peace in the Middle East: Project on Economic Transition.* Cambridge, MA: MIT Press.

Fisher, S., D. Rodrick, and E. Tuma. 1993. *The Economics of Middle East Peace: Views from the Region.* Cambridge, MA: MIT Press.

Forman, Shepard, and Derk Segaar. 2006. "New Coalitions for Global Governance: The Changing Dynamics of Multilateralism." *Global Governance* 12 (2): 205–26.

Frankel, J. A. 1997. *Regional Trading Blocs in the World Economic System.* Washington, DC: Institute for International Economics.

Frazier, Derrick V., and William J. Dixon. 2006. "Third-Party Intermediaries and Negotiated Settlements, 1946–2000." *International Interactions* 32: 385–408.

Freedman, Lawrence. 1998–99. "The Changing Forms of Military Conflict." *Survival* **40 (4).**

Galtung, Johan. 1996. *Peace by Peaceful Means: Peace and Conflict, Development and Civilization.* SAGE Publications.

Gartzke, Erik, Quin Li, and Charles Boehmer. 2001. "Investing in the Peace: Economic Interdependence and International Conflict." *International Organization* 55 (2): 391–438.

Gawerc, Michelle I. 2006. "Peace-building: Theoretical and Concrete Perspectives." *Peace and Change* 31 (4): 435–78.

Glaser, Barney G., and Anselm L.Strauss. 1967. *The Discovery of Grounded Theory: Strategies for Qualitative Research.* New York: Aldine, De Gruyter.

Goddard, S. E. 2012. "Brokering Peace: Networks, Legitimacy, and the Northern Ireland Peace Process." *International Studies Quarterly* 56: 501–15.

Goemans, H. E. 2000. *War and Punishment: The Causes of War Termination and the First World War.* Princeton: Princeton University Press.

Goetschel, Laurent. 2000. "Globalisation and Security: The Challenge of Collective Action in a Politically Fragmented World." *Global Society* 14 (2): 259–77.

Grugel, J. 2004. "New Regionalism and Modes of Governance—Comparing US and EU Strategies in Latin America." *European Journal of International Relations* 10 (4): 603–26.

Haacke, Jürgen. 2009. "The ASEAN Regional Forum: From Dialogue to Practical Security Cooperation?" *Cambridge Review of International Affairs* 22 (3): 427–49.

Haacke, Jürgen, and Paul D. Williams. 2011. "Regional Approaches to Conflict Management." In *Rewiring Regional Security in a Fragmented World*, edited by C. A. Crocker, F. O. Hampson, and P. Aall. Washington, DC: U.S. Institute of Peace Press.

Hall, Peter A. 1996. "Political Science and the Three New Institutionalisms." *Political Studies* 44: 936–57.

Hampson, Fen Osler, and Paul Heinbecker. 2011. "The New Multilateralism of the Twenty-First Century." *Global Governance* 17: 299–310.

Hancock, L. 2008. "The Northern Irish Peace Process: From Top to Bottom." *International Studies Review* 10: 203–38.

Hansen, Holley E., Sara McLaughlin MItchell, and Stephen Nemeth. 2008. "IO Mediation of Interstate Conflicts: Moving beyond the Global versus Regional Dichotomy." *Journal of Conflict Resolution* 52 (2): 295–325.

Harrison, E. Neil. 2006. "Thinking about the World We Make." In *Complexity in World Politics: Concepts and Methods of a New Paradigm*, edited by E. N. Harrison. Albany: State University of New York Press.

Harrison, John. 2006. "Re-reading the New Regionalism: A Sympathetic Critique." *Space and Polity* 10 (1): 21–46.

Hawkins, G. Darren, A. David Lake, L. Daniel Nielson, and J. Michael Tierney. 2006. "Delegation under Anarchy: States, International Organizations, and Principal-Agent Theory." In *Delegation and Agency in International Organizations*, edited by G. D. Hawkins, A. D. Lake, L. D. Nielson, and J. M. Tierney. Cambridge, UK: Cambridge University Press.

He, Kai. 2008. "Institutional Balancing and International Relations Theory: Economic Interdependence and Balance of Power Strategies." *European Journal of International Relations* 14 (3): 379–404.

He, Kai. 2010. "The Hegemon's Choice between Power and Security: Explaining US Policy toward Asia after the Cold War." *Review of International Studies* 36 (4): 1121–43.

Held, David, and Mathias Koenig-Archibugi. 2005. "Introduction." In *Global Governance and Public Accountability*, edited by D. Held and M. Koenig-Archibugi. Malden, MA: Blackwell Publishing.

Heller, Dominik. 2005. "The Relevance of the ASEAN Regional Forum (ARF) for Regional Security in the Asia-Pacific." *Contemporary Southeast Asia* 27 (1): 123–45.

Hemmer, Christopher, and Peter J. Katzenstein. 2002. "Why Is There No NATO in Asia: Collective Identity, Regionalism, and the Origins of Multilateralism." *International Organization* 56: 575–607.

Hentz, James, and Marten Bøås. 2003. *New and Critical Security and Regionalism.* Burlington, VT: Ashgate.

Hettne, Björn. 1999. "Globalization and the New Regionalism: The Second Great Transformation." In *Globalism and the New Regionalism*, edited by B. Hettne, A. Inotai, and O. Sunkel. New York: St. Martin's Press.

Hettne, Björn. 2000. "Development, Security, and World Order: A Regionalist Approach." *In Regions and Development: Politics, Security, and Economics*, edited by S. Page. London: Cass.

Hettne, Björn, and András Inotai. 1994. "The New Regionalism." The UN University and World Institute for Development Economics Research. Tokyo: Japan.

Hettne, Bjorn, and Fredrik Soderbaum. 2006. "The UN and Regional Organizations in Global Security: Competing or Complementary Logics?" *Global Governance* 12: 227–32.

Hoglund, Kristine, and Mimmi Soderberg Kovacs. 2010. "Beyond the Absence of War: The Diversity of Peace in Post-settlement Societies." *Review of International Studies* 36 (2): 367–90.

Horowitz, D. 1985. *Ethnic Groups in Conflict*. Berkeley: University of California Press.

Hurrell, Andrew. 1998. "Security in Latin America." *International Affairs* 74 (3): 529–46.

Hwang, Hokyu. 2006. "Planning Development: Globalization and the Shifting Locus of Planning." In *Globalization and Organization: World Society and Organizational Change*, edited by G. Driori, J. Meyer, and H. Hwang. New York: Oxford University Press.

International Crisis Group. 2011a. "Armenia and Azerbaijan: Preventing War." Europe Briefing no. 60: Tbilisi/Baku/Yerevan/Istanbul/Brussels. Accessed at www.crisisgroup.org/~/media/Files/europe/caucasus/B60%20Armenia%20and%20Azerbaijan%20---%20Preventing%20War.

International Crisis Group. 2011b. "Bosnia: What Does Republika Srpska Want?" Europe Report no. 214. Sarajevo/Istanbul/Brussels. Accessed at www.crisisgroup.org/en/regions/europe/balkans/bosnia-herzegovina/214-bosnia-what-does-republika-srpska-want.aspx.

Jafarova, Aynur. "Azerbaijan, Georgia and Turkey Mull Investments, Trade." *Azernews*, July 8, 2013. Accessed July 8, 2013, at www.azernews.az/business/54501.html.

Jarstad, Anna K., and Roberto Belloni. 2012. "Introducing Hybrid Peace Governance: Impact and Prospects of Liberal Peacebuilding." *Global Governance* 18: 1–6.

Jayasuriya, Kanishka. 2008. "Regionalising the State: Political Topography of Regulatory Regionalism." *Contemporary Politics* 14 (1): 21–35.

Jetly, Rajshree. 2003. "Conflict Management Strategies in ASEAN: Perspectives for SAARC." *Pacific Review* 16 (1): 53–76.

Jönsson, Christer. 1993. "International Organization and Co-operation: An Interorganizational Perspective." *International Social Science Journal* 45 (4): 463–78.

Judah, Tim. 2009. *Yugoslavia Is Dead: Long Live the Yugosphere*. London: European Institute, London School of Economics.

Kaldor, Mary, Mary Martin, and Sabine Selchow. 2007. "Human Security: A New Strategic Narrative for Europe." *International Affairs* 83 (2): 273–88.

Kathuria, Sanjay. 2008. *Western Balkan Integration and the EU: An Agenda for Trade and Growth*. Washington, DC: World Bank.

Katsumata, Hiro. 2006. "Establishment of the ASEAN Regional Forum: Constructing a 'Talking Shop' or a 'Norm Brewery'?" *Pacific Review* 19 (2): 181–98.

Katzenstein, Peter. 2005. *A World of Regions: Asia and Europe in the American Imperium*. Ithaca, NY: Cornell University Press.

Katzenstein, Peter J., Robert O. Keohane, and Stephen D. Krasner. 1998. "International

Organization and the Study of World Politics." *International Organization* 52 (4): 645–85.

Kaufmann, Daniel, Aart Kraay, and Massimo Mastruzzi. 2010. *The Worldwide Governance Indicators: Methodology and Analytical Issues.* World Bank Policy Research Working Paper no. 5430. Available at http://papers.ssrn.com/sol3/papers.cfm?abstract_id=1682130.

Keck, Margaret E., and Kathryn Sikkink. 1998. *Activists beyond Borders: Advocacy Networks in International Politics.* Ithaca, NY: Cornell University Press.

Kelly, Robert K. 2007. "Security Theory in the New Regionalism." *International Studies Review* 9: 197–229.

Kempe, I. 2013. "The Eurasian Union and the European Union Redefining Their Neighborhood: The Case of the South Caucasus." *Caucasus Analytical Digest* 51: 204. Available at http://www.css.ethz.ch/publications/DetailansichtPubDB_EN?rec_id=2598.

Keohane, R. O., and L. L. Martin. 1995. "The Promise of Institutionalist Theory." *International Security* 20 (1): 39–51.

Kirchner, Emil J., and Roberto Dominguez. 2011. "Regional Organizations and Security Governance." In *The Security Governance of Regional Organizations,* edited by E. J. Kirchner and R. Dominguez. New York: Routledge.

Klein, D., and O. Pentikainen. 2012. "Economy and Conflict in the South Caucasus: The Caucasus Business Development Network." In *Mediation and Dialogue in the South Caucasus,* edited by B. Kobakhia, J. Javakhishvili, L. Sotieva, and J. Schofield. London: International Alert.

Koppenjan, Joop, and Erik-Hans Klijn. 2004. *Managing Uncertainties in Networks.* New York: Routledge.

Kriesi, H., S. Adam, and M. Jochum. 2006. "Comparative Analysis of Policy Networks in Western Europe." *Journal of European Public Policy* 13 (3): 341–61.

Krikorova, Z. 2012. "The Phenomenon of the Caucasus Forum." In *Mediation and Dialogue in the South Caucasus,* edited by B. Kobakhia, J. Javakhishvili, L. Sotieva, and J. Schofield. London: International Alert.

Kumar, Chetan, and Jos De la Haye. 2012. "Hybrid Peacemaking: Building National Infrastructures for Peace." *Global Governance* 18: 13–20.

Kupchan, C. A. 2010. *How Enemies Become Friends: The Sources of Stable Peace.* Princeton: Princeton University Press.

Laffan, B., and J. O'Mahony. 2008. *Ireland and the European Union.* New York: Palgrave Macmillan.

Laffan, B., and D. Payne. 2001. *Creating Living Institutions: EU Programmes after the Good Friday Agreement.* Armagh: Centre for Cross Border Studies.

Lake, David A. 1997. "Regional Security Complexes: A Systems Approach." In *Regional Orders: Building Security in a New World,* edited by D. A. Lake and P. M. Morgan. University Park: Pennsylvania State University Press.

Lake, David A., and Patrick M. Morgan. 1997. "The New Regionalism in Security Affairs." In *Regional Orders: Building Security in a New World*, edited by D. A. Lake and P. M. Morgan. University Park: Pennsylvania University Press.

Lampe, J. 2006. *Balkans into Southeastern Europe: A Century of War and Transition*. Basingstoke, UK: Palgrave Macmillan.

Lederach, John Paul. 1997. *Building Peace: Sustainable Reconciliation in Divided Societies*. Washington, DC: U.S. Institute of Peace.

Lederach, John Paul. 2002. *A Handbook of International Peacebuilding: Into the eye of the Storm*. San Francisco: Jossey-Bass.

Leifer, Michael. 2000. *Singapore's Foreign Policy: Coping with Vulnerability*. New York: Routledge.

Lemke, Douglas. 2002. *Regions of War and Peace*. New York: Cambridge University Press.

LeoGrande, W. 1998. *Our Own Backyard: The United States in Central America, 1977–1992*. Chapel Hill: University of North Carolina Press.

Lepgold, J. 2003. "Regionalism in the Post-Cold War Era: Incentives for Conflict Management." In *Regional Conflict Management*, edited by P. F. Diehl and J. Lepgold. Boulder, CO: Rowman and Littlefield Publishers.

Libman, A. 2007. "Regionalisation and Regionalism in the Post-Soviet Space: Current Status and Implications for Institutional Development." *Europe-Asia Studies* 59 (3): 401–30.

Limaye, Satu P. 2007. "United States-ASEAN Relations on ASEAN's Fortieth Anniversary: A Glass Half Full." *Contemporary Southeast Asia* 29 (3): 447–64.

Lipschutz, Ronnie D. 1998. "Beyond the Neoliberal Peace: From Conflict Resolution to Social Reconciliation." *Social Justice* 25 (4): 5.

Mac Ginty, Roger. 2010. "No War, No Peace: Why So Many Peace Processes Fail to Deliver Peace." *International Politics* 47: 145–62.

Maftei, Loredana. 2012. "The Main Characteristics of the Romanian Illegal Drug Markets." *Eastern Journal of European Studies* 3 (1): 189–204.

Makim, Abigail. 2002. "Resources for Security and Stability? The Politics of Regional Co-operation on the Meking, 1957–2001." *Journal of Development and Environment* 11 (1): 5–52.

Manaut, R. B., and R. C. Macías. 2011. *Security Challenges in Mexico and Central America*. Washington, DC: U.S. Institute of Peace.

Mann, M. 2005. "Has Globalization Ended the Rise of the Nation-State?" In *The Global Transformations Reader: An Introduction to the Globalization Debate*, edited by D. Held and A. McGrew. Cambridge, UK: Polity Press.

Mansfield, Edward D., and Jack Snyder. 1995. "Democratization and the Danger of War." *International Security* 20 (1): 5–35.

Mazower, M. 2001. *The Balkans*. London: Phoenix.

McCall, Cathal. 1999. "Identity in Northern Ireland: Communities, Politics and Change." London: Macmillan.

McMahon, Patrice C., and Jon Western. 2009. "The Death of Dayton." *Foreign Affairs* 88 (5): 1–10.

Mertus, Julie, and Tazreena Sajjad. 2005. "When Civil Society Promotion Fails State-Building: The Inevitable Fault-Lines in Post-Conflict Reconstruction." In *Subcontracting Peace: The Challenges of the NGO Peacebuilding*, edited by Oliver P. Richmond and H. F. Carey. Burlington, VT: Ashgate.

Miller, Benjamin. 2005. "When and How Regions Become Peaceful: Potential Theoretical Pathways to Peace." *International Studies Review* 7: 229–67.

Milward, Alan. 1992. *The European Rescue of the Nation State*. London: Routledge.

Minić, Jelica. 2009. "A Decade of Regional Cooperation in South Eastern Europe: Sharing Guidance, Leadership and Ownership." In *Dialogues: Ownership for Regional Cooperation in the Western Balkan Countries*. Berlin: Friedrich-Ebert-Stiftung Foundation.

Mitchell, P. 1995. "Competition in an Ethnic Dual Party System." *Ethnic and Racial Studies* 18 (4): 773–96.

Mittelman, James. 2000. *The Globalization Syndrome: Transformation and Resistance*. Princeton: Princeton University Press.

Morgan, Clifton T., and Kenneth N. Bickers. 1992. "Domestic Discontent and the External Use of Force." *Journal of Conflict Resolution* 36 (1): 25–52.

Morgan, Patrick M. 1997. "Regional Security Complexes and Regional Orders." In *Regional Orders: Building Security in a New World*, edited by David A. Lake and Patrick M. Morgan. University Park: Pennsylvania State University.

Mouly, C. 2008. "Peace Constituencies in Peacebuilding: The Mesas de Concertación in Guatemala." In *Whose Peace? Critical Perspectives on the Political Economy of Peacebuilding*, edited by M. Pugh, N. Cooper, and M. Turner. New York: Palgrave Macmillan.

Nan, Susan Allen, Mary Mulvihill, and Anne Salinas. 2010. *Theories of Change and Indicator Development in Conflict Management and Mitigation*. Washington, DC: USAID.

Ness, Gayl D., and Stephen R. Brechin. 1988. "Bridging the Gap: International Organizations as Organizations." *International Organizations* 42 (2): 245–73.

Nguyen, Thi Hai Yen. 2002. "Beyond Good Offices? Regional Organizations in Conflict Resolution." *Journal of International Affairs* 55 (2): 468–79.

Nye, Joseph. 1968. "Introduction." In *International Regimes: Readings*, edited by J. Nye. Boston: Little, Brown.

Ohanyan, Anna. 1999. "Negotiation Culture in the Post-Soviet Context: An Interdisciplinary Perspective." *Conflict Resolution Quarterly* 17 (1): 83–104.

Ohanyan, Anna. 2002. "Post-Conflict Global Governance: The Case of Microfinance

Enterprise Networks in Bosnia and Herzegovina." *International Studies Perspectives* 3: 396–416.

Ohanyan, Anna. 2003. "Winning Global Policies: The Network-Based Operation of Microfinance NGOs in Bosnia and Herzegovina, 1996–2002." Ph.D. dissertation. Political Science Department, Syracuse University, Syracuse, NY.

Ohanyan, Anna. 2007. "On Money and Memory: Political Economy of Cross-Border Engagement on the Politically Divided Armenia-Turkey Frontier." *Conflict, Security and Development* 7 (4): 579–604.

Ohanyan, Anna. 2008. *NGOs, IGOs, and the Network Mechanisms of Post-conflict Global Governance in Microfinance.* New York: Palgrave Macmillan.

Ohanyan, Anna. 2009. "Network Model of NGO Behavior." *International Studies Review* 11 (3): 475–501.

Ohanyan, Anna. 2010. "The Effects of Global Policy Networks on Peacebuilding: Framework of Evaluation." *Global Society Journal: Journal of Interdisciplinary International Relations* 24 (4): 529–52.

Ohanyan, Anna. 2012. "Network Institutionalism and NGO Studies." *International Studies Perspectives* 13: 366–89.

Ohanyan, Anna. 2012. "Transfer Up or Down? Dialogue Groups between Turkish and Armenian Communities in the United States." *Conflict Resolution Quarterly* 29 (4): 433–60.

Ohanyan, Anna, and John Lewis. 2005. "Politics of Peace-Building: Critical Evaluation of Interethnic Contact and Peace Education in Georgian-Abkhaz Peace Camp, 1998–2002." *Peace and Change* 30 (1): 55–84.

Öjendal, Joakim. 2004. "Back to the Future? Regionalism in South-East Asia under Unilateral Pressure." *International Affairs* 80 (3): 519–33.

Özkan, B. 2008. "Who Gains from the No War No Peace Situation? A Critical Analysis of the Nagorno-Karabakh Conflict." *Geopolitics* 13: 572–99.

Paris, Roland. 2000. "Broadening the Study of Peace Operations." *International Studies Review* 2 (3): 27–44.

Paris, Roland. 2004. *At War's End: Building Peace after Civil Conflict.* New York: Cambridge University Press.

Parker, Rachel. 2007. "Networked Governance or Just Networks? Local Governance of the Knowledge Economy in Limerick (Ireland) and Karlskrona (Sweden)." *Political Studies* 55: 113–32.

Patrick, S. M. 2014. "The Unruled World." *Foreign Affairs* 93 (1, January/February): 58–73.

Pearson, Frederic S. 2001. "Dimensions of Conflict Resolution in Ethnopolitical Disputes." *Journal of Peace Research* 38 (3): 275–87.

Pease, Kelly-Kate. 2003. *International Organizations: Perspectives on Governance in the 21st Century.* Upper Saddle River, NJ: Prentice-Hall.

Perry, Valery. 2009. "At Cross Purposes? Democratization and Peace Implementation

Strategies in Bosnia and Herzegovina's Frozen Conflict." *Human Rights Review* 10: 35–54.

Peters, B. Guy. 1999. *Institutional Theory in Political Science: The New Institutionalism.* London: Pinter.

Peters, B. Guy, Jon Pierre, and Desmond S. King. 2005. "The Politics of Path Dependency: Political Conflict in Historical Institutionalism." *Journal of Politics* 67 (4): 1275–1300.

Pfeffer, Jeffery, and Gerald R. Salancik. 1978. *The External Control of Organizations: A Resource Dependence Perspective.* New York: Harper and Row.

Pierson, P. 1996. "The Path to European Integration: A Historical Institutionalist Approach." *Comparative Political Studies* 29 (2): 123–63.

Politi, Alessandro. 2001. "The Threat of Organized Crime in the Balkans." *Journal of Southeast European and Black Sea Studies* 1 (2): 39–63.

Papadopoulos, Yannis. 2007. "Problems of Democratic Accountability in Network and Multilevel Governance" *European Law Journal* 13 (4): 469-486.

Prezelj, Iztok. 2013. "Challenges of Multilateral Regional Security and Defence Cooperation in South East Europe." *European Perspectives* 5 (2): 83–112.

Prys, Miriam. 2010. "Hegemony, Domination, Detachment: Differences in Regional Powerhood." *International Studies Review* 12: 479–504.

Pugh, Michael, and Waheguru Sdhu, eds. 2003. *The United Nations and Regional Security: Europe and Beyond.* Boulder, CO: Lynne Rienner Publishers.

Rabushka, A., and K. Shepsle. 1972. *Politics in Plural Societies: A Theory of Democratic Instability.* Columbus, OH: Merrill.

Racioppi, L., and K. O'Sullivan See. 2007. "Grassroots Peace-building and Third-party Intervention: The European Union's Special Support Programme for Peace and Reconciliation in Northern Ireland." *Peace and Change* 32 (3): 361–90.

Ramsbotham, Alexander. 2012. "Building Peace across Borders." *New Routes: A Journal of Peace Research and Action* 17 (4): 6–8.

Regional Cooperation Council. 2012a. "Annual Report of the Secretary General of the Regional Cooperation Council on Regional Cooperation in South East Europe, 2011–2012." Sarajevo: Regional Cooperation Council.

Regional Cooperation Council. 2012b. "The Background Paper with Contributions of the RCC Secretariat's Operational Units: Annex 2." Sarajevo: Regional Cooperation Council.

Regional Cooperation Council. 2012c. "Self-assessment Report on the Implementation of the RCC Strategy and Work Programme 2011–2013." Brussels: Regional Cooperation Council.

Reinicke, Wolfgang, Francis Deng, Jan Martin Witte, Thorsten Benner, Beth Whitaker, and John Gershman. 2000. *Critical Choices: The United Nations, Networks, and the Future of Global Governance.* Ottawa: IDRD.

Reiter, Dan, and Allan C. Stam III. 2002. *Democracies at War*. Princeton: Princeton University Press.

Resmini, L. 2000. "The Determinants of Foreign Direct Investment in the CEECs: New Evidence from Sectoral Patterns." *Economics of Transition* 8 (3): 665–89.

Rhodes, R. A. W. 1990. "Policy Networks: A British Perspective." *Journal of Theoretical Politics* 2 (3): 293–317.

Rhodes, R. A. W. 1996. "The New Governance: Governing without Government." *Political Studies* 44: 652–67.

Richmond, Oliver P. 2005. "The Dilemmas of Subcontracting the Liberal Peace." In *Subcontracting Peace: The Challenges of the NGO Peacebuilding*, edited by O. P. Richmond and H. F. Carey. Burlington, VT: Ashgate.

Richmond, O. P. 2007. "Critical Research Agendas for Peace: The Missing Link in the Study of International Relations." *Alternatives* 32: 247–74.

Richmond, Oliver, and Jason Franks. 2009. "Between Partition and Pluralism: The Bosnian Jigsaw and an 'Ambivalent Peace.'" *Southeast European and Black Sea Studies* 9 (1–2): 17–38.

Robinson, Scott E. 2006. "A Decade of Treating Networks Seriously." *Policy Studies Journal* 34 (4): 589–98.

Ross, Marc Howard. 2000. "Creating the Conditions for Peacemaking: Theories of Practice in Ethnic Conflict Resolution." *Ethnic and Racial Studies* 23 (6): 1002–34.

Rotfeld, Adam Daniel. 1997. "Conflict Is within States, Not between Them." In *How Can Europe Prevent Conflicts?*, edited by M. Eyskens, D. Owen, M. Rocard, A. D. Rotfeld, G. Schroder, and A. Toukan. Brussels: Philip Morris Institute.

Ruane, J., and J. Todd. 2002. "The Northern Ireland Conflict and the Impact of Globalization." In *Ireland on the World Stage*, edited by W. Crotty and D. E. Schmit. New York: Longman, 111–26.

Rubin, B. R., and B. D. Jones. 2007. "Prevention of Violent Conflict: Tasks and Challenges for the United Nations." *Global Governance* 13: 391–408.

Ruiz-Dana, Alejandra, Peter Goldschagg, Edmundo Claro, and Hernan Blanco. 2009. "Regional Integration, Trade and Conflicts in Latin America." In *Regional Trade Integration and Conflict Resolution*, edited by S. Rafi Khan. New York: Routledge.

Rüland, J. 2011. "Southeast Asia Regionalism and Global Governance: Multilateral Utility or Hedging Utility?" *Contemporary Southeast Asia: A Journal of International and Strategic Affairs* 33 (1): 83–112.

Russett, Bruce, John Oneal, and David Davis. 1998. "The Third Leg of the Kantian Tripod for Peace: International Organizations and Militarized Disputes, 1950–1985." *International Organization* 52 (3): 441–67.

Sakwa, Richard. 2011. "The Clash of Regionalisms and Caucasian Conflicts." *Europe-Asia Studies* 63 (3): 467–91.

Saunders, Harold. 2000. "Interactive Conflict Resolution: A View for Policy Makers on

Making and Building Peace." In *International Conflict Resolution after the Cold War*, edited by P. C. Stern and D. Druckman. Washington, DC: National Academies Press.

Scharpf, F. W. 1997. *Games Real Actors Play: Actor-Centered Institutionalism in Policy Research*. Boulder, CO: Westview Press.

Schimmelfennig, Frank. 2005. "Strategic Calculation and International Socialization: Membership Incentives, Party Constellations, and Sustained Compliance in Central and Eastern Europe." *International Organization* 59 (4): 827–60.

Schnabel, Albrecht. 2002. "Post-conflict Peacebuilding and Second-generation Preventive Action." *International Peacekeeping* 9 (2): 7–30.

Schtonova, S. 1998. "Regional Co-operation and Strengthening Stability in Southeast Europe." In *NATO Research Fellowships Report*. NATO Office of Information and Press, Brussels.

Selby, J. 2008. "The Political Economy of Peace Processes." In *Whose Peace? Critical Perspectives on the Political Economy of Peacebuilding*, edited by M. Pugh, N. Cooper, and M. Turner. New York: Palgrave Macmillan.

Shor, Francis. 2012. "Declining US Hegemony and Rising Chinese Power: A Formula for Conflict?" *Perspectives on Global Development and Technology* 11 (1): 157–67.

Siverson, Randolph M. 1996. "Thinking about Puzzles in the Study of International War." *Conflict Management and Peace Science* 15 (2): 113–32.

Skocpol, Theda. 1992. *Protecting Soldiers and Mothers: The Political Origins of Social Policy in the United States*. Cambridge, MA: Belknap.

Slaughter, Anne-Marie. 2004. *A New World Order*. Princeton: Princeton University Press.

Smith, Edwin M., and Thomas G. Weiss. 1997. "UN Task-sharing: Towards or away from Global Governance?" *Third World Quarterly* 18 (3): 595–619.

Söderbaum, Fredrik. 2004. "Modes of Regional Governance in Africa: Neoliberalism, Sovereignty Boosting, and Shadow Networks." *Global Governance* 10: 419–36.

Soesastro, Hadi. 1994. "Pacific Economic Cooperation: The History of an Idea." In *Asia Pacific Regionalism: Readings in International Economic Relations*, edited by R. Garnaut and P. Drysdale. Sydney, Australia: Harper Educational Publishers.

Solioz, Christophe, and Paul Stubbs. 2009. "Emergent Regional Co-operation in South East Europe: Towards Open Regionalism?" *Southeast Europe and Black Sea Studies* 9 (1–2): 1–16.

Solis, L. G. 1995. "Peace Equation: The Need for Further Regional Cooperation." *Harvard International Review* 17 (2): 26–30.

Stefanova, Boyka. 2009. "OSCE and the Balkan Security." *Journal of Balkan and Near Eastern Studies* 11 (1): 43–60.

Stubos, George, and Ioannis Tsikripis. 2007. "Regional Integration Challenges in South East Europe: Banking Sector Trends." *Southeast European and Black Sea Studies* 7 (1): 57–81.

Swanström, Niklas. 2002. *Regional Cooperation and Conflict Management: Lessons from the Pacific Rim.* Uppsala: Uppsala Universitet.

Sylvester, C. 2006. "Bare Life as Development/Post-Colonial Problematic." *Geographical Journal* 172 (1): 66–77.

Tamminen, Tanja. 2004. "Cross-border Cooperation in the Southern Balkans: Local, National or European Identity Politics?" *Southeast European and Black Studies* 4 (3): 399–418.

Tannam, E. 2012. "The European Union and Conflict Resolution: Northern Ireland, Cyprus and Bilateral Cooperation." *Government and Opposition* 47 (1): 49–73.

Tanner, Fred. 2010. "Addressing the Perils of Peace Operations: Toward a Global Peacekeeping System." *Global Governance* 16: 209–17.

Tavares, Rodrigo. 2008. "Understanding Regional Peace and Security: A Framework for Analysis." *Contemporary Politics* 14 (2): 107–27.

Taylor, Ian. 2005. "Globalisation Studies and the Developing World: Making International Political Economy Truly Global." *Third World Quarterly* 26 (7): 1025–42.

Ter-Gabrielyan, G. 2012. "The Experience of the Caucasus Forum: An Experiment in Holistic Peacebuilding." In *Mediation and Dialogue in the South Caucasus*, edited by B. Kobakhia, J. Javakhishvili, L. Sotieva, and J. Schofield. London, International Alert.

Thakur, Ramesh, and Luk Van Langenhove. 2006. "Enhancing Global Governance through Regional Integration." *Global Governance* 12: 233–40.

Thelen, Kathleen. 1999. "Historical Institutionalism in Comparative Politics." *Annual Review of Political Science* 2: 369–404.

Themnér, Lotta, and Peter Wallensteen. 2013. "Armed Conflicts, 1946–2012." *Journal of Peace Research* 50 (4): 509–21.

Thomas, George, John Meyer, Francisco Ramirez, and John Boli. 1987. *Institutional Structure: Constituting the State, Society and the Individual.* Newbury Park, CA: Sage.

Thompson, William R. 1973. "The Regional Subsystem: A Conceptual Explication and a Propositional Inventory." *International Studies Quarterly* 17: 89–117.

Todorova, Maria. 1997. *Imagining the Balkans.* New York: Oxford University Press.

Trimçev, Eno. 2009. "Foreign Policy, Elites and Regional Identity." In *Dialogues: Ownership for Regional Cooperation in the Western Balkan Countries*, sponsored by Friedrich-Ebert-Stiftung Foundation, Berlin.

Varshney, Ashutosh. 2001. "Ethnic Conflict and Civil Society: India and Beyond." *World Politics* 53: 362–98.

Väyrynen, Raimo. 1984. "Regional Conflict Formations: An Intractable Problem of International Relations Theory." *Journal of Peace Research* 21: 337–59.

Väyrynen, Raimo. 2003. "Regionalism: Old and New." *International Studies Review* 5: 25–51.

Vucetic, Srdjan. 2001. "The Stability Pact for South Eastern Europe as a Security Community-building Institution." *Southeast European Politics* 2 (2): 109–34.

Weaver, C. 2010. "Black Sea or Black Lake? How US-Russian Tensions Are Affecting EU Policy." In *The Black Sea Region and EU Policy,* edited by K. Henderson and C. Weaver. Burlington, VT: Ashgate.

Weichert, Michael. 2009. "Introduction." In *Dialogues: Ownership for Regional Cooperation in the Western Balkan Countries,* sponsored by Friedrich-Ebert-Stifung Foundation, Berlin.

Williams, Paul D., and Jurgen Haacke. 2011. "Regional Approaches to Conflict Management." In *Rewiring Regional Security in a Fragmented World,* edited by C. A. Crocker, F. O. Hampson, and P. Aall. Washington, DC: U.S. Institute of Peace Press.

Wooten, Melissa, and Andrew J. Hoffman. 2008. "Organizational Fields: Past, Present and Future." In *The SAGE Handbook of Organizational Institutionalism,* edited by R. Greenwood, C. Oliver, K. Sahlin, and R. Suddaby. Los Angeles: SAGE.

World Bank. 2013. "Central America, Expanding Trade Horizons in Order to Diversify" February 7, 2013. http://www.worldbank.org/en/news/feature/2013/02/07/diversifica-cion-en-centroamerica Accessed on Oct 28, 2014.

Yakobashvili, T. 2013. "Is the South Caucasus a Region?" *Caucasus Analytical Digest* 51–52 (17 June): 5–8. Available at http://www.css.ethz.ch/publications/pdfs/CAD-51-52.pdf.

Zurn, Michael. 2005. "Global Governance and Legitimacy Problems." In *Global Governance and Public Accountability,* edited by D. Held and M. Koenig-Archibugi. Malden, MA: Blackwell Publishing.

Zysman, J. 1994. "How Institutions Create Historically Rooted Trajectories of Growth." *Industrial and Corporate Change* 3 (1): 243–83.

Interviews Conducted by the Author

Allen, Susan H. Associate Professor at George Mason University. June 10, 2013. Yerevan, Armenia.

Anonymous. Senior Official from OSCE. August 29, 2012. Sarajevo, Bosnia and Herzegovina.

Anonymous. International NGO representative. June 12, 2013. Yerevan, Armenia.

Anonymous. Official from the Georgian Ministry of Foreign Affairs. August 3, 2012. Tbilisi, Georgia.

Anonymous. Senior Official from the United Nations. September 1, 2012. Yerevan, Armenia.

Anonymous. Senior Official from the EU Delegation in Armenia. September 24, 2012. Yerevan, Armenia.

Anonymous. Senior Official from the EU Delegation in Bosnia and Herzegovina. August 28, 2012. Sarajevo, Bosnia and Herzegovina.

Anonymous. Senior OSCE Official. September 26, 2012. Yerevan, Armenia.

Anonymous. Senior Western Diplomat. June 25, 2013. Yerevan, Armenia.

Anonymous. Senior Western Diplomat. March 18, 2013. Yerevan, Armenia.

Anonymous. Governmental Official in Bosnia and Herzegovina. August 21, 2012. Sarajevo, Bosnia and Herzegovina.

Anonymous. Mid-level Official from the Ministry of Economy, Armenia. November 6, 2012. Yerevan, Armenia.

Babayan, Aneta. Ministry of Economy, Armenia. November 6, 2012.

Bagratyan, Hrant. Former Prime Minister in the Republic of Armenia and current member of the Parliament. July 17 2013. Yerevan, Armenia.

Bekirski, S. President, Tosp. November 6, 2012. Yerevan, Armenia.

Biščević, Hidajet. Secretary General, Regional Cooperation Council. Sarajevo, Bosnia and Herzegovina. August 28, 2012.

Broers, Laurence. Conciliation Resources, Caucasus Projects Manager. June 15, 2013. Yerevan, Armenia.

Christensen, Camrin. Eurasia Partnership Foundation Tbilisi. July 30, 2012. Tbilisi, Georgia.

Francis, Jonathan. Embassy of Sweden in Bosnia and Herzegovina. August 29, 2012. Sarajevo, Bosnia and Herzegovina.

Gegeshidze, Archil. Senior Fellow, Georgian Foundation for Strategic and International Studies. July 25, 2012. Tbilisi, Georgia.

Giragosian, Richard. Director, Regional Studies Center in Armenia. November 22, 2012. Yerevan, Armenia.Harutyunyan, Noune. Rotating Executive Director, Regional Environmental Centre for the Caucasus. July 1, 2013. Yerevan, Armenia.

Huseynov, Tabib. Conciliation Resources. August 1, 2012. Tbilisi, Georgia.

Isazade, Azad. Journalist. November 2012. Yerevan, Armenia.

Iskandaryan, Alexander. Director, Caucasus Institute. November 13, 2012. Yerevan, Armenia.

Ivan-Cucu, Virgil. Senior Expert, Head of Justice and Home Affairs Unit, Secretariat of the Regional Cooperation Council. August 13, 2012. Sarajevo, Bosnia and Herzegovina.

Kapetanovich, Amer. Official from the Ministry of Foreign Affairs of Bosnia and Herzegovina. August 14, 2012. Sarajevo, Bosnia and Herzegovina.

Makaryan, Gagik. Director, Union of Manufacturers and Businessmen Employers of Armenia. July 2, 2013. Yerevan, Armenia.

Margaryan, M. Ministry of Foreign Affairs. September 25, 2012. Yerevan, Armenia.

Mebuke, Manana. Director, Union of Wives of Invalids and Lost Warriors. July 26, 2012. Tbilisi, Georgia.

Minić, Jelica. Deputy Secretary General and Head of Expert Pool, Regional Cooperation Council. August 24, 2012. Sarajevo, Bosnia and Herzegovina.

Mišlović, Blaženka, and Jelica Grujić. Foreign Investment Promotion Agency. August 28, 2012. Sarajevo, Bosnia and Herzegovina.

Oliphant, Craig. Senior Advisor on Europe and Central Asia Programme at Saferworld. June 12, 2013. Yerevan, Armenia.

Sahakyan, D. Projects Specialist at the Regional Environmental Centre for the Caucasus. July 1, 2013. Yerevan, Armenia.

Shougarian, Rouben. Former Ambassador of the Republic of Armenia to the United States. May 1, 2014. Medford, MA.

Ter-Gabrielyan, Gevorg. Country Director, Eurasia Partnership Foundation in Armenia. May 31, 2013. Yerevan, Armenia.

Terterov, Marat. Director, European Geopolitical Forum. November 19, 2012. Yerevan, Armenia.

Torosyan, Tigran. Former Speaker of the Parliament, Republic of Armenia. June 27, 2013. Yerevan, Armenia.

Westergaard, Palle. Director, TACO. August 30, 2012. Sarajevo, Bosnia and Herzegovina.

Yedigaryan, Anoush. Senior Advisor on Public Sector Reforms, Public Finance Management in the South Caucasus Project, GIZ. July 18, 2013. Yerevan, Armenia.

Zakareishvili, Paata. Minister for Reconciliation and Civil Equity, Republic of Georgia. June 15, 2013. Yerevan, Armenia.

Index